The Acquisition of English Grammar and Phonology by Cantonese ESL Learners

Chan's exploration of the acquisition of English grammar and phonology by Cantonese learners of English as a Second Language (ESL) offers insights into the specific challenges that learners often encounter and posits ways to help them overcome those challenges. Possible sources of the challenges are also examined.

The book covers the basic differences between English and Cantonese grammar as well as those between English and Cantonese phonology. Chan discusses the kinds of grammatical and phonological problems that Cantonese ESL learners often have in their acquisition of English. In terms of grammar, various structures are reviewed, including errors which are clearly due to L1 interference and also those which may not be directly L1-related. Learners' common misconceptions about relevant concepts are also revealed. In terms of phonology, both speech perception and speech production problems at the segmental and suprasegmental levels are examined. For learner problems which may be the result of L1 interference, a contrastive approach is adopted in analysing the cause and nature of the errors. Chan also offers readers pedagogical insights to target common grammatical problems, including the use of an algorithmic approach, the use of a discovery-based consciousness-raising approach and the use of metalinguistic explanations. As far as the learning of English phonology is concerned, she argues that the training of speech production should go hand-in-hand with that of speech perception. Future research can experiment with the proposed teaching ideas with Cantonese ESL learners and learners of other native languages.

Researchers and ESL teaching professionals will find the insights and research contained within this volume invaluable when encountering or researching Chinese ESL learners.

Alice Yin Wa Chan (PhD) is Associate Professor in the Department of English at City University of Hong Kong. She gained her BA in linguistics from the University of Lancaster, UK, her MPhil in computer speech and language processing from the University of Cambridge, UK, and her PhD in linguistics from the University of Hong Kong, Hong Kong. Before joining CityU, she had taught at different local universities in Hong Kong. She has published in various international journals, and contributed to edited books, professional magazines and conference proceedings. Her research and teaching interests include second language acquisition, English grammar, English phonetics and phonology, and lexicography.

Routledge Research in Language Education

The *Routledge Research in Language Education* series provides a platform for established and emerging scholars to present their latest research and discuss key issues in Language Education. This series welcomes books on all areas of language teaching and learning, including but not limited to language education policy and politics, multilingualism, literacy, L1, L2 or foreign language acquisition, curriculum, classroom practice, pedagogy, teaching materials, and language teacher education and development. Books in the series are not limited to the discussion of the teaching and learning of English only.

Books in the series include:

Pluricentric Languages and Language Education
Pedagogical Implications and Innovative Approaches to Language Teaching
Edited by Marcus Callies and Stefanie Hehner

The Acquisition of English Grammar and Phonology by Cantonese ESL Learners
Challenges, Causes and Pedagogical Insights
Alice Yin Wa Chan

Using Digital Portfolios to Develop Students' Writing
A Practical Guide for Language Teachers
Ricky Lam and Benjamin Luke Moorhouse

Enhancing Beginner-Level Foreign Language Education for Adult Learners
Language Instruction, Intercultural Competence, Technology, and Assessment
Edited by Ekaterina Nemtchinova

Taboos and Controversial Issues in Foreign Language Education
Critical Language Pedagogy in Theory, Research and Practice
Edited by Christian Ludwig and Theresa Summer

For more information about the series, please visit www.routledge.com/Routledge-Research-in-Language-Education/book-series/RRLE

The Acquisition of English Grammar and Phonology by Cantonese ESL Learners

Challenges, Causes and
Pedagogical Insights

Alice Yin Wa Chan

LONDON AND NEW YORK

First published 2023
by Routledge
4 Park Square, Milton Park, Abingdon, Oxon OX14 4RN

and by Routledge
605 Third Avenue, New York, NY 10158

Routledge is an imprint of the Taylor & Francis Group, an Informa business

British Library Cataloguing-in-Publication Data
A catalogue record for this book is available from the British Library

ISBN: 978-1-032-17251-4 (hbk)
ISBN: 978-1-032-17255-2 (pbk)
ISBN: 978-1-003-25249-8 (ebk)

DOI: 10.4324/9781003252498

Typeset in Times New Roman
by Apex CoVantage, LLC

Contents

5 Learner Problems in the Acquisition of English Grammar II: English Article Errors

8   Learner Problems in the Acquisition of English Phonology II: Speech Perception

9   Cantonese ESL Learners' Acquisition of Grammar and Phonology: L1 Influence?

Figures

Tables

Abbreviations

A	Answer
ADJ	Adjective
AH	Accessibility Hierarchy
AI	Artificial Intelligence
ASP	Aspect Marker
ASR	Automated Speech Recognition
BELF	English as a Business Lingua Franca
CAPT	Computer-assisted Pronunciation Training
CL	Classifier
CLT	Communicative Language Teaching
C/U	Countable/Uncountable
DDL	Data-Driven Learning
EFL	English as a Foreign Language
EIL	English as an International Language
ELF	English as a Lingua Franca
ESL	English as a Second Language
DO	Direct Object
FonF	Focus on Form
FonFs	Focus on Forms
GA	General American
GEN	Genitive
HKE	Hong Kong English
HKSAR	Hong Kong Special Administrative Region
I	Instruction
IO	Indirect Object
ISCH	Interlanguage Structural Conformity Hypothesis
L1	First Language
L2	Second Language
L2LP	Second Language Linguistic Perception
MDH	Markedness Differential Hypothesis
NL	Native Language
NLM	Native Language Magnet Model
NLM-e	Native Language Magnet Theory Expanded

NOM	Nominalizer
OBL	Oblique
OCOMP	Object of Comparison
PAM	Perceptual Assimilation Model
POSS	Possessive Marker
Prep Comp	Prepositional Complement
PRT	Particle
Q	Question
Q-A	Question–Answer
RP	Received Pronunciation
S	Subject
SC	Subject Complement
SCH	Structural Conformity Hypothesis
SLM	Speech Learning Model
SLM-r	Revised Speech Learning Model
TL	Target Language
UR	Usage Rules
V	Verb
VP	Verb Phrase

Acknowledgements

The majority of the grammatical and phonology problems discussed in this book come from published or unpublished findings of different research projects I conducted (some with my research collaborators) at City University of Hong Kong. The support of the City University of Hong Kong and that of the Hong Kong Research Grants Council are acknowledged. I would like to express my gratitude to my research collaborators, Dr. David C. S. Li and Dr. Becky S. C. Kwan, and all my research assistants/associates, Hang Chan (Dr.), Christy Chau, Billy Cheung, James Lambert (Dr.), Candy Law, Emily Law, Carmen Lee, Jim Lo, Vanessa Tse, Amy Wong and Mira Wong. My thanks are also due to my husband, Szeto Chi Yuen, who assisted me in the technicalities involved in the drawing of the figures. Last but not least, I would like to thank all the participants who participated in the different research studies concerned.

1 Introduction

This book offers a comprehensive account of English grammar and phonology acquisition by Cantonese English as a Second Language (ESL) learners. It is a research-oriented book examining learners' grammar acquisition and phonology acquisition using empirical data from relevant research studies. The book also explores the probable causes of learner problems from different theoretical perspectives and provides practical pedagogical suggestions with concrete illustrative examples demonstrating effective ways of helping learners overcome their learning problems. In this introductory chapter, the purpose of the book and the target group of learners will be discussed. A brief description about the use of English in China today, as well as justifications for the importance of understanding ESL learners' problems in their acquisition of English grammar and phonology, will be presented. The focuses and organization of the book will also be outlined.

Objectives of the Book

This book has three main objectives. It aims to:

i   Provide a detailed account of the problems that Cantonese ESL learners often encounter and/or the errors that they often make in their acquisition of English grammar and phonology;
ii Examine the nature and probable causes of the problems identified;
iii Offer practical pedagogical suggestions on ways to help Cantonese ESL learners overcome their problems with their learning of English grammar and phonology.

Target Group of Learners

The target group of learners under discussion in this book is Cantonese ESL learners. The Chinese language has many regional varieties, of which Cantonese is one. Being the mother tongue of most Cantonese speakers in Hong Kong[1] and in the Guangdong area, Cantonese is a widely known and influential variety of Chinese. Cantonese speakers constitute a large subset of Chinese speakers in many areas of the globe. There exist fundamental differences between English and Cantonese

DOI: 10.4324/9781003252498-1

(see Chapters 2 and 3), and these differences may impact on Cantonese ESL learners' learning of English. Cantonese ESL learners' acquisition of English is, thus, appealing and worth attending to.

English in China Today

As an international language, English is used as a lingua franca (ELF) in many parts of the world and among speakers of different native languages (NL). In contemporary China, much importance has also been attached to this language. In Hong Kong, where most of the research studies cited in this book were situated, English is used as a second language (L2). It is compulsorily taught at all secondary and primary schools and is used as the medium of instruction in many primary, secondary and tertiary institutions. Although English is one of the two official languages of Hong Kong, daily communication among ESL learners is basically conducted in Chinese. The status of English in Hong Kong is not just a second language but also a value-added language important for both upward and outward mobility (Li, 1999). After the return of Hong Kong to China's sovereignty in 1997, the economic role of English in the city has remained strong (Hansen Edwards, 2015).

In other parts of China, English is used as a foreign language (EFL). The language has become more and more important after China's implementation of the official policy of reform and opening in the late 1970s (Yao & Du-Babcock, 2020). In terms of the number of learners, English is the most popular foreign language (Wei & Su, 2012). It plays a significant role for people in their pursuit of further education or better careers (He, 2010), and the study of English has been promoted on a national scale (Wang, 2007). English is also an important resource for international companies in China, and English as a Business Lingua Franca (BELF) has been widely used as the medium of workplace communication in China (Kankaanranta & Lu, 2013).

Importance of Understanding ESL Learners' Errors

It is well known that learners often encounter difficulties and make errors in learning a second or foreign language. Areas of difficulty can vary, ranging from the phonology and syntax of the target language (TL) to its morphology, semantics and even pragmatics. There have often been lamentations from the teaching sector regarding the handling and rectification of students' errors. In order to help learners overcome their second language learning problems, ESL teachers need to have a good understanding of the cognitive and psycholinguistic mechanisms that are at work in learners' learning processes.

Exploring learners' learning processes by investigating the errors that they often make can help enrich teaching curricula and guide teaching practices. Although errors often result from learners' lack of linguistic competence, they are not signs of inhibition. Instead, they are evidence of learners' strategies of learning (Corder, 1967), as they indicate the knowledge of the language that learners are acquiring and provide us with evidence of learners' learning development (Corder, 1981).

Learners cannot self-correct their own errors until they receive relevant input, implicit or explicit, and convert that input into intake (James, 1998). Teachers need to be aware of the nature and causes of learner errors in order to be able to design appropriate remedial instructional materials. With enhanced understanding of how far learners have progressed in their process of learning a second or foreign language, teachers will be better informed of how much to teach, what to focus on, what can be ignored and how to teach effectively. When teachers know more about the way a learner learns, they may be able to adapt to learners' needs instead of imposing on learners their own preconceptions of how, what and when learners ought to learn (Corder, 1967).

Scope of the Book

Many aspects of learning are important for our understanding of second language acquisition and are worth detailed discussion, especially interlanguage grammar and interlanguage phonology. Grammar and phonology are important domains within linguistics. Both native speakers and language learners need a certain level of grammatical and phonological competence in order to have effective communication in the language concerned. Thus, this book focuses on Cantonese ESL learners' acquisition of English grammar and phonology.

Important though they are, grammar and phonology are by no means the only aspects of learning worth attending to. Other domains within linguistics – such as pragmatics, which is regarded as a domain complementary to grammar (Leech, 1983) – should also be important to our understanding of second language learning. Devising learning activities to help learners notice the pragmalinguistic and sociopragmatic[2] constraints on L2 pragmatic acquisition should also be crucial to ESL teachers (Norouzian & Eslami, 2016). However, comprehensive discussions of interlanguage pragmatics and of other aspects of learning may warrant the space of another book. Due to limited space, this book will focus only on grammar and phonology.

Sources of Data

Most of the data included in this book come from published or unpublished findings of research studies conducted by the author and her research collaborators, including both research into Cantonese ESL learners' acquisition of English grammar (e.g. Chan, 2000, 2003, 2004a, 2004b, 2004c, 2004d, 2010c, 2016, 2017a, 2017b, 2019a, 2019b, 2022; Chan, Kwan & Li, 2002a, 2002b, 2003; Chan & Li, 2002; Chan, Li & Kwan, 2003; Kwan, Chan & Li, 2003; Li & Chan, 1999, 2000, 2001) and research into Cantonese ESL learners' acquisition of English phonology (e.g. Chan, 2006b, 2006c, 2007, 2009a, 2010a, 2010b, 2011, 2012, 2013, 2014; Chan & Li, 2000). More in-depth and thorough analyses of the data with elaborating details, as well as enriched and deepened discussions with novel insights, will be provided in this book. Though covering a wide range of aspects of L2 grammar and phonology acquisition by the target group of learners, the data from the author's own studies are not exhaustive and will, where necessary, be supplemented with findings from relevant research studies on Cantonese learners conducted by other researchers in Hong Kong and elsewhere (see Chapters 4–9). The pedagogical recommendations targeting the identified learner problems (see Chapters 10 and 11) are also adapted from the author's related studies (e.g. Chan, 2006a, 2008, 2009b, 2015, 2021) and are augmented with innovative suggestions which are pertinent to the contemporary learning environments. Pedagogical proposals advocated in other studies, where relevant, will also be discussed to supplement the author's own ideas.

Intended Audience of the Book

This book is intended for three major categories of audience: The first category of intended audience includes academics and researchers working in the ESL fields, with particular interest in second language grammar and second language phonology. The second category includes ESL teaching professionals. The third category of intended audience consists of linguistics students who are interested in English grammar, English phonetics and phonology, and second language acquisition. Although most of the studies from which the data in this book come involved Cantonese ESL learners in Hong Kong, the learner problems, theoretical discussions and pedagogical insights are also useful to learners and/or academics, teaching professionals and researchers working with Cantonese ESL/EFL learners in other parts of China and of the world. Many of the findings/discussions included in this book are also relevant to individuals having other Chinese dialects as their first languages (L1).

Organization of the Book

Given the focuses and objectives of the current book, Cantonese ESL learners' problems in their acquisition of English grammar and phonology are discussed here. In the study of learner errors, the role of one's native language is of interest to many researchers. Learner difficulties have often been attributed to the NL, and in particular to the differences between the NL and the TL, although there have also been arguments that differences between languages do not always lead to learning difficulties (Odlin, 1989). Therefore, before presenting a detailed examination of learner errors, this book will examine the major grammatical structures and the phonological systems of English and Chinese (typically the Cantonese dialect) from a contrastive perspective. Regarding learners' grammatical problems, the book will explore not only L1-related and non-L1-related errors, but also learners' common misconceptions about important concepts, such as those about the English article system. With regard to phonology, both speech perception and speech production problems at the segmental and suprasegmental levels will be discussed. The extent of first language influence, as well as probable non-L1 related factors, on Cantonese ESL learners' acquisition of English grammar and phonology will be examined. Other probable causes of L2 grammatical problems and those of L2 phonology problems will be discussed from different theoretical perspectives. A comprehensive discussion of L2 acquisition would be incomplete without referring to pedagogical insights, so suggested teaching strategies targeting the identified learner problems in grammar and phonology will also be provided. It will be argued that form-focused instruction, including the incorporation of an algorithmic approach, the use of discovery-based consciousness-raising techniques, and the use of metalinguistic explanations will be effective in advancing learners' understanding and use of relevant grammatical structures. As far as the learning of English phonology is concerned, it will be argued that the training of speech production should go hand-in-hand with that of speech perception.

The organization of the book is as follows: The two chapters that follow this introductory chapter will give some general descriptions of the basic differences between English and Chinese grammar (Chapter 2) and those between English and Cantonese phonology (Chapter 3). Chapters 4, 5 and 6 will discuss the most common grammatical problems encountered by Cantonese ESL learners. While Chapter 4 discusses the most common interlingual errors, Chapter 5 discusses problems related to English articles, and Chapter 6 deals with errors which may not be directly L1-related. The two chapters that follow are devoted to speech production and speech perception, with Chapter 7 detailing the kinds of speech production problems that learners commonly make, and Chapter 8 detailing their speech perception problems. Chapter 9 will analyse the probable sources of the grammatical and phonological problems discussed previously. Chapters 10 and 11 will provide pedagogical insights into effective means of helping learners overcome some of the identified grammatical and phonological problems, respectively. The last chapter (Chapter 12) reviews some concerns about the representativeness and coverage of the findings reported in the book and proposes future research in the areas of L2 grammar and L2 phonology.

Notes

1 Hong Kong is a special administrative region of China (known as the HKSAR). In this book, Hong Kong is used to refer to HKSAR.
2 Pragmalinguistics refers to learners' knowledge of the strategies for realizing speech intentions and their use of appropriate linguistic forms to express these speech intentions. Sociopragmatics, on the other hand, refers to learners' knowledge of the social conditions governing language use (Leech, 1983).

2 English and Chinese-Cantonese Grammar in Contrast

This chapter will adopt a contrastive approach to examine English and Chinese-Cantonese grammar (see the section "The English Language and the Chinese Language" for an explanation of the term *Chinese-Cantonese*). It will review the basic elements of a sentence and the various clausal or phrasal constituents of English and Chinese-Cantonese. Although structural similarities exist between English and Chinese, there are many more disparities between them. A full contrastive English Chinese grammar may warrant the space of a whole book (e.g. Li & Luk, 2017), so this chapter will focus on only some of the most significant differences between the two languages, especially those which may help explain the learner problems to be discussed in subsequent chapters. Areas of discussion include the language families that the two languages belong to, the use of topic in Chinese-Cantonese vs. the use of subject in English, the use and/or structures of English and Chinese-Cantonese verbs/verb phrases, nouns/noun phrases, adjectives/adjective phrases and prepositions, as well as the clause combining strategies in the two languages.

The English Language and the Chinese Language

English and Chinese are from typologically distant language families and share very few linguistic features in common. English is a Germanic language, alongside Danish, German and Swedish, within the Indo-European language family (Yule, 2017). Chinese, on the other hand, belongs to the Sino-Tibetan language family (Li & Thompson, 1981), to which languages such as Thai and Burmese also belong. Cantonese, being a dialect of Chinese and the mother tongue of most Cantonese speakers in Hong Kong and in the Guangdong area, is the most widely known and influential variety other than Mandarin, the official language of China. Cantonese is essentially a spoken language. The written form that educated Cantonese speakers use in most contexts is Standard Written Chinese, which is based on Mandarin. When written down, Cantonese is heavily affected by Standard Written Chinese. Written Cantonese also includes many exclusively Cantonese words and expressions, but many colloquial Cantonese words do not have a standard written form (Matthews & Yip, 2011).

In this book, the term *Chinese* refers to the standard language in China and its written form. The term *Cantonese* refers to the dialect and its spoken form,

DOI: 10.4324/9781003252498-2

including pronunciation. Because written Chinese used by native speakers of Cantonese is often a mixture of spoken Cantonese and Standard Written Chinese (Snow, 2004), the term *Chinese-Cantonese* is used in this book to refer to this special medium, including lexical items and constructions (phrases, clauses or sentences) written in Standard Written Chinese but read in spoken Cantonese (e.g. sentence (1)). The term is also used to refer to constructions containing lexical items which are exclusively Cantonese and used widely in spoken Cantonese but written in Cantonese characters (e.g. 屋企 (home) in sentence (2)), as well as constructions with a syntactic structure which is typically Cantonese (also sentence (2)).

(1) 我 回 家 吃 飯。
    ngo5 wui4 gaa1 hek3 faan6[1]
    I back home eat rice
    (I go home to have lunch/dinner.)

(2) 我 返 屋 企 食 飯。
    ngo5 faan1 uk1 kei2 sik6 faan6
    I back home eat rice
    (I go home to have lunch/dinner.)

Basic Sentence Constituents: English Subject vs. Chinese-Cantonese Topic

One major difference between English and Chinese is that the former is a subject-prominent language while the latter is a topic-prominent language (Li & Luk, 2017). In a subject-prominent language, the basic elements are the grammatical units of subject and predicate. The subject is an obligatory constituent. Omission of the subject in an English sentence which is not in the imperative mood[2] is unacceptable, as in example (3). When there is no notional subject, a dummy subject (e.g. *it*) is needed to fill the subject position, as in sentence (4).

(3)   *is raining.
(4)   **It** is cold.

In a topic-prominent language, the basic elements are the information units of topic and comment. The topic is the subject matter that a sentence talks about, and the comment is what the speaker/writer of the sentence says about the topic (Han, 2019). The topic also specifies the place, time or circumstances to which the rest of the sentence applies (Chafe, 1976; Matthews & Yip, 2011). Sentences (5) and (6) show some examples of Chinese-Cantonese sentences with a topic.

(5)   **這 些 電影** 我已經 看 過 了。
    this CL[3] movie I already see ASP[4] PRT[5]
    (I have already seen these movies.)

(6) 這　　本　　書　　內容　　很　　豐富 。
    this   CL   book   content   very   rich
    (The content of this book is very rich.)

The subject is not an obligatory constituent in a topic-prominent language like Chinese. There are many subject-less sentences in Chinese-Cantonese, and no pronoun corresponding to the English dummy subject is needed to fill the subject position, as in sentence (7).

(7) 下　　雨　　啦 。
    down rain PRT
    (It is raining.)

Within Chinese grammar, the subject-predicate construction is a special case of topic-comment, as the notion topic-comment includes the notion subject-predicate (Chao, 1968). The topic can be different from the subject and the two elements can co-exist in the same sentence (e.g. sentences (5) and (6)). In a sentence with no topicalized element, the subject is the topic by default (e.g. 媽媽 in sentence (8)).

(8) 媽媽　愛　　我 。
    mother love me
    (Mom loves me.)

English and Chinese-Cantonese Verbs/Verb Phrases

A number of differences in English and Chinese-Cantonese exist with regard to the use of verbs. The following sections will examine some of the major differences.

Finiteness and Nonfiniteness in English and Chinese-Cantonese

There are both finite and nonfinite verbs in English. Finite verbs carry a contrast in tense and may be marked for number and person agreement (e.g. *wants*, *went* and *am* in sentences (9–11)).

(9)   He **wants** a book.
(10) She **went** out.
(11) I **am** a girl.

The nonfinite forms of English verbs are infinitive with or without *to* (e.g. *to have* and *go* in sentences (12–13)), *-ing* participle (e.g. *taking* in sentence (14)) or past participle (e.g. *beaten* in sentence (15)).

(12) I want **to have** my lunch now.
(13) He let me **go**.

(14) She prefers **taking** a taxi.
(15) **Beaten** by his mom, the little boy feels desperate.

Chinese does not have overt morphological marking to systematically distinguish between finiteness and non-finiteness (Hu, Pan & Xu, 2001). Multiple verbs in a Chinese sentence can appear in the form of bare verbs without any morphological markers but with an optional aspect marker, such as 了 (perfective aspect) (Tang, 2020), as in sentences (16). These constructions with a chain of verbs are regarded as serial verb constructions in the literature (Li & Thompson, 1981).

(16) 他 **換**　　了　　衣服　**上**　班。
　　　he change ASP clothes up work
　　　(He got changed to go to work.)

Serial verb constructions with a number of verbs in the same sentence are not difficult to find, especially in spoken Cantonese (Li & Luk, 2017). Sentence (17) has a total of nine verbs.

(17) 我 **打算** 而家 **換**　　衫　　**落**　　樓　　買　餸　　返　　屋企
　　　I plan now change clothes down floor buy food back home
　　　煮　　飯　**食**　完　　**去返**　　工　。
　　　cook rice eat ASP　go return work
　　　(Now I plan to get changed and go down to buy food for cooking at home. After eating, I will go to work.)

It is ungrammatical to have two or more English finite verbs juxtaposed in the same sentence without any intervening marker such as a conjunction (e.g. sentence (18)). Therefore, in English, subjects or objects which are clauses have to be nonfinite clauses (e.g. *working late at night* and *being scolded by her parents* in sentences (19 and 20)).

(18) *He **changed** his clothes **went** to work. (cf. He changed his clothes *and* went to work).
(19) **Working late at night** results in lack of sleep.
(20) She hates **being scolded by her parents**.

On the other hand, in Chinese-Cantonese, the verb in a clausal/verbal subject or object is simply a bare verb (e.g.探望 (visit) and 吃 (eat) in sentences (21) and (22)).

(21) 你們 **探望**我 令　　我 十分 興奮。
　　　you　visit me make　me　very excited.
　　　(Your visiting me makes me very excited.)
(22) 我不 喜歡**吃** 早餐。
　　　I not like eat breakfast
　　　(I don't like eating breakfast.)

Tense vs. Aspect in English and Chinese-Cantonese

Some significant differences exist between the representation of temporal relations in English and Chinese-Cantonese. Of relevance are the concepts of tense and aspect.

Tense indicates the time when an event happens/happened. Under the grammatical category of tense, a basic distinction is made between absolute tense and relative tense. Absolute tense locates a process in time relative to the present moment (i.e. past, present or future), and relative tense further locates the process relative to the absolute tense. The reference point for relative tense is some point in time given by the context, which is not necessarily the present moment (Comrie, 1985). For example, the absolute and relative tenses for the English verb *have sent* (in a sentence such as *I have sent the parcel*) are present and past respectively. The past is in a sense viewed from the present and can be glossed as *past in the present*.[6] English marks every finite verb for absolute tense irrespective of whether the time orientation would be clear with or without a time adverbial (e.g. sentences (23) and (24) and sentence (25) respectively) (Lock, 1996).

(23) She **worked** till midnight yesterday. (Past tense)
(24) She **will come** tomorrow. (Future tense)
(25) She **works** in a factory. (Present tense)

Aspect refers to the different ways of viewing the internal structure of a situation. It has to do with how a process is viewed by the speaker (Brinton & Brinton, 2010; Comrie, 1976) instead of how the process is located in time. A process can be viewed as a whole or complete (e.g. perfective aspect) or not complete (e.g. progressive aspect). Chinese-Cantonese makes use of a number of aspect markers, such as 了 (perfective aspect; e.g. sentence (26)), 過 (experiential aspect; e.g. sentence (27)) and 在 (progressive aspect; e.g. sentence (28)).

(26) 我 看 **了** 一 部 電影。
      I   see ASP one CL movie
      (I saw a movie.)
(27) 我 做 **過** 老師。
      I   do ASP teacher
      (I was once a teacher.)
(28) 我**在** 做 功課。
      I ASP do homework
      (I am doing homework.)

Chinese-Cantonese lacks distinctions of tense, so the notions of past, present and future are not represented grammatically in the verb. Temporal relations are typically expressed by the use of time adverbials (e.g. 昨天 (yesterday), 以前 (before)) and/or aspect markers (e.g. 了, 過) (see sentences (29) and (30)).

(29) 我 **昨天** 看 **了** 一 部 電影。
     I yesterday see ASP one CL movie
     (I saw a movie yesterday.)

(30) 我 **以前** 做 **過** 老師。
     I   before do ASP teacher
     (I was once a teacher.)

Contextual factors also help express temporal relations (Matthews & Yip, 2011). Thus, time-sensitive information in Chinese-Cantonese can often be deduced from the context without the existence of time adverbials. For example, sentences (26) and (27) clearly indicate the past by the use of the aspect markers 了 and 過 without the need for using a time adverbial.

Passive Constructions in English and Chinese-Cantonese

Sentences with a transitive verb can be used in the active voice or in the passive voice. An essential typological difference between English and Chinese-Cantonese passive constructions lies in the fact that English passive is a derived voice which involves passivization, whereas Chinese-Cantonese passive is a pragmatic voice. There are two passive forms in English, the unmarked *be-* passive (*be* + past participle; e.g. sentence (31)) and the marked *get-*passive (*get* + past participle; e.g. sentence (32)). Although the *get-*passive is regarded as a marked choice, it is very commonly used in informal written genres (Xiao & McEnery, 2010). In an English passive sentence, the agent of the action can be expressed overtly (e.g. *his parents* in sentence (31)), but it can also be omitted (e.g. sentence (32)).

(31) The boy **was beaten** by his parents.

(32) My car **got stolen** a few days ago.

In Chinese-Cantonese, a wide range of devices is employed to express passive meanings. The most important passive marker is 被 (BEI), which can be used to mark passive constructions with or without an agent (e.g. sentences (33) and (34) respectively).

(33) 他 **被** 鄰居 殺 了。
     he BEI neighbour kill ASP
     (He was killed by his neighbour.)

(34) 他 **被** 殺 了。
     he BEI kill ASP
     (He was killed.)

The 被 passive is traditionally used for expressing adversity (Chappell, 1986).[7] To avoid using the passive in many cases, Chinese-Cantonese uses a topicalized structure with the object of a transitive verb (e.g. 書 (book) and 這件大衣 (this overcoat) in sentences (35) and (36) respectively) as the topic and the focus.

Although these topicalized structures are best translated with an English passive, it is unacceptable to use the 被 passive in such Chinese-Cantonese sentences, as in sentences (37) and (38).

(35) 書　　已經　　出版　　了。
book already publish ASP
(This book has already been published.)

(36) 這　件　大衣　　已經　　洗　　了。
this CL overcoat already wash ASP
(This overcoat has already been washed.)

(37) *這　件　大衣　　已經　　**被**　洗　　了。
this CL overcoat already BEI wash ASP
(This overcoat has already been washed.)

(38) *這　件　大衣　　已經　　**被**　她　洗　　了。
this CL overcoat already BEI she wash ASP
(This overcoat has already been washed by her.)

English and Chinese-Cantonese Noun Phrases

English and Chinese-Cantonese noun phrases also exhibit a number of differences, including the structures of determiners and post-modifiers.

English and Chinese-Cantonese Determiners

A typical English noun phrase consists of a head noun (e.g. *boys*). There are optional elements preceding and/or following the head noun. The first constituent of a noun phrase is, if present, a determiner, which introduces the noun phrase. In English, there are different kinds of determiners, of which articles, namely *a/an, the* and *ZERO* (no explicit article) are the most common (e.g. examples (39–42)). Other determiners include demonstratives (e.g. *this* in example (43)), possessives (e.g. *his* in example (44)) and others. Determiners are not the only constituents before the head noun. A head noun can also be pre-modified by other constituents such as an adjective phrase (e.g. *very beautiful* in example (45)) or a noun phrase (e.g. *glass* in example (46)), or by different combinations of both (e.g. example (47)), which, if present, come after the determiners.

(39) **a** boy
(40) **an** apple
(41) **the** boy
(42) **(ZERO)** boys
(43) **this** boy
(44) **his** books
(45) a **very beautiful** girl
(46) a **glass** container
(47) a **big glass** container

In Chinese-Cantonese, demonstratives (e.g. 這 (this), 那 (that)) serve to introduce a noun phrase, as in examples (48) and (49).

(48) 這　個　人
　　　this　CL　person
　　　(this person)
(49) 那　棵　樹
　　　that　CL　tree
　　　(that tree)

Articles and demonstratives are distinct grammatical items. Articles (in English only) can be used to show different types of references: generic reference (e.g. *the computer*, *(ZERO) dinosaurs* and *a computer* in sentences (50–52)), definite reference (e.g. *the bell* in sentence (53)), indefinite reference (e.g. *a boy* in sentence (54)). The same article (e.g. *the*) can be used to express different types of reference (e.g. sentence (50) vs. sentence (53)), and the same reference (e.g. generic) can be represented by different articles (e.g. *the*, *ZERO* and *a* in sentences (50–52)) (For more details about the English article system, see Chapter 5).

Generic Reference

(50) **The computer** is an advanced invention.
(51) **(ZERO) Dinosaurs** are extinct.
(52) **A computer** is an advanced invention.

Definite Reference

(53) He rang **the bell**.

Indefinite Reference

(54) **A boy** is coming.

Demonstratives (in English or in Chinese-Cantonese) serve a deictic function indicating the proximity of the referents (i.e. whether the referents are near or far), as in sentences (55–58).

(55) **This** book is mine. (referent is near)
(56) **That** book is mine. (referent is far)

(57) 這　件　大衣　　很　漂亮。 (referent is near)
　　　this　CL　overcoat　very　pretty
　　　(This overcoat is very pretty.)
(58) 那　件　大衣　　很　漂亮。 (referent is far)
　　　that　CL　overcoat　very　pretty
　　　(That overcoat is very pretty.)

Although demonstratives are often associated with definite reference and may have an anaphoric function comparable to the most common function of the English definite article *the* (Chan, 2004b), they do not show other types of references, such as generic reference. For example, *that computer* and 那 (頭) 獅子 (that lion) in sentences (59) and (60) can only have definite reference.

(59) ?**That computer** is an advanced invention.
(60) **那   (頭) 獅子** 什麼 都   吃。
      that CL lion   what also eat
      (That lion eats everything.)

The English definite article, on the other hand, does not show proximity like what demonstratives (in English or in Chinese-Cantonese) can do, as sentence (61) shows:

(61) **The** book is mine. (no proximity information)

Chinese-Cantonese Classifiers

In a Chinese-Cantonese noun phrase, there is another important constituent, known as the classifier (or measure word), before the head noun, such as 件 and 頭 in examples (57) and (60) shown earlier. Classifiers, which are based on distinctive features of shape, natural kind and function, perform the function of individuating entities (Matthews & Yip, 2011). Although it has been argued that Chinese classifiers are equivalent to the definite article (in English) (Cheng & Sybesma, 1999, 2005), counterarguments against that position exist (e.g. Wu & Bodomo, 2009): While determiners (such as the definite article) are functional morphemes devoid of semantic content, classifiers are contentful morphemes used to indicate the semantic classes of nouns and carry information beyond the information carried by their associated nouns (Zhang, 2007). There are, thus, no structural equivalents of English articles in Chinese-Cantonese.

English and Chinese-Cantonese Relative Structures

The differences between English and Chinese-Cantonese relative structures are worth mentioning in any discussion of English–Chinese-Cantonese contrastive grammar related to the structures of the noun phrase. The differences lie not only in the structure of the clauses but also in the position of the clauses. While English relative clauses (e.g. *who loves me* in example (62)) are post-modifying occurring after the head noun (e.g. *boy*), Chinese-Cantonese relative structures (e.g. 喜歡我 的 (who likes me) in example (63)) are pre-modifying occurring before the head noun (e.g. 人(person)). Most importantly, Chinese-Cantonese relative structures are typically realized by nominalizations, which may be formed by the addition of the nominalizer (NOM) 的 (or 嘅 in spoken Cantonese) to a clause (e.g. example (63)) or to an attributive adjective (e.g. example (64)).[8] Unlike English, which has a number of relative pronouns such as *which, who* and *whom* and relative adverbs such as *where*, Chinese-Cantonese does not have relative pronouns or relative adverbs.

(62) The boy **who loves me**
(63) 喜歡 我 的   人
     like   me NOM person
     (the person who likes me)
(64) 一   個 美麗   的   女孩子
     one CL beautiful NOM girl
     (a beautiful girl)

Because of the pre-modifying position, Chinese-Cantonese relative structures are essentially restrictive, which is an important difference between Chinese-Cantonese relative structures and English relative clauses, as the latter can be restrictive or non-restrictive. A restrictive relative clause (e.g. *who has just left* in sentence (65)) helps to restrict or define the head noun, whereas a non-restrictive relative clause (e.g. *who has just left* in sentence (66)) only gives additional information about the head noun.

(65) The girl **who has just left** is called Helen.
(66) The girl, **who has just left**, is called Helen.

In Chinese-Cantonese, it is acceptable to have a resumptive pronoun (e.g. 佢 (him)) in a pre-modifying relative structure to refer forward to the head noun (e.g. 同學 (coursemate) in sentence (67) and 朋友 (friend) in sentence (68)), especially in complex constructions where the resumptive pronoun is the object of a verb (e.g. 請 (invite) in example (67)) taking a complement clause (e.g. 食飯 (to have lunch)); or where the resumptive pronoun is the object of a preposition (e.g. 同 (with) in example (68)) (Matthews & Yip, 2011). Resumptive pronouns are more common in spoken Cantonese than in written Cantonese.

(67) 我 請   佢 食 飯   嘅   同學
     I   invite him eat lunch NOM coursemate
     (The coursemate whom I treated to lunch)
(68) 我 同   佢 睇 戲   嘅   朋友
     I   with him see movie NOM friend
     (The friend whom I saw a movie with)

On the other hand, resumptive pronouns are unacceptable in English, so constructions such as examples (69) and (70) are ungrammatical.

(69) *The boy **whom I love him**.
(70) *The boy **who he loves me**.

English and Chinese-Cantonese Adjectives/Adjective Phrases

In English, adjectives and verbs are two distinct categories. The distinction between adjectives and verbs in Chinese-Cantonese is, however, not categorical (Matthews & Yip, 2011). Many adjectives in Chinese-Cantonese can serve verbal functions. In traditional Chinese grammars, adjectives are classified as a subclass of verbs (e.g. Chao, 1968; Li & Thompson, 1981). Predicative adjectives[9] in Chinese-Cantonese, thus, do not require a verb, such as the copula.

Like verbs, Chinese-Cantonese adjectives can take aspect markers. Sentences (71) and (72), in which the predicative adjectives 瘦 (thin) and 漂亮 (pretty) are used, and sentence (73), in which the verb 看 (see) is used, demonstrate the similar syntactic behaviour of adjectives and verbs in this respect.

(71) 她　瘦　了。
　　 she thin ASP
　　 (She has become thin.)
(72) 她　曾經　**漂亮**　**過**。
　　 she once pretty ASP
　　 (She was once pretty.)
(73) 我　**看**　**了**　一　部　電影。
　　 I　see ASP one CL movie
　　 (I saw a movie.)

Like stative verbs,[10] Chinese-Cantonese adjectives can be pre-modified by intensifiers such as 很 (very) and 十分 (very), as in sentences (74) and (75) (cf. sentence (76)).

(74) 我　**很**　瘦 。
　　 I　very thin
　　 (I am very thin.)
(75) 她　**十分** 漂亮 。
　　 she very　pretty
　　 (She is very pretty.)
(76) 我　**很**　**喜歡** 你 。
　　 I　very like　you
　　 (I like you so much.)

Although English adjectives can also be used with most intensifiers in more or less the same ways as Chinese-Cantonese adjectives, there is a significant difference between the two languages with regard to the English intensifier *too* and the Chinese-Cantonese equivalent 太 (too): In English, *too* shows an unwanted excessive degree of meaning with a negative implication of *so [adj] that* the subject cannot/should not/does not perform the action denoted by the verb (Li & Chan, 2000), as in sentences (77) and (78).

(77) I am **too tired to walk**.
      (cf. I am so tired that I **cannot walk**.)
(78) He is **too busy to help you**.
      (cf. He is so busy that **he cannot help you**.)

In Chinese-Cantonese, 太 (too) is often used with adjectives or stative verbs to suggest a positive and high degree of meaning conveyed by the adjective (e.g. sentence (79)) or the verb (e.g. sentence (80)).

(79) 她　**太　漂亮**　了。
      she too pretty PRT
      (She is so pretty. She is very, very pretty.)
(80) 我　**太　喜歡**　你　了　。
      I   too like   you PRT
      (I like you so much. I like you very, very much.)

As far as comparisons of adjectives are concerned, in Chinese-Cantonese, the words 更 (*more*) and 最 (*best*) are typically added before an adjective for expressing comparatives and superlatives respectively, such as 更大 (*bigger*) in sentence (81) and 最大 (*biggest*) in sentence (82).

(81) 這　間　公司　　比　　　那　間　規模 **更　　大**。
      this CL company compare that CL scale more big
      (This company has a bigger scale than that one.)
(82) 他　年紀　**最　　大**。
      He age   most big
      (He is the oldest.)

English also uses the equivalents of Chinese-Cantonese words 更 (*more*) and 最 (*best*) for expressing comparatives and superlatives, as in sentences (83) and (84).

(83) Peter is **more handsome** than John.
(84) Peter is the **most handsome** guy.

However, for regular adjectives with one or two syllables, English typically uses the suffixes -*er* and -*est* to form comparatives and superlatives respectively (e.g. sentences (85) and (86)).

(85) Peter is **taller** than John.
(86) Peter is **the tallest**.

It is unacceptable to have *more* and -*er* or *most* and -*est* co-occur in the same English expression (e.g. sentences (87) and (88)).

(87) *Peter is **more taller** than John.
(88) *Peter is the **most tallest**.

English Prepositions and Chinese-Cantonese Coverbs

English prepositions have a relating function, establishing relations (e.g. of location, direction or time) between nominal units (e.g. noun phrases) and other units in the surrounding discourse (Downing, 2015), as can be seen in sentences (89–91).

(89) I am sitting **in** the room.
(90) I will meet you **at** 5 o'clock.
(91) Mary is watching a movie **with** John.

In Chinese-Cantonese, prepositions do not form a clearly distinct class of words. The ideas expressed by many English prepositions are instead expressed by verbs (Wang, 2020). The term *coverb* has been used in the literature to refer to such expressions (Li & Thompson, 1974). A coverb (e.g. 幫 (help/for) and 用 (use/with) in sentences (92) and (93)), as the name suggests, typically occurs with another verb (e.g. 做 (do) and 吃 (eat) in sentences (92) and (93)). Coverbs behave like verbs in many respects, so Chinese-Cantonese sentences with a coverb often resemble serial verb constructions. But coverbs also behave like prepositions, expressing spatial relations of location and direction, as well as non-spatial relationships such as time.

(92) 她　**幫**　我　**做**　飯。
　　　she help me do rice
　　　she for   me do rice
　　　(She helps me cook/She cooks for me.)
(93) 她　**用**　手　**吃**　飯。
　　　she use   hand eat rice
　　　she with hand eat rice
　　　(She uses her hand to eat/She eats with her hand.)

Clause Combining Strategies: Parataxis vs Hypotaxis

Another major difference between English and Chinese is their use of clause-combining strategies. English makes greater use of hypotaxis, while Chinese makes greater use of parataxis in combining clauses (Li & Luk, 2017). Hypotaxis is "the subordination of one proposition to another by use of subordinating conjunctions" (Kirkpatrick & Xu, 2012: 120), as in sentences (94) and (95).

(94) **If** you have any news, please inform me.
(95) **Because** it is raining heavily now, we won't go out today.

Parataxis is "the juxtaposition of clauses and propositions, both coordinate and subordinate, without the use of connectors" (Kirkpatrick & Xu, 2012: 119–120), as can be seen in sentences (96) and (97).

(96) 你　有　消息　通知　我　。
　　　you have news inform me.
　　　(If/When you have news, inform me.)

(97) 雨　太　大，　今天　不　出　去　了。
　　 rain too big　 today no out go PRT
　　 (Because the rain is too heavy, we won't go out today.)

In parataxis, the status of the two combined clauses is more symmetrical, and the use of double conjunctions (e.g. 因為 . . . 所以 (because . . . so); 雖然 . . . 但是 (although . . . but)) is acceptable, as in sentences (98) and (99)).

(98) 他 **因為**　遲　了　起床，**所以** 遲　了　出　門。
　　 he because late ASP up bed　so　 late ASP out door
　　 (Because he got up late, he went out late.)
(99) **雖然**　我很　窮，**但是** 我很　快樂。
　　 although I very poor but　I very happy
　　 (Although I am very poor, I am very happy.)

In English, on the other hand, the use of double conjunctions such as *because . . . so* or *although . . . but* is not acceptable, as in sentences (100) and (101).

(100) ***Because** he got up late, **so** he went out late.
(101) ***Although** I am very poor, **but** I am very happy.

Conclusion

"English and Chinese belong to two typologically different language families, and the typological distance between them is huge" (Li & Luk, 2017: x). Many structural disparities exist between the two languages. In this chapter, we have examined some of the major differences between English and Chinese-Cantonese grammars, including the basic sentence elements such as subject vs. topic and the structures of different phrases and clauses, as well as the use of different clause-combining strategies in the two languages. This chapter has not presented all the major differences between the two languages, nor has it presented all the characteristic syntactic features of either language: It has discussed only those elements that provide a solid foundation for understanding the rest of this book.[11] No attempt has been made to suggest that all grammatical problems which Cantonese ESL learners encounter can be attributed to the contrastive differences presented in this chapter (see Chapter 9), nor are the differences adequate in explaining all L1-related learner problems. However, a basic understanding of the major differences will facilitate our subsequent discussions. The next chapter will examine the major differences between English and Cantonese phonology.

Notes

1 The Chinese characters in sentences (1) and (2) are transliterated using the Jyutping system promoted by the Linguistic society of Hong Kong (Tang, Fan, Lee, Lun, Luke, Tung & Cheung, 2002) as a way of showing how the Chinese-Cantonese sentences are read in Cantonese. The number at the end of each transliterated Cantonese syllable is a tone mark indicating one of the six distinctive tones in Cantonese. (Some linguists

analyse Cantonese as having nine distinctive tones instead of six; see Chapter 3). For simplification purposes, no transliterations will be given for other sentences given in this chapter and in the rest of the book. Only Chinese characters will be given.

2 Examples of sentences in the imperative mood include *Open the door* and *Don't close the windows*. The subject in an imperative sentence is understood to be *you*, such as *You open the door* and *You don't close the windows*.

3 CL stands for classifier (see the section "Chinese-Cantonese Classifiers").

4 ASP stands for aspect marker (see the section "Tense vs. Aspect in English and Chinese-Cantonese").

5 PRT stands for particle. Chinese-Cantonese makes use of different particles, many of which are used at the end of a sentence as sentence final particles.

6 An alternative analysis of English tenses exists, which interprets verb forms such as *have gone* or *was doing* as realizing a combination of tense and aspect. For example, *have gone* is interpreted as present tense (*have*) + perfect aspect (*gone*) and *was doing* is interpreted as past tense (*was*) + progressive aspect (*doing*) (e.g. DeCapua, 2008; Ogihara, 1989) (see the discussion of aspect in the next paragraph).

7 Under the influence of the English passive, non-adversative use of 被 is becoming more widespread in Standard Written Chinese (Li & Luk, 2017).

8 Attributive adjectives are adjectives used as pre-modifiers of nouns, such as *beautiful* in *a beautiful girl*. Chinese "attributive adjective + 的" structures are often analysed as relative structures in the literature (e.g. Duanmu, 1998). In this book, Chinese-Cantonese "attributive adjective + 的/嘅" structures are also analysed as relative structures, although counterarguments against such an analysis exist (e.g. Waltraud, 2005).

9 Predicative adjectives are adjectives that are used as subject complements or object complements instead of as pre-modifiers of nouns, such as *beautiful* in *She is beautiful*, or *clever* in *I consider him clever*.

10 Stative verbs refer to a state or a condition which is not likely to change. Mental verbs such as liking or disliking are some examples of stative verbs.

11 Because of space limitation, only a simplified account of some select aspects of English and Chinese-Cantonese grammars and the differences between the two languages in those aspects have been presented in this chapter. For a more comprehensive account of English–Chinese contrastive grammar, see Li and Luk (2017); of English grammar, see Quirk, Greenbaum, Leech and Svartvik (1985); of Cantonese grammar, see Matthews and Yip (2011); and of Mandarin Chinese grammar, see Li and Thompson (1981).

3 English and Cantonese Phonology in Contrast

In this chapter, the English and Cantonese phonological systems will be discussed from a contrastive perspective. A lot of differences exist between the English and Cantonese phonological systems. At the segmental level, not only are the inventories of English and Cantonese phonemes different, but so are the ways of production. At the suprasegmental level, English and Cantonese have different rhythms and tone patterns. Both major differences between English and Cantonese at the segmental and suprasegmental levels will be reviewed in this chapter.[1]

In the discussion of phonology, it is important to first establish the dialect or accent in focus. English, as used in this chapter and the rest of the book when phonology is at issue, refers to Received Pronunciation (RP) English. RP English is the accent which is regarded as the standard for British English, and it is most often recommended for learners who want to learn British English (Roach, 2009). Cantonese, as discussed in Chapter 1, is the Chinese dialect widely spoken in Hong Kong and in the Guangdong area.

The English and Cantonese Consonant Systems

Consonants can be classified according to manner of articulation, place of articulation and the state of the glottis when the consonants are produced (Roach, 2009). There are 24 consonants in RP English and 19 consonants in Cantonese. Table 3.1 gives an overview of their places and manners of articulation.

Plosives/Stops

In both English and Cantonese, there are six plosive stops: bilabial plosives /p, b/, alveolar plosives /t, d/, and velar plosives /k, g/. In English, /p, t, k/ are voiceless, whereas /b, d, g/ are voiced. In Cantonese, however, there are no voiced plosives; all plosives are voiceless. The feature that distinguishes between /p, t, k/ and /b, d, g/ is aspiration, that is, "whether or not a burst of air is emitted immediately after oral release in the process of articulation" (Matthews & Yip, 2011: 19), where the former are aspirated and the latter are unaspirated.[2] Table 3.2 shows some examples of words with a plosive in word-initial position:[3]

DOI: 10.4324/9781003252498-3

Table 3.1 An overview of English and Cantonese consonants

Places of Articulation/ Manners of Articulation		Bilabial	Labio-dental	Dental	Alveolar	Palato-(Post) Alveolar	Palatal	Velar	Labio-Velar	Glottal
Plosives/Stops	E	p b			t d			k g		
	C	p b			t d			k g	kʷ gʷ	
Fricatives	E		f v	θ ð	s z	ʃ ʒ				h
	C		f		s					h
Affricates	E					tʃ dʒ				
	C				ts dz					
Nasals	E	m			n			ŋ		
	C	m			n			ŋ		
Lateral	E				l					
	C				l					
Approximants	E	w				r	j			
	C	w					j			

Table 3.2 Examples of words with a plosive in word-initial position

Plosives	English		Cantonese
/p/	pin	/pɪn/	怕 'frightened' /pa:/
/t/	ten	/ten/	他 'he' /ta:/
/k/	cold	/kəuld/	卡 'obstacle' /ka:/
/b/	bin	/bɪn/	爸 'father' /ba:/
/d/	den	/den/	打 'hit' /da:/
/g/	gold	/gəuld/	家 'family' /ga:/

Table 3.3 Examples of words with a plosive in word-final position

Plosives	English		Cantonese
/p/	rope	/rəup/	鴨 'duck' /a:p/
/t/	lit	/lɪt/	發 'prosper' /fa:t/
/k/	back	/bæk/	屋 'house' /uk/
/b/	robe	/rəub/	—
/d/	lid	/lɪd/	—
/g/	bag	/bæg/	—

In terms of distribution, all the plosives in English may occur in initial or final position of a syllable. In contrast, only /p, t, k/ in Cantonese may occur in syllable-final position, as illustrated in Table 3.3.

It should be noted that unlike plosives in English,[4] Cantonese plosives in word-final position are unreleased. For example, in the word 鴨 ('duck' /a:**p**/), the lips are closed in the formation of /p/ but not opened again, so no air can be released; in the word 發 ('prosper' /fa:**t**/), the tongue tip touches the alveolar ridge in the formation of /t/ but clings to the alveolar ridge without air being released; and in the word 屋 ('house' /u**k**/), the back of the tongue touches the velum in the formation of /k/ but remains there without air being released. Such an articulation, in effect, neutralizes the contrast between aspirated and unaspirated plosives, since unreleased plosives will not be aspirated.[5]

Cantonese has two other stops which do not exist in English, namely /kʷ, gʷ/. They are both voiceless labio-velar stops, with the former being aspirated and the latter unaspirated. They are coarticulated consonants because the velar sound /k/ or /g/ is articulated simultaneously with the bilabial /w/, that is, the back of the tongue is held against the velum for the production of /k/ or /g/, and at the same time the lips are rounded for the production of /w/.[6] Table 3.4 shows a minimal pair containing these two stops.

Fricatives

English makes much greater use of fricatives than Cantonese. There are nine fricatives in English but only three in Cantonese. The English fricatives are:

Table 3.4 Examples of words with a labio-velar stop

Labio-Velar Stops	Cantonese
/kʷ/	誇 'boast' /kʷaː/
/gʷ/	瓜 'melon' /gʷaː/

Table 3.5 Examples of words with a fricative in word-initial position

Fricatives	English		Cantonese
/f/	fan	/fæn/	花 'flower' /faː/
/v/	van	/væn/	—
/θ/	thin	/θɪn/	—
/ð/	this	/ðɪs/	—
/s/	sip	/sɪp/	沙 'sand' /saː/
/z/	zip	/zɪp/	—
/ʃ/	ship	/ʃɪp/	—
/ʒ/	genre	/ʒɑːnrə/	—
/h/	hat	/hæt/	蝦 'shrimp' /haː/

labio-dental /f, v/; dental /θ, ð/; alveolar /s, z/; palato-alveolar or post-alveolar /ʃ, ʒ/; and glottal /h/. Of these, /f, θ, s, ʃ, h/ are voiceless whereas /v, ð, z, ʒ/ are voiced. The Cantonese fricatives are: labio-dental /f/, alveolar /s/ and glottal /h/. Being all voiceless, they are articulated in ways very similar to their English counterparts. Since there are neither voiced fricatives nor dental and palato-alveolar fricatives in Cantonese, the inventory of Cantonese fricatives is much smaller than that of English.

In terms of distribution, all English fricatives may appear in syllable-initial position, though words which begin with /ʒ/ tend to be lexical borrowings from French (e.g. *genre* /ʒɑːnrə/). In syllable-final position, all English fricatives except /h/ can be found. By contrast, Cantonese fricatives may only occur in syllable-initial position. In other words, no Cantonese syllables end with a fricative. Table 3.5 shows some examples of words with a fricative in word-initial position.

Affricates

Both English and Cantonese have a pair of affricates. The English affricates /tʃ, dʒ/ are palato-alveolar, with the former being voiceless and the latter being voiced. Their production is characterized by lip-rounding. The Cantonese affricates /ts, dz/, in contrast, are alveolar and are characterized by lip-spreading. Like plosives in Cantonese, both Cantonese affricates are voiceless. The difference between the two is again one of aspiration, with the former being aspirated and the latter being unaspirated.

In terms of distribution, both English affricates may appear in syllable-initial and syllable-final positions, whereas the Cantonese affricates are restricted to the

Table 3.6 Examples of words with an affricate in word-initial position

Affricates	English	Cantonese
/tʃ/	church /tʃɜːtʃ/	—
/dʒ/	George /dʒɔːdʒ/	—
/ts/	—	叉 'fork' /tsaː/
/dz/	—	渣 'residue' /dzaː/

Table 3.7 Examples of words with a nasal in word-initial position

Nasals	English	Cantonese
/m/	mouse /maʊs/	媽 'mother' /maː/
/n/	nurse /nɜːs/	拿 'take' /naː/
/ŋ/	—	我 'I' /ŋɔ/

Table 3.8 Examples of words with a nasal in word-final position

Nasals	English	Cantonese
/m/	some /sʌm/	心 'heart' /sam/
/n/	son /sʌn/	新 'new' /san/
/ŋ/	sing /sɪŋ/	生 'life' /saŋ/

syllable-initial position. Table 3.6 shows some words in English and Cantonese beginning with an affricate.

Nasals and Lateral

Both English and Cantonese have three nasal consonants: bilabial /m/, alveolar /n/ and velar /ŋ/. The productions of the English nasals are very similar to those of the Cantonese nasals. All Cantonese nasals may appear in both syllable-initial and syllable-final positions, whereas the English velar nasal /ŋ/ cannot appear in syllable-initial position. Table 3.7 shows some examples of words with a nasal in word-initial position, and Table 3.8 shows some examples of words with a nasal in word-final position.

Only one lateral appears in both the English and Cantonese phonological systems, namely the voiced alveolar lateral /l/. In English, /l/ has two allophones in complementary distribution: the clear [l], which occurs before vowels (e.g. *live* /lɪv/), and the dark [ɫ], which occurs after vowels (e.g. *dull* /dʌl/). Clear [l] has a quality rather similar to that of an [i] vowel with the front of the tongue raised, while dark [ɫ] has a quality rather similar to that of an [u] vowel with the back of the tongue raised.[7] In Cantonese, however, only the pre-vocalic clear [l] exists: There is no dark [ɫ], as no laterals may occur in post-vocalic or syllable-final

Table 3.9 Examples of words with a lateral in word-initial or word-final position

Lateral	English	Cantonese
/l/	live /lɪv/ dull /dʌl/	來 'come' /lɔi/ —

Table 3.10 Examples of words with an approximant in word-initial position

Approximants	English	Cantonese
/r/	run /rʌn/	—
/j/	yes /jes/	也 'also' /jaː/
/w/	warm /wɔːm/	雲 'cloud' /wan/

position. Some examples showing the lateral in word-initial (in English and in Cantonese) or word-final position (only in English) are shown in Table 3.9.

There is a tendency for Cantonese speakers, especially younger ones, to substitute the clear [l] for an initial /n/ in a Cantonese word, thereby neutralizing their opposition. Thus, for example, the initial /n/ of 拿 ('take' /naː/) is often pronounced as [l], making [naː] and [laː] free variants of this lexical item. Such variations, however, rarely give rise to communication problems, as the intended meaning may usually be disambiguated by the context at large.

Approximants

There are three approximants in English: /r, j, w/. The post-alveolar approximant /r/ is formed by having the tongue approaching the alveolar area but not making contact with any part of the roof of the mouth. The palatal approximant /j/ and the bilabial approximant /w/ are also commonly known as semi-vowels, because the articulations of /j/ and /w/ are practically the same as those of the close front vowel /iː/ and the close back vowel /uː/ respectively, except that the approximants are very short. In Cantonese, /r/ does not exist, whereas /j/ and /w/ are articulated in much the same way as their English counterparts. A few words containing an approximant are shown in Table 3.10.

As can be seen from the preceding contrastive description, English and Cantonese consonants differ not only in their inventories but also in terms of their articulatory features and distribution within a syllable. In particular, English consonants are subject to relatively fewer distributional restrictions, whereas in Cantonese, only the nasals /m, n, ŋ/ and the plosives /p, t, k/ may occur in syllable-final position.

The English and Cantonese Vowel Systems

The previous section gave a brief overview of the differences between the English and Cantonese consonant systems. In this section, the differences between the English and Cantonese vowel systems will be discussed.

Pure Vowels

Vowels can be classified according to tongue height (i.e. whether the body of the tongue is high or low), frontness or backness of the vowel (i.e. whether the front or the back of the tongue is raised) and the shape of the mouth (i.e. whether the lips are rounded or spread) (Roach, 2009). There are 12 and 8 pure vowels in English and Cantonese respectively, including both short and long ones. The 12 English vowels comprise seven short vowels, /ɪ, e, æ, ʊ, ɒ, ʌ, ə/, and five long vowels, /iː, uː, ɔː, ɑː, ɜː/. Of these 12 vowels, the schwa /ə/ is by far the most frequent. The eight Cantonese vowels include /i, e, y, u, ɔ, œ, a, aː/, of which only /aː/ is long in contrast to /a/. Figures 3.1 and 3.2 give an overview of English and Cantonese vowels.

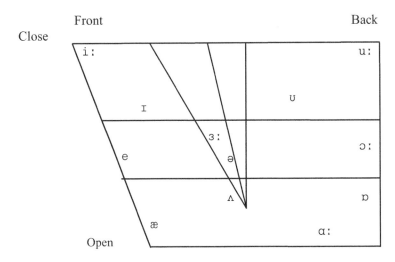

Figure 3.1 An overview of English vowels

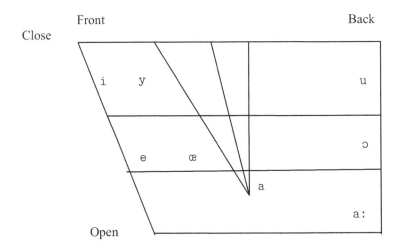

Figure 3.2 An overview of Cantonese vowels

English has two close front vowels, the long /iː/ and the short /ɪ/; two close back vowels, the long /uː/ and the short /ʊ/; and two open back vowels, the long /ɔː/ and the short /ɒ/. In contrast, Cantonese has only one close front vowel, /i/, one close back vowel, /u/, and one open back vowel, /ɔ/,[8] all of which lie somewhere between the respective long and short vowel pairs in English.

The English /e/ and /æ/ are rather similar in articulation, except that the former is less open than the latter. In Cantonese, however, there is only /e/, which is similar to the English /e/, with the mouth not widely open. The English central vowel /ɜː/, which is articulated with neutral lip position, has a similar counterpart in Cantonese, /œ/, which is articulated with lip-rounding. The English vowels /ʌ/ and /ɑː/ are similar in articulation to the Cantonese /a/ and /aː/ respectively, in that the English /ʌ/ and the Cantonese /a/ are both centralized vowels, while the English /ɑː/ and the Cantonese /aː/ are both back vowels.

It should be noted that although there are only eight vowel phonemes in Cantonese, there are altogether 13 vowel allophones.[9] The vowels /i/, /e/, /œ/, /u/ and /ɔ/ all have long and short allophones depending on the contexts in which they appear. For example, the two allophones of /i/ are [iː] and [ɪ] respectively. The former occurs before labials and alveolars such as /m/, /p/, /n/ or /t/, while the latter occurs before velars such as /ŋ/ or /k/. The two allophones of /u/, [uː] and [ʊ] occur before alveolars such as /n/ or /t/ and velars such as /ŋ/ or /k/ respectively. The long and short allophones of /ɔ/, namely [ɔː] and [o], occur before alveolars and velars such as /n/, /ŋ/ and /k/, and before labial semivowels, namely /w/, respectively. Tables 3.11 and 3.12 show some examples of words with different vowels as the peak, and Table 3.13 shows the phonological environments for the allophones of Cantonese /i, u, ɔ/.

Diphthongs

Diphthongs are "sounds which consist of a movement or glide from one vowel to another" (Roach, 2009: 17). There are eight diphthongs in English: /ɪə, eə, ʊə,

Table 3.11 Examples of words with different English vowels

/ɪ/	/e/	/æ/	/ʊ/	/ɒ/	/ʌ/	/ə/	/iː/	/uː/	/ɔː/	/ɑː/	/ɜː/
sit	bed	bad	foot	cot	cup	about	seat	food	caught	car	bird
/sɪt/	/bed/	/bæd/	/fʊt/	/kɒt/	/kʌp/	/əbaut/	/siːt/	/fuːd/	/kɔːt/	/kɑː/	/bɜːd/

Table 3.12 Examples of words with different Cantonese vowels

/i/	/e/	/y/	/u/	/ɔ/	/œ/	/a/	/aː/
絲	靚	書	夫	落	唱	新	山
'silk'	'pretty'	'book'	'husband'	'descend'	'sing'	'new'	'hill'
/si/	/leŋ/	/sy/	/fu/	/lɔk/	/tsœŋ/	/san/	/saːn/

Table 3.13 Phonological environments for the allophones of Cantonese /i, u, ɔ/ (Chan, 2012: 17)

Environments Phonemes/ Allophones	Before Velars	Before Alveolars	Before Labials	Before Labial Semi-Vowel /w/
/i/	[ɪ]	[iː]	[iː]	
/u/	[ʊ]	[uː]		
/ɔ/	[ɔː]	[ɔː]		[o]

Table 3.14 Examples of words with different English diphthongs

/ɪə/	/eə/	/ʊə/	/eɪ/	/aɪ/	/ɔɪ/	/aʊ/	/əʊ/
peer /pɪə/	pear /peə/	poor /pʊə/	bay /beɪ/	buy /baɪ/	boy /bɔɪ/	cow /kaʊ/	go /gəʊ/

Table 3.15 Examples of words with different Cantonese diphthongs

/ei/	/ai/	/aːi/	/ɔi/	/ui/	/au/	/aːu/	/iu/	/ou/	/œy/
四 'four' /sei/	西 'west' /sai/	乖 'well-behaved' /gʷaːi/	菜 'vegetable' /tsɔi/	杯 'cup' /bui/	夠 'enough' /gau/	教 'teach' /gaːu/	跳 'jump' /tiu/	好 'good' /hou/	水 'water' /sœy/

eɪ, aɪ, ɔɪ, aʊ, əʊ/, and ten diphthongs in Cantonese: /ei, ai, aːi, ɔi, ui, au, aːu, iu, ou, œy/. In both English and Cantonese, the second element of a diphthong denotes the direction towards which the tongue moves, but the tongue seldom reaches the position specified by the second element.

There are three possible final elements for diphthongs in both languages. In English, the three elements are /ə, ɪ, ʊ/. Since /ə/ is a central vowel and /ɪ/ and /ʊ/ are close vowels, diphthongs gliding towards /ə/ are termed "centring diphthongs" while those gliding towards /ɪ/ or /ʊ/ are termed "closing diphthongs". For Cantonese diphthongs, the three possible final elements are /i, u, y/.[10] Tables 3.14 and 3.15 illustrate some words containing the diphthongs under discussion.

Another significant difference between English and Cantonese is that Cantonese diphthongs are not followed by any of the final consonants /m, n, ŋ, p, t, k/, whereas English diphthongs can be followed by many different final consonants.

The English and Cantonese Syllable Structures

English has a relatively complex syllable structure. There can be a maximum of three consonants before a vowel and a maximum of four consonants after a vowel (Abercrombie, 1967), viz.:

(C) (C) (C) V (C) (C) (C) (C)

Table 3.16 Examples of words showing all possible configurations of C and V in Cantonese

Syllable structures	Examples
V	/ɔ/ 哦 'exclamation showing surprise'
CV	/fu/ 夫 'husband'
VC	/aːn/ 晏 'late'
CVC	/faːt/ 發 'prosper'

One such example is *strengths* /strɛŋkθs/.[11] The syllable structure of Cantonese, in contrast, is rather simple: The possible combinations of sounds are severely restricted (Bauer, 1995). Unlike English, there are no consonant clusters in Cantonese. The maximal syllable structure is as follows:

(C) V (C)

Thus, in terms of possible configurations of V and C, English clearly outnumbers Cantonese, the latter being limited to V, CV, VC, and CVC as exemplified in Table 3.16.

The English and Cantonese Tones

Cantonese is a tone language. This means that "every morpheme-word unit in its citation form has a lexical tonal pattern" (Fok Chan, 1974: 1). In addition, tones are distinctive in Cantonese: a change in tone will result in a change in lexical meaning. The Cantonese dialect is well known for being relatively rich in tones. According to the traditional Chinese classification system, there are a total of nine basic tones in Cantonese. The first six tones (tones 1–6) capture words ending with no consonants or with any of the three nasal consonants /m, n, ŋ/, whereas the last three tones (tones 7–9, also known as "entering tones") capture words ending with the unreleased plosives /p, t, k/.

More recent works on Cantonese phonology, however, regard tones 7, 8 and 9 as carrying the same tone (or distinctive pitch level) as those of the three level tones 1, 3 and 6 respectively. Seen from this perspective, Cantonese is analysed as having six instead of nine tones (e.g. Matthews & Yip, 2011; Zhang & Zhang, 1987). Table 3.17 shows some examples of words with different tone levels and their tone contours.

Unlike Cantonese, English is an intonation language. This means that a change in tone will not result in a change of lexical meaning (Roach, 2009), but it may show a difference in attitude. For example, saying the word *yes* with a fall-rise tone may show limited agreement or response with reservations, while a rise-fall tone may signal rather strong feelings of approval and a level tone tends to indicate a feeling of boredom.

Since every syllable in a Chinese-Cantonese sentence carries a tone, a sentence with five syllables such as 他是男孩子 /taː si   naːm   haːi   dzi/ ('He is a boy') has five independent tones, and each word is regarded as an

Table 3.17 Examples of Cantonese words with different tone levels

Tone Levels	Tone Contours	Examples	Tone Levels	Tone Contours	Examples
1	high-level	/si1/ 絲 'silk'	7	high-level	/sik1/ (/sik7/) 色 'colour'
2	high-rising	/si2/ 史 'history'			
3	mid-level	/si3/ 試 'try'	8	mid-level	/sek3/ (/sek8/) 錫 'kiss'
4	low-falling	/si4/ 時 'time'			
5	low-rising	/si5/ 市 'market'			
6	low-level	/si6/ 事 'thing'	9	low-level	/sik6/ (/sik9/) 食 'eat'

independently variable item (Roach, 2009). In English, on the other hand, tones can only be identified on one prominent syllable in a tone group, which can be as short as a monosyllabic word or as long as a phrase or even a whole sentence. The whole tone group has only one tone, or more precisely, one intonation pattern. For example, in the sentence *He is a diligent student*, there is only one tone group – the whole sentence itself – so there can be only one syllable which carries the tone, and the tone will probably fall on the first syllable of the word *diligent* or *student*, depending on the speaker's intended meaning.

The English and Cantonese Rhythmic Patterns

English has stress-timed rhythm. This implies that stressed syllables will tend to occur at relatively regular intervals whether they are separated by unstressed syllables or not. All the unstressed syllables that come between stressed ones have to be squeezed into the allotted time (Forbes, 1993). Cantonese, in contrast, has syllable-timed rhythm. This means that all syllables, whether stressed or unstressed, tend to occur at regular intervals. Thus, in English, unstressed syllables will be spoken much faster and shorter when compared with stressed syllables, whereas in Cantonese, there is practically no reduction in terms of vowel length during the pronunciation of each syllable. For example, in the English word *international*, only the first and third syllables (the underlined ones) are stressed, while the unstressed syllables are weaker and spoken faster. In contrast, in the corresponding Cantonese expression 國際 /gʷɔk dzai/, the two syllables are spoken with more or less equal duration.

Words in Connected Speech

Weak Forms

Many English words have both a strong and a weak form. These words are called *function words* – words that do not have a dictionary meaning in the way that we normally expect nouns, verbs, adjectives or adverbs to have. These function words include auxiliary verbs (e.g. *have*, *is*), prepositions (e.g. *of*, *from*), conjunctions

Table 3.18 Common English function words and their strong and weak forms

Function Words	*the*	*a, an*	*and*	*but*
Strong forms	/ðiː/	/eɪ/ and /æn/ respectively	/ænd/	/bʌt/
Weak forms	/ðə/ before consonants /ðɪ/ before vowels	/ə/ before consonants /ən/ before vowels	/ən/	/bət/

(e.g. *and*, *but*), and the like. Table 3.18 contains some English function words which exhibit strong and weak forms.

When spoken in isolation, function words are normally pronounced in their strong forms. In connected speech, these words tend to be spoken in their weak forms. This phenomenon of reducing the pronunciations of function words to their weak forms in connected speech has no parallel in Cantonese.

Linkage

In English connected speech, words are sometimes linked together. This often happens when two vowels occur next to each other across word boundaries. A "linking r" is often introduced for this purpose. For example, the words *four* and *far* do not have an /r/ sound when they are spoken in isolation in RP English,[12] but when they occur before another word which begins with a vowel, an [r] is introduced to link the two words together, for example, *four eggs* [fɔːregz] and *far away* [fɑːrəweɪ].

In English, if two words are in the same tone group and the first ends with a consonant while the second begins with a vowel, the consonant is simply carried forward to the next syllable. Thus, the preferred pronunciation pattern of the phrase *pick it up* should be [pɪkɪtʌp]. In contrast, neither of these linking phenomena is found in Cantonese.

Conclusion

This chapter provided a discussion of the major differences between the RP English and Cantonese phonological systems. It can be seen that English and Cantonese differ not only in their phonemic inventories but also in the characteristics of the sounds, the distributions of phonemes, and the permissible syllable structures and rhythms. These differences are important in understanding and explaining the most common speech production and perception difficulties encountered by Cantonese ESL learners (see Chapters 7 and 8).

Notes

1 All the materials included in this chapter except the introductory paragraphs and the conclusion are reproduced from Chan and Li (2000) (visit www.tandfonline.com), with some slight adaptations to ensure smooth integration of the reproduced materials into

the current chapter. Some modifications and additions are also made to ensure comprehensiveness and recency of information.

2 Because no Cantonese plosives are distinctively voiced, some linguists prefer to use the symbols /pʰ, tʰ, kʰ/ to represent the aspirated plosives /p, t, k/ and preserve the symbols /p, t, k/ to represent the unaspirated plosives /b, d, g/ (e.g. Bauer & Benedict, 1997; Lee, 1976).

3 Since the cognitively salient phonetic unit in all Han-Chinese varieties is a syllable, which often but not always has morphemic status, this unit is variously referred to as "syllabo-morpheme" or "morpho-syllable". Put another way, a Cantonese syllable has more than a chance probability of being a word, but it may also be sub-morphemic. For the sake of convenience, in this chapter we will give illustrations of Cantonese syllables which have morphemic status wherever possible (cf. Bauer, 1995; DeFrancis, 1984, 1989).

4 The production of English plosives is characterized by three phases. The first is the closing phase, when the articulators (e.g. the upper lip and the lower lip for the production of /p/) move together to form an obstruction. The second is the hold phase, when air is compressed, and the third is the release phase, when the articulators (e.g. the two lips) move apart to allow air to escape (Gimson & Ramsaran, 1989). All the three phases are obligatory when an English plosive is in initial position. Final singleton plosives in English isolated words are also normally, though not obligatorily, released.

5 English word-final plosives tend to be unreleased in many dialects, so the voiced/voiceless distinction is not clear either (see Chapter 7).

6 There is some disagreement as to whether /kʷ/ and /gʷ/ should be analysed as consonant phonemes or consonant clusters. In this chapter, they are treated as unitary consonants since they are coarticulated sounds with simultaneous articulation at both the velar and the labial regions. These two sounds are sometimes classified as semi-vowels instead of stops (e.g. Fok Chan, 1974) because they consist of the semi-vowel /w/.

7 [i] and [u] are primary cardinal vowels instead of vowels of a particular language. [i] is defined as "the vowel which is as close and as front as it is possible to make a vowel without obstructing the flow of air enough to produce friction noise", while [u] is "fully close and back" (Roach, 2009: 13).

8 Strictly speaking, the English /ɔː/ and the Cantonese /ɔ/ are not open vowels, as they lie between the half-open and half-close regions. In this chapter they are treated as open vowels to facilitate discussion.

9 The description of Cantonese vowels has received different treatments because there is more than one way of analysing vowel contrasts. Alternative analyses reduce the number of vowel phonemes to seven (e.g. Chao, 1947). Others argue that there should be 14 vowel allophones instead of 13 (e.g. Zee, 1993).

10 The description of Cantonese diphthongs has also received different treatments. Some linguists (e.g. Bauer & Benedict, 1997) argue that they comprise a nuclear vowel followed by either /y/ or one of the final approximants /w, j/, so they are not described as sequences of two vowels as diphthongs in English are. In this chapter Cantonese diphthongs are treated as sequences of two vowels (cf. Fok, 1974).

11 Depending on the speaker, the words *strength* and *strengths* may be pronounced with or without the /k/ sound before /θ/.

12 In American English and some accents of British English (known as rhotic accents), words like "four" and "far" are pronounced with /r/ at the end.

4 Learner Problems in the Acquisition of English Grammar I: Interlingual Errors

In Chapter 2, some similarities and differences between English and Chinese-Cantonese grammar were presented. In this chapter and Chapters 5 and 6, we will examine Cantonese ESL learners' problems in their acquisition of English grammar. As argued in Chapter 1, it is more than expected that learners make errors in their process of acquiring a second language. Errors should not be viewed negatively, as they are often indicative of a learner's interlanguage. We can understand learners' acquisition of English by analysing their interlanguage output, as interlanguage is a learner's developing second language knowledge. It may have features which are characteristic of the learner's first language, features which are characteristic of the second language, as well as those which have some general characteristics that tend to occur in all or most interlanguage systems (Lightbown & Spada, 2021). Although some learner errors may be seen as solely L1- or solely L2-related, many are the results of a complex interplay between L1- and L2-related factors (Li & Chan, 1999). Errors which can be seen as a result of L1 interference are termed interlingual errors. On the other hand, intralingual errors are due to the language being learned and are independent of the L1 (Gass, Behney & Plonsky, 2013). These errors reflect general characteristics of rule learning, including inaccurate generalization of rules, inappropriate or incomplete application of rules (Richards, 1971).

A number of research studies have been carried out to investigate the kinds of grammatical errors made by Cantonese ESL learners (e.g. Budge, 1989; Chan, 2000, 2003, 2004a, 2004b, 2004c, 2004d, 2006a, 2010c; 2017a, 2017b, 2019a, 2019b, 2022; Chan, Kwan & Li, 2002a, 2002b, 2003; Chan & Li, 2002; Chan, Li & Kwan, 2003; Gisborne, 2002; Green, 1991; Kwan, Chan & Li, 2003; Li & Chan, 1999, 2000, 2001; Webster & Lam, 1991; Webster, Ward & Craig, 1987; Yip & Matthews, 1991; Yu & Atkinson, 1988a, 1988b). This chapter will give a thorough analysis of the kinds of common interlingual errors made by Cantonese ESL learners. All the example errors presented in this chapter, except otherwise stated and acknowledged, come from unpublished data of Chan (2010c).[1]

Lexical Level

It has been observed that L1 interference is at work at all the lexical, syntactic and discoursal levels with speakers of different proficiency levels (Chan, 2010c).

DOI: 10.4324/9781003252498-4

Interlingual errors at the lexical level are not prevalent among Cantonese ESL learners. Only a few error types have been identified. These errors are regarded as errors at the lexical level because the items affected are just individual lexical items and may have no direct impact on the syntactic patterns of the sentences they are in. Although lexical errors are far from being ubiquitous, the effects of L1 transfer are easily noticeable.[2]

Inaccurate Directionality

Errors with inaccurate directionality (e.g. sentence (1)) are characterized by an inappropriate substitution of an English word for another English word where the Chinese-Cantonese equivalent of the target English word and that of the English substitute share the same Chinese-Cantonese character.

(1)   *I borrowed money from my friends and **borrowed** the money to him. (cf. lent) (Chan, 2010c: 301)

If translated to Chinese-Cantonese, sentence (1) will read:

(2)   我 問 朋友 **借**　　錢　 並 **借** 錢　　 給 他。
　　 I   ask friend borrow money and lend money to him
　　 (I borrowed some money to my friend and lent him some money.)

As can be seen from sentence (2), the Chinese-Cantonese equivalent 借 of the English substitute *borrow* and that of the target English word *lend* share the same character with no indication of the directionality of the actions involved (Chan, 2010c), so irrespective of whether the agent of the action is the payer or the payee, the same Chinese-Cantonese word is used. On the other hand, the English words *borrow* and *lend* are converse antonyms (or relational opposites) expressing a converse meaning of each other, i.e. if X *lends* money to Y, then Y *borrows* money from X, or vice versa (Yule, 2017).

Although this kind of inaccurate directionality problems are limited to individual lexical items and are more common among elementary learners, proficient learners may also sometimes make similar slips of the tongue in speaking.

Synonym Confusion

Synonymy is a relationship about "sameness of meaning". However, it is well known that strict synonymy does not exist (Yule, 2017), so two words which are synonyms or near-synonyms of each other are not interchangeable in all possible contexts, and contexts often exist in which one lexical item is appropriate whereas its (near) synonyms may not be appropriate (Jackson & Amvela, 2007). Learners may not be able to differentiate the differences in usage between a pair of (near) synonyms and the contexts in which either should be used. When the L1 equivalents of these English synonyms or near-synonyms share the same Chinese-Cantonese words, learners' confusion will be compounded.

Take the English words *fight* and *hit* as an example. While the two words have some common semantic features (e.g. both involve some violent physical actions), it is doubtful whether they are synonyms of each other and whether they are interchangeable or substitutable, as the former typically denotes a two-way reciprocal action involving more than one entity, whereas the latter typically denotes a one-way action. However, they share the same Chinese-Cantonese translation 打 (or have 打 as a constituent character of the corresponding Chinese-Cantonese translation, as in 打架 (fight)). By the same token, the English synonyms *study* and *learn* also share the same Chinese-Cantonese translation 學習, although the two English words are by no means interchangeable in all contexts. Errors showing such synonym confusion can be seen as results of L1 influence, as demonstrated in sentences (3–5)).

(3)   *But my mother have not **fight** me, and very kind with me. (cf. hit)
(4)   *I very very afraid, because I afraid my mother **fight** but she not **fight** me. (cf. hit)
(5)   *Moreover, she send me to **study** piano seeing that **studying** piano is a long-term investment. (cf. learn)

Synonym confusion may appear similar to inaccurate directionality, given that an inappropriate English word is used to substitute for a target English word which has the same Chinese-Cantonese translation as the English substitute. In effect, this error type is different from inaccurate directionality, because the two English lexical items are not converse antonyms with opposite directionality. On the contrary, the target word and its substitute are often (near) synonyms of each other in English.

Vocabulary Compensation

The third type of lexical interlingual errors can be termed vocabulary compensation, as can be illustrated in sentences (6–8).

(6)   *They **found** the money to me. (cf. earned)
(7)   *Then my brother is **let** me. (cf. compromise with)
(8)   *She is so **nervous** me and she is so tried to cook the lunch, the dinner and do the housework. (cf. concerned about)

In this type of vocabulary compensation errors, some form of lexical relation between the substitutes and the target words is apparent, but the lexical relation holds only in Chinese-Cantonese. In English, the substitutes and the target words (word groups) are two unrelated words with very different meanings and usage. For example, in sentence (6), the English substitute *found* and the target word *earned* do not share any common meanings. The pairs of English words (word groups) *let* and *compromise* in sentence (7) and *nervous* and *concerned about* in sentence (8) do not mean the same either. However, the Chinese-Cantonese equivalents of each of these pairs of words share the same character or share at least one same character, i.e. 搵 for *found* and 搵錢 for *earned,* 讓 for both *let* and *compromise,* 緊張 for both *nervous* and *concerned about.* Though sharing the same written form, these Chinese-Cantonese word pairs have very different meanings, so they should be regarded as homographs instead of synonyms. Given the diverse meanings of these pairs of words in both English and Chinese-Cantonese, the extent of L1 influence is apparent: In order to compensate for their inability to use an appropriate L2 lexical item (e.g. *compromise*) for expressing a certain intended meaning, learners simply use another L2 vocabulary item (e.g. *let*) which shares the same L1 character (e.g. 讓) as the intended L2 word on the basis of an inappropriate L1-to-L2 direct word translation.

Syntactic Level

Interlingual errors at the syntactic level are prevalent. They are regarded as syntactic because the erroneous items span more than one word, affecting constituents larger than individual words, such as within a certain phrase, or across different constituents of a clause/sentence.

Be + *Base Form*

The *be + base form* error is a very common interlingual error made by Cantonese ESL learners at the syntactic level. This error type is characterized by the co-existence of the verb *be* with the base form of the main verb (e.g. *use, need* and *exist* in sentences (9–11)), with or without an intervening adverb in between (e.g. *still* in sentence (11)).

(9)   *The police and postmen **are use** machines to work.
(10) *Every student **is need** to face the HKCEE.
(11) *There are no land transports in Hong Kong in 2047 but the MTR **is** still **exist**.

This error can be seen as a result of L1 interference. In Chinese-Cantonese, it is common to use the verb 是 (is)[3] as a marker of special affirmation, linking the two major constituents of a sentence, typically the subject and the object of the main verb, to mean "it is true that" (Li & Thompson, 1981) (see sentences (12) and (13), which are the idiomatic Chinese-Cantonese translations of sentences (9) and (10)). The Chinese-Cantonese 是 structure is also commonly found in clauses/sentences without an object, such as the second clause in sentence (14).

(12) 警員   和 郵差   **是用** 機器   工作 的。
      policeman and postman is use machine work PRT
      (Policemen and postmen use machines for their work.)
(13) 每   個 學生   都 **是 需要** 面對 中學會考 的。
      every CL student all is need face HKCEE PRT
      (Every student needs to do HKCEE.)

(14) 2047 年　香港　　　　沒　有　　陸路　運輸，　　　　但　港鐵　**是**
仍然**存在**　的。
2047 year Hong Kong   no have land   transportation but MTR is
still exist   PRT
(There will be no land transportation in Hong Kong in 2047, but the MTR
will still exist.)

Be + -ed/-en

Other than the inappropriate use of *be + base* form, *be* is also often misused with
the past or past participle form of the main verb (e.g. sentences (15–17)).

(15)   *The young children **was** in the park **played** the society service.
(16)   *I was a happy child. Because my father and mother **were** very **loved** me.
They look after me carefully.
(17)   *And I **was grown up** under her influences.

For these errors, it is not clear whether the form of the verb after *be* is the past form
or the past participle form when the verb concerned has identical past and past participle forms (e.g. the past and past participle forms of *play* are both *played*, and the
past and past participle forms of *love* are both *loved*). It is sometimes also unclear
why the *-ed* (or *-en*) form is used instead of the base form (cf. *be + base form* earlier)
(Chan, 2010c). L1 interference is arguably one major cause of the error, also because
of the customary use of 是 (*is*) in Chinese-Cantonese for special affirmation (Chinese-
Cantonese translations of sentences (15–17)) omitted to avoid redundancy).

Calquing

Calquing (also known as loan-translation) is a type of borrowing (a word-formation
process) where each morpheme of a word or each word of a word group in the
source language is translated into the equivalent morpheme or word in the borrowing language (Richards & Schmidt, 2010). The English phrase *the moment
of truth* is believed to be an example of a calque from the Spanish expression
el momento de la verdad, and the Chinese 男朋友 can be seen as an example of
a calque from the English word *boyfriend* (Yule, 2017). The individual words/
morphemes in the borrowing language semantically match the individual words/
morphemes in the source language.

Calquing is a technique commonly employed by Cantonese ESL learners, especially elementary ones, in their construction of English sentences. Constituents
affected are not necessarily limited to individual words but may often span different phrases or even clauses (e.g. sentences (18–20)).

(18)   *My teacher often **said me very strong**.
(19)   * It is because **no they no me**.
(20)   * **From Hong Kong fly to America just need** 15 minutes and the rocket is
more safe.

Sentences (21–23) are probably the Chinese-Cantonese sentences from which sentences (18–20) come.

(21)　我的　老師　　常常　**說　我　很　　堅強**。
　　　my　teacher　often　say　I　very　strong
　　　(My teacher often said that I was very strong.)
(22)　那　是　因為　**沒　有　他們　沒　有　我**。
　　　that　is　because　no　have　they　no　have　I
　　　(It is because I wouldn't have been born without them.)
(23)　**從　　香港　　　飛　往　美國　　只　需**　15　分鐘，....。
　　　from　Hong Kong　fly　to　America　just　need　15　minute ...
　　　(It only takes 15 minutes to fly to America from Hong Kong, ...)

Inappropriate calques can sometimes be difficult to understand. Sentence (24), which is apparently a direct translation of sentence (25), is a good example.

(24)　*That dog was **father in my birthday for mine**.
(25)　那　隻　狗　是　**父親　在我　生日　　給　　我　的**。
　　　that　CL　dog　is　father　in me　birthday　give/for me　PRT
　　　(That dog was given to me by my father on my birthday.)

Because 給 is a coverb (cf. Chapter 2) in Chinese-Cantonese and can be used as a verb (meaning *give*) or a preposition (meaning *for*), and the combination 我 + 的 can express *me + PRT* or *mine*, the inappropriate calque *for + mine*, together with the inappropriate placement of the adverbial *in my birthday*, has rendered the structure (and probably meaning) of the resultant English sentence opaque.

Double Correlatives/Conjunctions

In Chapter 2, we saw the characteristic use of parataxis in Chinese-Cantonese and the acceptability of using double conjunctions, such as 因為 ... 所以 (because ... so) or 雖然 ... 但是 (although ... but) in the same Chinese-Cantonese sentence. Learner errors with the redundant use of both an English subordinating conjunction and an English coordinating conjunction, such as *although* and *but* in sentences (26) and (27), are very common. Occasionally, words other than conjunctions, such as adverbs functioning as connectives (e.g. *therefore* in sentence (28)) may be inappropriately used in place of one of the target English conjunctions.

(26)　***Although** you can see your partner is look like through telephone, **but** you cannot meet him or her.
(27)　***Although** she always shouts at me and cleans my flat, **but** I also feel that she is treat me very good.
(28)　***Because** my family is very poor at that time, **therefore** four member lived in a small room at the flat.

Duplicated Comparatives or Superlatives

As discussed in Chapter 2, English adjectives with three syllables or more require the addition of *more* and *most* before them for showing comparatives and superlatives respectively (e.g. *more beautiful, most beautiful*), but those with one or two syllables typically have -*er* and -*est* added to express the same concepts (e.g. *happier, happiest*). Chinese-Cantonese also uses the words 更 (more) and 最 (best) before an adjective to express the same concepts. The following learner errors, with *more* and *most* added before comparatives and superlatives respectively, are very common (sentences (29–31)).

(29) *I think that dog is **more better** than dinosaurs.
(30) *It's because China is not well-developed and the privilege of the people is **much more lower** than HK locals.
(31) *This is the **most unhappiest** event in my life.

Although the corresponding Chinese-Cantonese sentences (32–34) do not have duplicated comparatives and superlatives, the need to add an extra lexical item in front of an adjective for expressing comparatives and superlatives in both English and Chinese-Cantonese may have resulted in learners' overgeneralization of using *more* or *most* with English adjectives which are already in their comparative or superlative forms due to a (false) resemblance between the two languages.

(32) 我　認為　狗　比　　　恐龍　　**更**　**好**。
　　　I　think　dog　compare　dinosaur　more　good
　　　(I think dogs are better than dinosaurs.)
(33) 人民　的　　特權　　　比　　　香港　　　　本地　人　**更**　**低**。
　　　people POSS[4] privilege compare Hong Kong local man more low
　　　(The privilege of the people is much lower than that of HK locals.)
(34) 這　是　我　一　生　**最**　**不快樂**　的　　一　件　事。
　　　this is I one life most unhappy NOM one CL thing
　　　(This is the most unhappy event in my life.)

Incorrect Order of Adverbs

Incorrect order of adverbs is exemplified in the following examples, where an adverb, such as *very*, is placed immediately before a verb, such as *enjoy, love* or *care* (sentences (35–37)).

(35) *I like play basketball, so I **very enjoy** it.
(36) *I **very love** the food.
(37) *She **very care** my brother and me.

In English, an adverb is typically used to modify a verb, an adjective or another adverb. Although it is acceptable for an adverb functioning as a sentential adverbial to appear before a verb, as in *I **usually** do my homework in the evening*, it is not acceptable to use an intensifier, such as *very*, immediately before a verb to modify it. On the other hand, in Chinese-Cantonese, the intensifiers 很 (very) or 非常 (very) can be used not only before predicative adjectives (e.g. 很有用 (very useful), as in sentence (38)) but also before verbs (e.g. 很喜愛 (very enjoy), 非常喜歡 (very love), 非常關心 (very care) in sentences (39–41)) to intensify the degree of feelings denoted by the verbs. Direct translation from the L1 to the L2 in learners' production of English sentences with an intensifier pre-modifying a verb is, thus, evident.

(38) 這　本　書　**很**　**有用**。
　　　 this CL book very useful
　　　 (This book is very useful.)

(39) 我喜歡打 籃球，　　所以我**很**　**喜愛**它 。
　　　 I　 like hit basketball so　I very enjoy it
　　　 (I like playing basketball, so I enjoy it very much.)

(40) 我　**非常**　**喜歡**　這　些　食物。
　　　 I　 very love　 this CL food
　　　 (I love the food very much.)

(41) 她　**非常**　**關心**　我的　兄弟　 和　我。
　　　 She very care　 my　 brother and me
　　　 (She cares for my brother and me a lot.)

Independent Clause as Subject or Object/Complement

The independent clause as subject or object/complement structure is characterized by the use of a finite, independent clause (e.g. *I can't get better marks*) as the subject (e.g. sentences (42–44)) or object/complement of a sentence (e.g. sentences (45–47)), resulting in a series of finite verbs in the same sentence (see the section "Serial Verb Constructions" later in this chapter).

As Subject:

(42) *__I can't got better marks__ make her disappoint.
(43) *__She do this thing__ is my most important thing in my life.
(44) *__They only eat a little sweet__ is O.K.

As Object/Complement:

(45) *In 2047, we have to celebrate __Hong Kong return to China for 50 years__.
(46) *The main difference was __the Legco have full of elected member__ when compare before in 1985 was none of them.
(47) *So overlapping the membership in the two councils could be a reason to explain __the relationship between Exco and Legco was harmonious before 1985__.

The structures of the erroneous sentences can be traceable to Chinese-Cantonese grammar. In Chinese-Cantonese, it is acceptable to have the first verb phrase/ clause of a sentence be the subject of the whole sentence without any change in the form of the first verb or the use of a complementizer comparable to the English *that* (e.g. sentence (48)). It is also acceptable to have the second verb phrase/ clause of a sentence be the object/complement of the whole sentence without the use of any intervening constituents (e.g. a conjunction) or a change in the form of the second verb (e.g. sentences (49)) (see Chapter 2). L1 interference is again evident.

(48) 我 不能 得 到 更 好 的 分數 令 她 失望。
     I   cannot obtain arrive more good NOM marks make her disappointed
     (That I can't get better marks makes her disappointed.)
(49) 在 2047, 我們 必須 慶祝 香港 回歸 中國 五十 年。
     in 2047 we   have to celebrate Hong Kong return China 50   years
     (In 2047, we have to celebrate the fact that Hong Kong has returned to China for 50 years.)

In-*Prepositional Phrases*

Prepositional phrases in English are often used as adjuncts for denoting the place, the time, etc., under which an event occurs. However, prepositional phrases are not the only choice for denoting such circumstantial information. Noun phrases and adverbs are also very common, such as *twelve years ago* and *yesterday*. For these adjuncts, Cantonese ESL learners have a tendency to use an unwanted preposition, typically *in*, to introduce the phrases, resulting in erroneous *in*-prepositional phrases such as **in twelve years ago, in every Tuesday, in long ago* as in sentences (50–52).

(50) ***In twelve years ago**, I was one year old.
(51) ***In every Tuesday**, he and I always go to practise badminton.
(52) ***In long ago**, I remembered to my mother very young.

Although the Chinese-Cantonese equivalents of the above *in*-prepositional phrases do not obligatorily require the presence of a preposition, it is acceptable to add 在 (in), a general-purpose marker of location or time in Chinese-Cantonese, to introduce the sentences. The erroneous English structures are thus traceable to their Chinese-Cantonese equivalents (sentences (53–55)).

(53) (在) 十二 年 前, 我 一 歲。
     in   twelve years ago I one year
     (I was one year old twelve years ago.)
(54) (在) 每 個 星期二, 他 和 我 時常 去 練習 羽毛球。
     in   every CL Tuesday he and I always go practice badminton
     (He and I practise badminton every Tuesday.)

(55) **(在) 很　久　以前,**　我　記得　　我母親　很　年輕。
in　very　long　ago　I　remember　I mother　very　young
(I remember my mom was very young a long time ago.)

The preposition *in* is also sometimes mistakenly chosen to introduce prepositional phrases which should better be introduced by other prepositions, such as *on, at* or *during*, as in sentences (56–58).

(56)　*In that day**, I was very happy. (cf. On that day, . . .)
(57)　*In one summer holiday**, I go to uncle home and stay here in one week (cf. During one summer holiday, . . .)
(58)　*In that time**, my mother should help my father to do the farming work. (cf. At that time, . . .)

Again 在, as a general-purpose marker of location or time, is the default choice for the corresponding Chinese-Cantonese prepositional phrases, as in examples (59–61)).

(59)　**(在)**那 天,　. . .。
in that　day . . .
(On that day, . . .),
(60)　**在**　一　個　暑假　　　裡,　. . .。
in　one　CL　summer holiday　in　　. . .
(During one summer holiday, . . .),
(61)　**(在)**那　時,　. . .　。
in that　time　. . .
(At that time, . . .).

The prevalence of the use of 在 in Chinese-Cantonese prepositional phrases is, thus, one major probable cause of erroneous *in*-prepositional phrases.

Misuse of Until/Till

The English word *until/till* is a commonly misused word. According to the *Collins Advanced English Dictionary* online, if something happens until a particular time, it happens during the period before that time and stops at that time (https://www.collinsdictionary.com/dictionary/english/until). On the other hand, if *until* is used with a negative, it emphasizes the moment in time after which the rest of the statement becomes true (Quirk, Greenbaum, Leech & Svartvik, 1985), as in the following sentences.

(62)　We will wait **till Peter arrives**.
(63)　We won't leave **until the rain stops**.

In sentence (62), the action of waiting continues and will stop at the time when Peter arrives. In sentence (63), the action of leaving will be actualized only when the rain stops. Before the rain stops, the action of leaving won't happen.

The use of *until/till* is sometimes not consistent even among native speakers. For example, in sentence (64), whether the specified date (23 October) is included in the leave period is sometimes controversial. According to the canonical use of the word, the specified date should not be within the leave period, so 23 October should be the date when the person involved has to resume duty. However, it is not uncommon to see the use of similar sentences to include the specified date in the leave period even by native speakers.[5]

(64) I will be on leave **until 23 October**.

The Chinese-Cantonese equivalents of *until/till*, namely 直到/直至, have a different usage. They are often used to emphasize the truth of the preceding or following statement at the time of speaking/writing, including the time denoted by the phrases/clauses that follow (Chan, 2003). Expressions such as 現在 (now), 永遠 (forever) are very commonly used in association with 直到/直至 for emphatic or confirmatory purposes, as in sentences (65) and (66).

(65) 我會　愛　　你，　　**直到　永遠**。
　　　I will love you   until   forever
　　　(I will love you forever.)
(66) 我　**直到　現在**　都　不　知道　他們的　關係。
　　　I   until now   all no know their   relationship
　　　(I still don't know their relationship now.)

Cantonese ESL learners often misuse English *until/till* in their English output (e.g. sentences (67–69)), as if the words share the same usage of their Chinese-Cantonese counterparts 直到/直至.

(67) *Some of friends communicated **until now**.
(68) *Of course I know there are many other people are important to me, but I'm sure the most important person is my father, **until forever**.
(69) ***Until I recovered**, then she relaxed.

Omission of Copula

Despite the prevalent use of sentences with a redundant *be* in *be* + base form and *be* + *-ed/-en* sentences for affirmative purposes (see earlier in this chapter), erroneous copulative clauses missing the verb *be* are also very common (e.g. sentences (70–72), especially when the clauses have a modal verb, such as *will* or *can*.

(70) *If I ^ **sick,** they **will** ^ very nervous.
(71) *We **will** ^ very busy to do some housework.
(72) *The cars **will** ^ beautiful and big.

Mother tongue interference is probably a major cause of this error, as in Chinese-Cantonese, the verb 是 (*is*) does not co-occur with many auxiliary verbs, such as 能 (*can*) or 會 (*will*) (Li & Thompson, 1981).

(73) 如果 我生病 了，   他們 **會**   非常 緊張。
      if   I sick PRT they will very nervous
      (If I am ill, they will be very worried.)

The fact that adjectives behave very much like verbs in Chinese-Cantonese may also be a probable reason for learners' omission of the copula. As discussed in Chapter 2, Chinese-Cantonese sentences with a predicative adjective do not require the use of the copula. Erroneous sentences with the copula omitted as seen previously may be due to the influence of such syntactic behaviour of Chinese-Cantonese adjectives.

Omission of Subject

The omission of subject problem is often found in complex or compound sentences where both the subordinate and main clauses (for complex sentences) or both the coordinated clauses (for compound sentences) share the same subject and the subject is already present in one of the clauses (e.g. sentences 74–76)).

(74) *When I was playing, ^ **always hurt myself careless**.
(75) *Every time I eat the breakfast, ^ **just feel warm in my heart**.
(76) *She always said ^ **hate me**.

Mother-tongue interference is evident in this kind of error. As discussed in Chapter 2, Chinese-Cantonese is characterized by topic-prominence whereas English is characterized by subject-prominence. It is acceptable for a Chinese-Cantonese sentence/clause to have no subject if the subject can be understood from the immediate context or can be identified from other clauses in the same discourse (Matthews & Yip, 2011). Although it is acceptable to use a co-referential pronoun for the co-referential subject, the pronoun is not obligatory (Li & Thompson, 1981). The Chinese-Cantonese translations of sentences (74–76) show that the subject can be omitted without affecting grammaticality or understanding (sentences (77–79)).

(77) 當   我 玩   的   時候，   **時常   不小心   傷害** 自己。
      when I play NOM time   always careless hurt   myself
      (Whenever I play, I hurt myself carelessly.)
(78) 每   次   我 吃 早餐，   **確實   感 到   心   裡 溫暖**。
      every time I eat breakfast indeed feel arrive in   warm
      (Every time when I have my breakfast, I am touched.)

(79) 她　時常　說　**恨　我**。
she always say hate me
(She always says she hates me.)

Pseudo-Tough Movement Structures

The pseudo-tough movement structure, which is characterized by the use of a tough adjective in an inappropriate context (Yip, 1995), has been regarded as a high-frequency erroneous structure for Cantonese ESL learners (Li & Chan, 1999). In this error, a tough adjective (e.g. *convenient*, *difficult* and *easy* as in sentences (80–82)) is inappropriately used to refer to the degree of facility or potentiality at which the subject (e.g. *people*, *you* and *this stage*) performs the action denoted by the verb in the *to + V* structure that follows (e.g. *to buy things or get informations*, *to see a countryside* and *to receive bad things*).

(80) *People are **more convenient to buy things or get informations from the website**.
(81) *You are **difficult to see a countryside** after forty-seven years.
(82) *This stage is **very easy to receive bad things**.

The Chinese-Cantonese equivalents of these three pseudo-tough movement structures are not only acceptable but also very common (sentence (83)), especially in spoken Cantonese (sentences (84) and (85)). L1 transfer is evident.

(83) 人們　更　方便　　購買 東西 或 從　網站　獲取 資訊。
people more convenient buy thing or from website get information
(It is more convenient for people to buy things or to get information from the web.)
(84) 四十七　　年　後，你 好 難　　見 到　　鄉村。
forty-seven years after you very difficult see arrive countryside
(It is very difficult for you to see the countryside in 47 years.)
(85) 呢　個 階段 好 容易 收　到　唔好 嘅　嘢。
this CL stage very easy receive arrive no good NOM thing
(It is very easy to receive bad things at this stage.)

Pseudo-Passives and Under-Generation of Passives

Pseudo-passives are erroneous sentences with a theme subject followed by a transitive verb in its active form. These sentences are regarded as pseudo-passives because the intended, canonical English structures are passive sentences (Yip, 1995). Sentences (86–88) are some examples.

(86) *But the sea in Hong Kong, and KLN, will not be there again. Because in 2020 **the people numbers can't control** (cf. can't be controlled).

(87) *I realized that **my best friends couldn't promote** to Form 6. (cf. couldn't be promoted).

(88) ***Her role** is very important and **cannot replace** to anyone else (cf. cannot be replaced).

As discussed in Chapter 2, English requires a distinct verb form (*be/get* + past participle) for showing passives, whereas Chinese-Cantonese does not require different forms of the verbs. There are many Chinese-Cantonese passive constructions without the explicit passive marker (被 (by)). The pseudo-passive is, thus, "a direct transfer of an L1 topic-comment structure with null subject" (Han, 2000: 91) and reflects the Chinese typological characteristic of topic-prominence. Sentences (89–91) demonstrate the effects of L1 transfer.

(89) ... 因為　　在 2020 年，　人民　　數目　**無　法　　控制**。
　　　 ... because in 2020 year people number no method control
　　　 (. . . because the number of people cannot be controlled in 2020.)

(90) 我 意識　到　　我 最　好　的　　朋友 **不能 升　　讀**　中六。
　　　 I　 realize arrive I　most good NOM friend cannot promote read F.6
　　　 (I realized that my best friend could not be promoted to F.6.)

(91) 她的　角色 非常 重要，　　　**不能　取代**。
　　　 her　role　very　important cannot replace
　　　 (Her role is so important that it cannot be replaced.)

Because learners fail to generate the full range of English passive constructions, pseudo-passive errors are also seen as cases of under-generation of the target passive (Yip, 1995).

The Somewhere Has Something *Problem*

The *somewhere has something* problem, which should have been expressed as *there* + *be* existential structures, is characterized by the use of a subject noun phrase (e.g. *the table, Mong Kok* in sentences (92) and (93)) indicating the location where something is found. The verb *have* is typically used as the main verb in such structures (Chan, Kwan & Li, 2002b).

(92) ***The table has** a lot of books.

(93) ***Mong Kok has** a lot of rubbish.

Alternatively, an adverbial of place (typically realized by a prepositional phrase, such as *in the park* in sentence (94)), is inappropriately used in the subject position as if the adverbial functions as the subject of the sentence (see the earlier section "*In*-Prepositional Phrases").

(94) ***In the park has** many children.

The Chinese-Cantonese equivalents (sentences (95–97)), with the subject realized by a phrase with or without 在 (in) indicating the location, as well as the use of the possessive verb 有 (have), are not only grammatical but also common, illustrating the effects of L1 interference on the *somewhere has something* problem.

(95) **桌子 上 有**　很多　書。
       table top have many books
       (There are many books on the table.)
(96) **旺角**　　**有**　很多　垃圾。
       Mongkok have many rubbish
       (There is a lot of rubbish in Mong Kok.)
(97) **在公園 裡**　　**有**　很多　孩子。
       in park   inside have many children
       (There are a lot of children in the park.)

The Too + Adj + to VP *Structure*

The following interlingual errors involving the use of *too + adj + to VP* (verb phrase)[6] in English are very common among Cantonese ESL learners.

(98) ?I am **too happy to see you**.
(99) ?He is **too excited to have a chance to meet the Chief Executive**.

To many Cantonese ESL learners, the *too + adj + to VP* structure functions in the same way as its Chinese-Cantonese counterpart, suggesting a positive and high degree of meaning conveyed by the adjective (e.g. *too happy* vs. *very very happy; too excited* vs. *very very excited*). Learners are often not aware that the adjectives in the corresponding *too + adj + to VP* English structures show an unwanted excessive degree of meaning with a negative implication of *so adj that . . . cannot/ should not/do not VP* (Li & Chan, 2000) (see Chapter 2).

It should be noted that Cantonese ESL learners' interlanguage output such as sentences (98) and (99) may not be grammatically incorrect but can be just semantically opaque. It is unclear whether the writer/speaker wants to convey an excessive degree of meaning in line with the negative implications expected of the canonical *too + adj + to VP* English structure, or whether a positive and intense meaning conveyed by the adjective corresponding to the Chinese-Cantonese use of the structure, is intended. Irrespective of the intended meanings, the influence of the L1 on such L2 output is also apparent.

There + Have *Existential Structures*

There + have existential structures are characterized by the misuse of the verb *have* for the target verb *be* in expressing an existential or presentative function (Chan, Kwan & Li, 2002a), as in sentences (100) and (101).

(100) ***There will have** many trees, birds, and some animals.
(101) ***There will not have** any paper.

L1 transfer is apparent, as the existential meaning is expressed by the verb 有 in Chinese-Cantonese, which can be literally translated to *have* in English (sentences (102) and (103)).

(102) **那裡 會 有**　許多　樹木，　鳥類　和　一些　動物。
　　　　there will have many trees　　birds and some animals
　　　　(There will be many trees and birds and some animals.)
(103) **那裡 會 沒 有**　任何　紙張。
　　　　there will no have any　　paper
　　　　(There won't be any paper.)

This kind of *there + have* existential structures are also commonly found in sentences with an *in*-prepositional phrase denoting the location, as in sentences (104–106).

(104) *In every place, **there will have** a computer.
(105) *In Disneyland, **there have** anything to play and anything to eat.
(106) *In the swimming pool **there have** many toy here so I want to play this.

Although the Chinese-Cantonese translations of sentences (104–106) do not require the word 那裡 (there) to co-exist with the verb *have* in the main clause (see the "*Somewhere Has Something* Problem" section), L1 interference is still one major cause of the error as evidenced by learners' customary use of *there + have* for expressing an existential function. It may be argued that the *somewhere has something* problem and the *there + have* existential structures are variant manifestations of L1 interference on Cantonese ESL learners' production of English existential sentences.

Transitivity Pattern Confusion

There are many pairs of English and corresponding Chinese-Cantonese verbs which differ in their transitivity patterns. Cantonese ESL learners who model their use of English verbs on the transitivity patterns of the corresponding Chinese-Cantonese equivalents often make transitivity pattern errors, where an English transitive verb is inappropriately used with the direct object embedded in a prepositional phrase (e.g. sentences (107–109)), or where an English intransitive verb is inappropriately followed by a direct object (e.g. sentences (110–112)).

(107) *When I was doing my homework, Peter **telephone to me**.
(108) *She decided to **divorce with him**.
(109) *I tried doing my best to **contact with my schoolmate**.
(110) *We always smile when we **listen the funny things**.

(111) * When I **arrived the Museum**, I paid the fee by using computer outside the door.

(112) * She has never **complained this thing**.

The effects of L1 transfer can be seen from the translations of the verbs in question: the transitive verbs *telephone*, *divorce* and *contact* are all intransitive in Chinese-Cantonese (examples (113–115)), whereas the intransitive verbs *listen*, *arrive* and *complain* are all transitive in Chinese-Cantonese (examples (116–118)).

(113) . . . ,   彼得 **致電**   **給** 我。
　　　　 . . .   Peter telephone to   me
　　　　 (. . . Peter telephoned me.)

(114) 她   決定 **和**   他   **離婚**。
　　　　 she decide with him divorce
　　　　 (She decided to divorce him.)

(115) . . . **與**   我的 同學   **聯繫**。
　　　　 . . . with my   coursemate contact
　　　　 (. . . to contact my coursemates.)

(116) . . . **聽**   有趣 的   事情。
　　　　 . . . listen funny NOM thing
　　　　 (. . . listen to funny things.)

(117) 當   我 **到達** 博物館   , . . .
　　　　 when I   arrive   museum
　　　　 (When I arrive at the museum, . . .)

(118) 她   從來 沒 有 **投訴**   這   件   事。
　　　　 she ever no have complain this CL thing
　　　　 (She has never complained about this.)

Serial Verb Constructions

Serial verb constructions are characterized by the incorrect use of two or more finite verbs/verb clauses juxtaposed in the same English sentence/clause without any intervening markers such as a conjunction (e.g. *and, when*). The clauses juxtaposed in the same sentence normally share the same subject (e.g. sentences (119–121)).

(119) *I remember I broke a vase and **play balls broke the windows**.

(120) *When I play this toy I cut my finger, so **my brother** punish me, and **bring me go home**.

(121) *When **they finish homework use computer send it** to their teacher.

As discussed in Chapter 2, in Chinese-Cantonese, there is no distinction between finite and nonfinite verbs, and serial verb constructions without any intervening markers are very common. The erroneous English sentences with a chain of finite verbs resemble, to a certain extent, such acceptable constructions in Chinese-Cantonese (Chinese-Cantonese translations of erroneous sentences omitted).

Discoursal Level

Interlingual errors at the discoursal level can be defined as errors related to how learners combine sentences or clauses into a broader text. They are also associated with learners' misuse of "expressions within a text to refer to some portion of the discourse containing that text" (Chan, 2010c: 309). Like errors at the lexical level, discoursal-level interlingual errors are not ubiquitous. Two particular types of errors are worth mentioning: one has to do with the misuse of the connective *on the contrary*, and the other is known as periphrastic-topic constructions.

Misuse of "On the Contrary"

Cantonese ESL learners, including advanced learners, tend to misuse the connective *on the contrary* when making a contrast between the previous portion of a text/discourse and the subsequent portion of the text/discourse, as in examples (122) and (123).

(122) *Tim is very fat. **On the contrary**, his brother is very thin.
(123) *John is a very diligent student. **On the contrary**, Mary is very lazy.

Learners are often unaware that *on the contrary* should be used when we have just said that something is not true and are going to say that the opposite is true (https://www.collinsdictionary.com/dictionary/english/on-the-contrary), as in examples (124) and (125).

(124) It is not expensive. **On the contrary**, it is very cheap.
(125) Mary is not ugly. **On the contrary**, she is very pretty.

The effects of L1 transfer are apparent: The Chinese-Cantonese dictionary definition of *contrary* is 相反地, which fits into the context of the corresponding Chinese-Cantonese translations (examples (126) and (127)). Learners may thus be misled into thinking that the English connective *on the contrary* is functionally synonymous with the target connectives, such as *in contrast* or *by contrast* (Chan & Li, 2002).

(126) 蒂姆很　胖。　**相反地，**　他的　哥哥　　很　　瘦。
   Tim very fat contrary his brother very thin
   (Tim is very fat. By contrast, his brother is very thin.)
(127) 約翰是　　一　個　非常　　勤奮　　的　　學生。**相反地**，
   John is one CL very diligent NOM student contrary
   瑪麗很　　懶。
   Mary very lazy
   (John is a very diligent student. In contrast, Mary is very lazy.)

Errors with the misuse of *on the contrary* are not limited to the connection between two sentences or two clauses. Sometimes the connective is wrongly used to connect two paragraphs or even elements larger than single paragraphs.

Periphrastic-Topic Constructions

According to Yip (1995), periphrastic-topic constructions are constructions with a topic-comment structure where a subject noun phrase or pronoun is redundantly used to repeat a fronted topic. For example, the topics *my father* and *parents who have their own emotional sickness* in sentences (128) and (129) are unnecessarily repeated by the pronouns *he* and *they*, which refer to the same entities as the entities denoted by the respective topics. In sentence (130), on the other hand, the topic *Social Welfare Chief* is embedded in a fronted adverbial beginning with *according to*. The topic is redundantly repeated by the subject *Mr. Leung* in the main clause.

(128) *But **my father he** always get my mother's money and go out every day.
(129) ***Parents who have their own emotional sickness, they** will express their sickness or transmit it to their children.
(130) ***According to Social Welfare Chief, Mr. Leung** said that Hong Kong's elderly population is set to "double" to 1.62 million by 2011, there will be "14 elderly people out of every 100".[7]

As discussed in Chapter 2, topic-comment structures are very common in Chinese-Cantonese. The corresponding Chinese-Cantonese translations (examples (131) and (132)) both contain acceptable topic-comment structures, thus inviting verbatim transfer of the Chinese-Cantonese constructions to the English realizations and resulting in the erroneous sentences (128–129) (Kwan, Chan & Li, 2003).

(131) 但是 **我 父親 他** 總是 拿 我 媽媽的 錢,
       but   I   father he always take I   mother's money
       每   天 出去。
       every day go out
       (But my father always takes my mother's money and goes out every day.)
(132) **自己 有 情緒   病   的   父母**, **他們** 會 表達
       self have emotional illness NOM parents they will express
       他們的 . . . 。
       their   . . .
       (Parents who have emotional problems will express their . . .)

The written Chinese-Cantonese translation of sentence (130) with a topic-comment structure may, however, not be idiomatic, but the spoken Cantonese translation also typically contains a topic-comment structure, providing evidence for the effects of L1 interference, as can be seen in example (133).

(133) 根據   **社會福利總署 署長   梁生**   佢   話   呢,
       香港   嘅   長者   人口 . . . 。
       according to Social Welfare Chief Leung Mr he   said PRT
       Hong Kong POSS elderly population
       (According to Mr. Leung, Chief of Social Welfare, the elderly population in Hong Kong . . .)

Table 4.1 A taxonomy of interlingual errors

	Lexical Level	*Syntactic Level*	*Discoursal Level*
Error Types	• Inaccurate directionality • Synonym confusion • Vocabulary compensation	• *Be* + base form • *Be* + *-ed/-en* • Calquing • Double correlatives/conjunctions • Duplicated comparatives or superlatives • Incorrect order of adverbs • Independent clause as subject or object/complement • *In*-prepositional phrases • Misuse of *until/till* • Omission of copula • Omission of subject • Pseudo-tough movement structures • Pseudo-passives and under-generation of passives • The *somewhere has something* problem • The *too + adj + to VP* structure • *There + have* existential structures • Transitivity pattern confusion • Serial verb constructions	• Misuse of *on the contrary* • Periphrastic-topic constructions

A Taxonomy of Interlingual Errors Made by Cantonese ESL Learners

Table 4.1 summarizes the different kinds of interlingual errors that have been discussed in this chapter.

Conclusion

In this chapter, we have examined some common interlingual errors made by Cantonese ESL learners. The list is not meant to be exhaustive, but it has captured many of the most common errors. It is evident from the analyses that L1 interference is at work in learners' production of written (and spoken) output, spanning all the lexical, syntactic and discoursal levels. However, L1 transfer is not necessarily the only source of problems for the interlingual errors discussed in this chapter. Non-L1-related factors may also be at work. For example, the incorrect order of adverbs, the independent clause as subject or object/complement problem, the *somewhere has something* problem, the pseudo-tough movement structure, and the *there + have* existential structure have all been explained in the literature as having a trace of L2-related influence, such as learners' inadequate knowledge of the L2 system and overgeneralization (e.g. Chan, Kwan & Li, 2002a, 2002b, 2003; Chan & Li, 2002; Chan, Li & Kwan, 2003). L1-related and L2-related factors often interact intricately, and in our discussions of interlingual errors, it is undesirable to isolate other probable L2-related causes from L1-related causes (see Chapter 9 for a detailed discussion about the interplay between L1-related and non-L1-related factors). In the following two chapters, errors which are largely non-L1-related will be discussed.

Notes

1 All of the error types discussed in this chapter, except the *somewhere has something* problem, the *too + adj + to VP* structure and the misuse of *on the contrary* problem, have been briefly discussed in Chan (2010c). These three errors are included in this chapter alongside all the other errors because they are also seen as results of L1 interference and are findings of the author's other research studies (with her collaborators).
2 The sequence of errors discussed in this chapter (at each of lexical, syntactic and discoursal levels) follows alphabetical order, not error prevalence.
3 The corresponding verb in spoken Cantonese is 係 (is).
4 POSS stands for a possessive marker.
5 The argument is based on the author's own observation in her email communication with her colleagues.
6 Strictly speaking, the expression following the adjective is a *to*-clause instead of a *to + VP*, but VP has been used to describe the structure in the literature (e.g. Li & Chan, 2000).
7 Whether sentences (128–130) are regarded as ungrammatical or just stylistically undesirable is a controversial issue. Sentences (128) and (129) may be acceptable if the topics are meant to signal a topic shift from previous topics in a conversational discourse.

5 Learner Problems in the Acquisition of English Grammar II: English Article Errors

In the previous chapter, we examined Cantonese ESL learners' grammatical errors which are largely due to L1 interference. There are, however, many learner errors which are not necessarily L1-related but which are also worth our attention. In this chapter and in the next chapter, learner errors which are largely non-L1-related will be examined. Some of the most prevalent errors that learners make are related to the English article system. Learners' errors in their use of English articles will be examined in this chapter. A typology of article errors will be presented, the problems learners have with the representation of different references, their confusion between specificity and definiteness, their difficulties with the definite generic, as well as their misconceptions about the English article system, will be scrutinized.

English Articles and Reference Representation

As discussed in Chapter 2, English articles, *a/an, the* and *ZERO* (no explicit article), are among the most common function words in English, yet they are not just function words for filling a grammatical slot to achieve grammaticality. They are also used for showing definite (e.g. sentence (1)), indefinite (e.g. sentences (2) and (3)), or generic reference (e.g. sentences (4–6)).

Definite Reference

(1) I saw **the boy who hit Mary**.

Indefinite Reference

(2) **A boy** is coming.
(3) I can see (**ZERO**) **ants** everywhere in the room.

Generic Reference

(4) **The dinosaur** is extinct.
(5) **A computer** is a machine which can help us work faster.
(6) (**ZERO**) **Dinosaurs** are extinct.

DOI: 10.4324/9781003252498-5

Generic reference refers to a whole class of entities, and definite reference refers to an identified subset of a class, whereas indefinite reference refers to an unidentified subset of a class (Lock, 1996). There is no one-to-one relationship between the choice of an article and its interpretation. The same article (e.g. *the*) can be used to represent different references (e.g. definite or generic; sentences (1) and (4)), and the same reference (e.g. generic) can be represented by different articles (e.g. *the, a/an, ZERO*; sentences (4–6)). Generic reference is among the most varied, as all the different English articles can be used to represent this reference.

The use of English articles has often been found to be difficult for ESL students (Huebner, 1983; Master, 1987; Murphy, 1997; Parrish, 1987; Pica, 1985; Robertson, 2000; Thomas, 1989; Zobl, 1980), especially for learners whose mother tongue does not have articles, like Chinese (Ionin, Zubizarreta & Maldonado, 2008; Luk & Shirai, 2009). English article use is, thus, one major obstacle to these learners, and article errors are ubiquitous. Although article errors may not impede communication, for learners who aim at having a good control of the language, errors in articles need to be attended to and addressed (Chan, 2021).

Typology of English Article Errors

Many research studies have investigated ESL learners' errors in the use of English articles and have established different typologies (e.g. Han, Chodorow & Leacock, 2006; H. Mizuno, 1986; M. Mizuno, 1999; Ouertani, 2013). Chan (2022), which focused on Hong Kong Cantonese ESL learners' problems in their acquisition of English articles and adopted a taxonomy similar to that of M. Mizuno (1999), classifies article errors according to the intended structures (i.e. which article should correctly be used in a certain context), and the intended reference of a sentence with an article error is also examined (i.e. whether a target sentence without an article error should have definite, indefinite or generic reference).

With regard to the intended structures, errors can be classified into over-extension of *the* for *ZERO* (e.g. sentences (7–9)) and of *a/an* for *ZERO* (e.g. sentences (10) and (11)); under-extension of *ZERO* for *a/an* (e.g. sentences (12–14)), and of *ZERO* for *the* (e.g. sentences (15–17)); substitution of *a/an* for *the* (e.g. sentences (18) and (19)) and of *the* for *a/an* (e.g. sentences (20–22)); co-occurrence (e.g. sentence (23)) and word-order errors (e.g. sentence (24)). Over-extension is characterized by the overuse of either *a/an* or *the* when no explicit article is needed, whereas under-extension is characterized by the presence of no explicit article when either *a/an* or *the* is needed in the respective sentences. Substitution, on the other hand, is characterized by the misuse of either *a/an* or *the* or even other determiners for the target. Co-occurrence errors are characterized by the inappropriate co-existence of both an article and another determiner (e.g. a possessive determiner such as *my*). In word-order errors, the positions of the chosen article (which can be correctly or incorrectly selected) and another determiner (e.g. *both, all*) are inappropriately interchanged. Over-extension and under-extension are the most predominant subtypes of article errors, whereas co-occurrence and word-order errors are rather rare (Chan, 2022).

The noun phrases in which an article error is found can serve different functions in the respective sentences, including subject (S), direct object (DO), indirect object (IO), subject complement (SC), prepositional complement (Prep Comp), and others. The following examples illustrate the different subtypes of article errors, with the functions of the erroneous noun phrases given in brackets after each example. All the examples of article errors included in this chapter, except those which are acknowledged with a source, come from unpublished data of Chan's (2022) study.

Over-Extension (the *for* ZERO)

(7)   *In the year 2047, Hong Kong will have advanced technology, then **the Hong Kong people** will not to do every works. (S)
(8)   *Playing with friends can create memories, as well as training **the children** their communication skills with others. (IO)
(9)   *In my childhood, it was very very happy, because in my one years old, my mother usually bought many many doll and **the toys** with me. (DO)

Over-Extension (a/an *for* ZERO)

(10) *Everyone will become **a rich people.** (SC)
(11) *In my childhood is a very happy, because I am in a holiday never with my dog went to a Ocean park play **a football**. (DO)

Under-Extension (ZERO *for* a/an)

(12)   *The whole choir was about one hundred and twenty, moreover, many past student and ^ **bass band** joined us. (S)
(13)   *I know me is ^ **very bad girl**. (SC)
(14)   *Because my brother was love me, in my birthday, he will buy ^ **gift** to me and my sister. (DO)

Under-Extension (ZERO *for* the)

(15)   *My father see I forgot the sweater, he didn't went work, he went my school gave me ^ **sweater**. (DO)
(16)   *Although some of you may criticize that the one who earn money to support the expenditure of a family is ^ **father**, generally speaking, the one who take care of us until we grow up is mother. (SC)
(17)   *I feel in my life ^ **most important person** is my mum. (S)

Substitution (a/an *for* the)

(18)   *I thought that my childhood was worse than **a life of a pet**. (Prep Comp)
(19)   *I need spent money on studying, eating, living, entertainment and learning **a piano**. (DO)

Substitution (the *for* a/an)

(20) *However, after the HKCEE, I tried to find **the summer job**, discovering I couldn't. (DO)

(21) *I loudly cried, then **the policeman** came and said to me "What happen for you?" (S)

(22) *When I was seven years old, I was across the road, then **the car** hurt with me, so I going to hospital. (S)

Co-Occurrence

(23) *This is **my the most important event in my life**. (SC)

Word-Order

(24) *In **the all tests** or exams, I always get bad result. (Prep Comp)

Given that English articles are used for showing different references, article errors are often linked with errors in reference representation. For example, in sentence (8), the intended noun phrase *(ZERO) children* should have indefinite reference, but the overuse of *the* for *ZERO* has rendered the resultant noun phrase (**the children*) definite. Similarly, the intended noun phrase *a summer job* in sentence (20) should have intended indefinite reference, whereas the incorrect use of *the* for *a* has also rendered the resultant noun phrase (**the summer job*) definite. The intended noun phrase *the life of a pet*, which functions as the prepositional complement of *than* in sentence (18), should have intended definite reference, yet the incorrect substitution of *a* for *the* has rendered the resultant noun phrase (**a life of a pet*) indefinite. Although it is often possible to interpret what the intended reference of an erroneous noun phrase should be, article errors may result in difficulties in reference interpretation. For example, it may be argued that the intended noun phrase in the very last part of sentence (15) is *a sweater* with intended indefinite reference, although the context does indicate a more plausible definite interpretation with the intended noun phrase *the sweater* referring to the same sweater that the writer has forgotten. Because of the writer's omission of an explicit article, his/her original intention could be difficult to arrive at, and misinterpretation or even miscommunication may arise (for more examples exploring the relations between error types and intended references, see Chan, 2022).

Cantonese ESL Learners' Confusion Between Specificity and Definiteness

The previous section presented a taxonomy of common English article errors analysed according to the intended structures and intended references. This section explores learners' confusion between two important concepts related to the use of English articles, namely specificity and definiteness. Two types of references are relevant to the discussion, namely specific reference and definite reference.

Specific reference and definite reference are two distinct concepts and should not be equated with each other. According to Ko, Ionin and Wexler (2010: 219), a specific noun phrase "intends to refer to exactly one individual", so there exists a property which the speaker regards as noteworthy in the context (Ionin, 2003, 2006). Definiteness, on the other hand, is related to the identifiability of referents in discourse and presupposes existence and uniqueness (Ko, Ionin & Wexler, 2010; Trenkic, 2008). Therefore, for a noun phrase to be specific, it has to refer to (a) certain individual(s), whereas for a noun phrase to be definite, the referent has to be identifiable by both the speaker and the hearer. While a noun phrase with definite reference is often specific (e.g. *the boy whom Mary loves* in sentence (25)), there are definite noun phrases which are not specific (e.g. *the student who gets the highest mark* in sentence (26)). On the other hand, although many indefinite noun phrases are non-specific (e.g. *a car* in sentence (27)), there are many indefinite noun phrases which are specific (e.g. *a boy* in sentence (28)).

(25) I met **the boy whom Mary loves**.
(26) After the test results are out, I will award **the student who gets the highest mark**.
(27) I want to buy **a car**.
(28) **A boy** is coming.

Cantonese ESL learners are not aware of the importance of identifiability for definiteness and often confuse definiteness with specificity. To them, *specific* is synonymous with *definite*, so a definite noun phrase is by default regarded as specific (or vice versa), whereas an indefinite noun phrase is by default regarded as non-specific (or vice versa) (Chan, 2016, 2017b). For example, although *a policeman* and *a beautiful girl* in sentences (29) and (30) are indefinite because their referents are not identifiable, many learners will misinterpret the two noun phrases as definite, as they are specific and refer to exactly one individual. Their confusion is even more acute when the indefinite but specific noun phrase in question is pre-modified or post-modified, as in sentences (31) and (32).

(29) I saw **a policeman**.
(30) **A beautiful girl** is coming,
(31) I found **a history textbook**.
(32) **A boy with long hair** is coming.

The classificatory modification of the pre-modifier *history* in *a history textbook* (sentence (31)) and the post-modification description *with long hair* in *a boy with long hair* (sentence (32)) are presumably mistaken by learners as information which helps identify the referents of the respective noun phrases (Chan, 2017b).

Confusion about specificity and definiteness is not limited to interpretation but is often extended to production: Learners have a tendency to overuse *the* in contexts which are specific but which are not necessarily definite. Substitution of *the* for target *a/an*, such as in sentences (21) and (22), is likely the result of such confusion, with learners incorrectly using the definite form to signal a specific salient referent which is actually not identifiable.

Problems With the Definite Generic

The English definite article, as its name suggests, is typically used to represent definite reference. However, definite reference is not the only reference type that can be represented by this article, as it can be used with a singular noun for representing generic reference, especially when generalizations are made about a class of entities which have clear defining characteristics (Lock, 1996), as in sentence (4). Such a structure is known as the definite generic (Snape, 2018) or NP-level generics (Krifka, Pelletier, Carlson, ter Meulen, Link & Chierchia, 1995) in the literature.

For the English definite article to have a generic interpretation, in addition to the feature [+ definite], the article must also have the feature [+ species] (Dayal, 2004; Ionin, Montrul, Kim & Philippov, 2011). In that sense, the generic noun phrase in question denotes the entire species instead of a single individual or a group of individuals (Snape, 2013), and the predicate in the sentence in question will be a kind predicate (Krifka, Pelletier, Carlson, ter Meulen, Link & Chierchia, 1995). As in example (4) earlier (repeated here as example (33)), where the definite generic is used, *the* in *the dinosaur* "induces a mass reading on the noun it combines with" (Chierchia, 1998: 383) and denotes the entire species of dinosaurs across all possible worlds instead of just one single dinosaur. The predicate *is extinct* denotes a feature describing the whole kind of dinosaurs.

(33) **The dinosaur** is extinct.

Although the definite generic is relatively rare in terms of use (Liu & Gleason, 2002; Parrish, 1987; Tarone & Parrish, 1988), it is the most likely choice when a noun phrase representing generic reference is in subject position, in the first sentence of a paragraph, in an introduction or in a conclusion, or when it marks the topic of a scientific essay (Master, 1987).

Cantonese ESL learners often encounter difficulties in the use of the definite generic. As far as productive use is concerned, the structure is very rarely attempted in free writing tasks (Chan, 2022). As far as interpretation is concerned, when learners are presented with a sentence with the definite generic, they often misinterpret the noun phrase concerned (e.g. *the elephant* in sentence (34)) as having definite reference rather than generic reference.

(34) I heard that **the elephant** often forgets (Chan, 2019b: 863).

Some learners may realize that a definite interpretation is unacceptable in such a context. However, instead of accepting the noun phrase as showing generic reference, they tend to reject the whole sentence and regard it as ungrammatical.[1] Some learners may even be inclined to "correct" such sentences using other generic forms, such as *ZERO* + plural, as in sentence (35).

(35) I heard that **elephants** never forget (Chan, 2019b: 867).[2]

Attempts to "correct" a sentence with the definite generic, however, often result in undesirable use of erroneous structures, including incorrect use of *the* + plural (e.g. sentence (36)) and of bare singular noun phrases (e.g. sentence (37)).

(36) *I heard that **the elephants** never forget (Chan, 2019b: 867).
(37) *I heard that **elephant** never forgets (Chan, 2019b: 867).

Cantonese ESL learners who use *the* + plural as showing generic reference (e.g. *the elephants* in sentence (36)) are apparently not aware of the number requirement of the definite generic, that it requires a singular head noun instead of a plural head noun. Unlike *the* + singular, *the* + plural is not used for representing generic reference, because *the* in English lexicalizes maximality (Chierchia, 1998; Dayal, 2004), meaning that the article picks out the maximal individual in the set of entities in a certain discourse situation. Therefore, if *the* is used with a plural noun, the noun phrase will denote the entire set of entities in that discourse situation, so *the elephants* in sentence (36) should denote the entire set of elephants in that discourse situation, not the whole species of elephants.

As for bare singular noun phrases (e.g. *elephant* in sentence (37)), it has been claimed that learners whose native languages do not have structural equivalents of English articles tend to favour bare noun phrases (Trenkic, Mirkovic & Altmann, 2014). This favouritism may help explain Cantonese ESL learners' tendency to use bare singular noun phrases for (incorrectly) representing generic reference. The widespread (correct) use of *ZERO* + plural/mass for generic reference may also lead to learners' confusion between the correct and incorrect structures for representing generic reference.

Problems With Noun Countability

The use of English articles is, to a certain extent, related to noun countability, and Cantonese ESL learners' problems with noun countability should not be ignored in any discussions about English article errors. Countability is a property applicable to all English common nouns, yet whether a noun is countable or uncountable is sometimes not as straightforward as it may seem, as many English nouns can be countable (e.g. *waters*) or uncountable (e.g. *water*) depending on the contexts in which they are used. There is no absolute constraint which will prevent a certain countable noun from functioning uncountably in a certain context, or vice versa (Allan, 1980; Dziemianko, 2012), although the countable use of uncountable nouns has been regarded as highly infrequent (Hall, Schmidtke & Vickers, 2013). While "English obliges us to make a distinction with regard to how a referent is cognitively perceived" (Downing, 2015: 365), the countable vs. uncountable distinction is "primarily arbitrary, unprincipled, or idiosyncratic" (Wisniewski, Lamb & Middleton, 2003: 585).

Noun countability is important for determining whether it is acceptable to use *a/an* with a certain noun in a certain context, or whether a certain noun should be pluralized in a certain context. While most uncountable nouns are not used with *a/an*, some uncountable nouns (e.g. *knowledge*) can be used with *a/an* when a singular sense is activated, such as *a good knowledge of English*. Learners' decisions on such article uses are often dependent on their intuitive judgements about noun countability (Yoon, 1993). Some common English errors, such as the redundant use of *a/an* with an uncountable noun (e.g. *a furniture, *an equipment), as well as the inappropriate pluralization of an uncountable noun (e.g. *furnitures, *equipments), are arguably the results of inappropriate countability judgements. Cantonese ESL learners also show problems in these aspects. The following examples illustrate the overuse of *a/an* with uncountable nouns (sentences (38) and (39)) and inappropriate pluralization of uncountable or plural nouns (sentences (40) and (41)).

(38)   *If we could pay **a great attention** in environment as early as possible, HK may not become a dead city.

(39)   *So, we should use this chance to give **a feedback** to our parent.

(40)   *Also, she give me **some advices on doing that thing**, but not just using the force in solving problems.

(41)   *The aeroplanes will be discarded because **many peoples** always travel spaceships.

Some Misconceptions About the English Article System

Other than the aforementioned errors associated with learners' actual use and/or interpretation of English articles, Cantonese ESL learners' knowledge of the English article system is also inadequate. Learners have some misconceptions about the system, including its inventory, the functions of its members and inappropriate mappings between articles and references. They have also formulated some inappropriate hypotheses about different constituents of a sentence containing an article.

Confusion Between Articles and Other Determiners

Although the English article system only consists of a few members: *a/an, the* and *ZERO*, Cantonese ESL learners have been found to lack precise knowledge of the inventory of the system. Some learners think that other determiners such as demonstratives (e.g. *this, that*), and even numerals (e.g. *one*) are also members of the system. On the other hand, *a/an* is sometimes regarded as a kind of quantifiers showing quantities comparable to the numeral *one* (Chan, 2016).

As is well known, different determiners in English have different functions. For example, possessive determiners refer to a possessor, whereas demonstratives signal the proximity of the referent. Articles, on the other hand, signal the scope of reference as to a whole class of entities (i.e. generic) or just a subset of a class (i.e. definite or indefinite). While demonstratives and possessives can be used to represent definite reference, they cannot be used to represent other reference types. On the other hand, while articles are used for representing different reference types, they cannot show proximity or possession (see Chapter 2). In addition, although *a/an* does signal that the referent is singular (or just one), it does not belong to the category of post-determiners of which quantifiers are members (Quirk, Greenbaum, Leech & Svartvik, 1985). Cantonese ESL learners' confusion between articles and other determiners show that they are not aware of the different ways in which different determiners particularize noun referents (Lock, 1996).

Inappropriate Mappings Between Articles/Determiners and References

Many Cantonese ESL learners tend to accord a one-to-one reference mapping to an article, thus attributing a "bona fide lexical meaning" to the article form (Trenkic, 2008: 10). For example, *a/an* is often mapped to non-specific reference, and *the* is considered definite by default (Chan, 2017b). Such inappropriate one-to-one mappings also help explain learners' confusion between specificity and definiteness and their rejection of the definite generic as discussed earlier in the chapter.

Cantonese ESL learners also have a misconception that noun phrases referring to all entities of a group must have generic reference irrespective of whether the group refers to a subgroup or designates a whole class. Therefore, when encountering a noun phrase with the pre-determiner *all*, they tend to have an incorrect assumption that the presence of the pre-determiner must render the noun phrase generic. The use of an article in the noun phrase is, thus, precluded (e.g. sentence (42)) irrespective of whether the sentence in question is intended to have a generic interpretation (where an article is not needed) or a definite interpretation (where *the* is needed) (Chan, 2017b).

(42) **All the?/ZERO? lenses** have individual markings (Chan, 2017a: 22).

Inappropriate Hypothesis About Subject Complement

Another misconception that Cantonese ESL learners have about the English article system is related to the subject complement of an identifying relational clause/sentence[3] and the subject of the clause/sentence (Chan, 2017b). For example, in sentence (43), the relation between the subject and the subject complement is one of equivalence, with the subject *the essence of advertising* being the carrier of the identifying attribute denoted by the subject complement *persuasion*. Such equivalent constituents are interchangeable, so sentence (43) can be rewritten as sentence (44).

(43) **The essence of advertising** is persuasion (Chan, 2017b: 25).
(44) Persuasion is **the essence of advertising**.

When confronted with an article selection decision, Cantonese ESL learners have a tendency to base their article selection simply on the equivalence relation between the subject and the subject complement, thus assigning definite reference to the subject noun phrase and selecting *the* for the subject noun phrase.[4] Although learners' article selection is often appropriate in such contexts, the reason underlying their selection shows that they are unaware of the distinction between identifiability and equivalence. Identifiability, as discussed earlier, is what is required for a noun phrase to be definite. The referent of the head noun *essence* in the definite noun phrase *the essence of advertising* is identifiable from the post-modifier *of advertising*, which provides cataphoric reference.[5] Therefore, it is the post-modifier *of advertising*, not the subject complement *persuasion*, which renders the referent of the head noun *essence* identifiable. Cantonese ESL learners are apparently unaware that the equivalence relation between an identifying attribute (i.e. *persuasion*) and the carrier of that attribute (i.e. *the essence of advertising*) does not contribute to the identifiability of the referent of the carrier, nor are they aware that an identifying attribute cannot help delimit the article choice of a carrier (Chan, 2017b).

Inappropriate Hypothesis About Post-Modifiers

A further misconception about the English article system that Cantonese ESL learners have is concerned with the presence of a post-modifier, which is often thought to necessitate the use of *the* for the head noun, because the mere occurrence of a post-modifier is thought to render a noun phrase definite (Chan, 2017b).

It is true that the post-modifier of a definite noun phrase often helps to provide cataphoric reference for identifying the referent of the head noun, as can be seen from *the essence of advertising* in sentence (43). However, not all post-modifiers help to achieve identifiability. A noun phrase with a post-modifier can be indefinite, such as *a boy with long hair* and *some boys with long hair* in sentences (45) and (46). Noun phrases with a post-modifier can even be generic (providing limited generic reference), such as *teachers in this era* in sentence (47).

(45) I met **a boy with long hair**.
(46) There are **some boys with long hair** in the class.
(47) **Teachers in this era** are less respected than those in the previous millennium.

Learners' undue default association of definite reference with the presence of a post-modifier sometimes results in their overuse of *the* in non-definite contexts, such as sentence (48).

(48) *I like reading very much, especially **the books about physics** (Chan, 2019b: 865).

Confusion Between English Articles and Similar L1 Linguistic Items

Although, as claimed in the introductory paragraph of this chapter, English article errors are largely non-L1 related because of the non-existence of articles in

Chinese-Cantonese, the effects of L1 transfer sometimes surface. Contrary to arguments against the effects of L1 transfer on English article use (e.g., Zdorenko & Paradis, 2012), recent research shows that Cantonese ESL learners sometimes inappropriately rely on Chinese-Cantonese in their selection of English articles based on ungrounded comparisons between Chinese-Cantonese and English (Chan, 2019a). They tend to formulate their thoughts in their native language when producing target language output, translating a target English construction (e.g. *during the three years of studies* in example (49)) into Chinese-Cantonese first and comparing the translated Chinese-Cantonese construction with the target English construction they want to produce. If the translated Chinese-Cantonese construction (e.g. example (50)) requires a Chinese-Cantonese item thought to be equivalent/closest to an English article (e.g. the demonstratives 嗰 (that) or 嗰啲 (those)), they tend to choose *the* in the target English construction.

(49) During **the** three years of studies, . . .
(50) 係 **嗰** 三 年 嘅 學習 裡面, . . .
      in that three years NOM study inside
      (During those three years of studies)

On the other hand, if the translated Chinese-Cantonese construction does not require a "thought-to-be-equivalent" Chinese-Cantonese item (e.g. example (51)), learners will not use an English article (or use *ZERO*) in the target English construction (e.g. sentence (52)) based on the comparison (Chan, 2019a, 2019b).

(51) 唔 好 用 **濕** **嘅** **手** 摸 插座
      not good use damp NOM hand touch socket
      (Don't use damp hands to touch the socket.)
(52) Don't use **(ZERO) damp hands** to touch the socket.

This kind of "translation and comparison" strategy is presumably rooted in learners' misconceptions about the two language systems. They have mistakenly equated a Chinese-Cantonese demonstrative with the English definite article, probably because of their shared function of showing definiteness in a sentence, as in sentences (53) and (54)). Such reliance on the L1 may result in correct English article selection, but the ungrounded comparisons that trigger the selection are undesirable.

(53) 那 個 人 很 高
      that CL man very tall
      (That man is very tall.)
(54) The man is very tall.

Conclusion

In this chapter, we examined the problems that Cantonese ESL learners often have with the use of English articles. Different problems have been identified, including production and interpretation problems. A typology of article errors has been presented, and learners' confusion between specificity and definiteness and their ignorance of the definite generic, as well as some common misconceptions that they have about the English article system, have been explored. Learners' correct article selection may have been led by misidentification of reference types or misdetection of information to identify referents, resulting in deceptive target-like article uses that often escape teachers' attention (Chan, 2017b). The effects of L1 transfer are not to be totally ignored, as learners tend to use a special kind of "translation and comparison" strategy to guide their article selection. Therefore, although article errors may not result in communication breakdown, pedagogical efforts should be invested in advancing learners' explicit knowledge of the English article system. Even if learners' production output does not demonstrate deviations from the target language norms, their knowledge of the English article system and their metalinguistic awareness of the functions, uses and reference representations of English articles still deserve pedagogical attention (see Chapter 10 for more details about the teaching of the English article system). In the next chapter, more errors which are largely non-L1-related will be explored.

Notes

1 The arguments put forward in this section are based on the results of Chan (2019b), which required participants to do a grammaticality judgement task determining the grammaticality of a number of sentences with or without an article error.
2 In Chan (2019b), participants were also required to correct the sentences they considered ungrammatical. Sentences (35–37) are examples of their "corrections".
3 An identifying relational clause is a clause in which the subject complement is equated with the subject and the former serves to define the identity of the latter, as in sentence (43) (Lock, 1996).
4 The discussion in this section is based on the results of Chan (2017b), which required participants to provide a suitable article for different noun phrases in a text and to give the reason behind each selection.
5 Cataphoric reference means that the information necessary to identify the referent of the head noun in a definite noun phrase has to be found forwards after the head.

6 Learner Problems in the Acquisition of English Grammar III: Other Errors

In the previous two chapters, we looked at the most common interlingual errors made by Cantonese ESL learners as well as their problems in the use of English articles. In this chapter, we will examine other errors commonly made by Cantonese ESL learners. Focus will be put on errors which are largely non-L1-related. Errors at all the morphological, lexical, syntactic and discoursal levels will be discussed, the nature of the errors will be scrutinized in detail, and the probable cause(s) of the errors will be put forward. Like the interlingual errors discussed in Chapter 4, the majority of the error types in this chapter are based on Chan's (2010c) study. Unless otherwise stated and acknowledged, the examples used for illustration all come from unpublished data of the study.[1]

Morphological Level

Errors at the morphological level are those concerned with the misuse of a bound morpheme. Bound morphemes are morphemes which cannot stand alone as independent words, such as prefixes (e.g. *un-*; *dis-*) or suffixes (e.g. *-able*; *-ful*), which are collectively known as affixes (Yule, 2017). In Chapter 4, no interlingual errors at the morphological level have been identified, as most Chinese-Cantonese words consist of one single morpheme which cannot be further analysed into component morphemes, and L1 interference is not apparent (Chan, 2010c). However, for intralingual errors, misuse of affixes, including inappropriate selection and overuse, is not uncommon.

Inappropriate Selection of Affixes

Sentences (1–3) show some examples of errors with affixes mis-selected. For these errors, an affix is indeed needed for the target English words, and the meanings of the mis-selected affixes (e.g. *un-* in *unobedient* and *unseparatable* in sentences (1) and (2)) and the target affixes (e.g. *dis-* in *disobedient* and *in-* in *inseparable*) often share similar meanings or are different allomorphs of the same morpheme.[2] Not only are prefixes sometimes mis-selected, but errors in suffix selection are also found, such as substitution of *-able* for the target suffix *-ing* (e.g. *disturbable* vs. *disturbing* in sentence (3)). The most probable cause of this error

DOI: 10.4324/9781003252498-6

is learners' inadequate mastery of and confusion about English word-formation processes and about the use of different affixes.

(1)   *But I always **unobedient**. (cf. disobedient)
(2)   *That's our **unseparatable** relationship. (cf. inseparable)
(3)   *No **disturbable** noise will be found and good security is seen. (cf. disturbing)

Overuse of Affixes

Overuse of affixes is characterized by the redundant use of an unnecessary affix (e.g. *-ly, -ful*) to a stem which does not require an affix (e.g. *often, overall, kind* in sentences (4–6)). The redundant affix is often commonly used for a certain function. For instance, *-ly* is a highly productive suffix in the formation of an adverb from an adjective, such as from *kind* to *kindly*; *-ful* is also a productive suffix in the formation of an adjective from a noun, such as from *thought* to *thoughtful*. Learners may be so used to using such affixes that they are unaware that without an additional affix, the thought-to-be "stems" already suffice, as the words already belong to the target grammatical category (e.g. *overall* and *often* are already adverbs, and *kind* is already an adjective).

(4)   *I probably think it was the place where I can find my answers and so I **oftenly** go there.
(5)   *Well, I should say my childhood was full of happiness **overally**.
(6)   *And her appearance attract me, so beautiful, **kindful** and helpful is she that she is my important person in my mind.

Lexical Level

Only one interlingual error type at the lexical level has been attested, namely synforms.

Synforms

Synforms are lexical items inappropriately selected because of some kinds of resemblance between the target items and the mis-selected lexical items (Hall, 2002; Laufer, 1997). In examples (7–9), the mis-selected words *lift, them* and *robber* (for the target items *life, team* and *robots* respectively) are some examples of synforms.

(7)   *The most important event in my **lift**. It is a football. (cf. life).
(8)   *In the **them** there had a good teacher. (cf. team)
(9)   *They are **robber**, the robber can wash the dishes. (cf. robots)

The major cause of this type of error is probably due to learners' inadequate knowledge of both the target words and the corresponding mishits, which resemble each other in spelling or, to a lesser extent, in pronunciation. The meanings of the target words and mishits are often distinct, and there is no evidence that the mishits are "easier" to learners than the targets. Misspellings due to carelessness may also be a probable reason for such mishits.

It may be argued that inappropriate selection of affixes and overuse of affixes at the morphological level discussed in the previous section can also be categorized as synforms, as the resultant words (e.g. *unobedient*, *overally*) also resemble, to a certain extent, the target words in spelling and/or in pronunciation (e.g. *disobedient*, *overall*). Those errors are regarded as separate error types in this chapter for two reasons. First, the constituents affected (e.g. *un-* vs. *dis-*; *-ly*) are bound morphemes always attached to another morpheme rather than free morphemes which can be used as independent words (e.g. *life* vs. *lift*; *team* vs. *them*). Second, the majority of the resultant words after mis-selection or overuse of affixes are non-words in English (e.g. *unobedient, overally*), whereas synforms are real English words (e.g. *lift, them*) with meanings which can differ greatly from the target items.

There are occasional cases of affix overuse where the resultant word after addition of an unwanted affix is a real English word (e.g. *procession*), as in sentence (10).

(10) *New policy proposals were always put before various advisory committees, whereas everything was predictable in the **procession** of policy making because of the overlapping membership in the two councils.

In these cases, indeterminacy in categorization may exist, as it is unclear whether the resultant word is a lexical mishit or a word with an unnecessary affix. There is reason to believe that such cases are overuse of affixes rather than synforms, as the target word *process* is apparent after removal of the unnecessary affix and is acceptable in the context in question. More research is needed to ascertain the categorization.

Syntactic Level

A number of syntactic errors which are largely non-L1-related have been attested. This section will discuss the various error types in detail. As there is often a complex interplay between different causes of an error, L1 interference is not completely ignored and will be brought up for discussion where appropriate.

Concord Problems

Different kinds of concord errors can be found in Cantonese ESL learners' L2 output, including concord between the determiner and head noun of a noun phrase, as well as concord between the subject and subject complement of a sentence.

For concord problems between determiners and head nouns, not only are determiners inviting plural head nouns used with singular head nouns (e.g. sentences

(11–13)), but determiners inviting singular head nouns are also used with plural nouns (e.g. sentences (14–16)).

(11)   *Now I have **a lot of thing** to think and to do.
(12)   *And then it will have **a lot of room: ten bedroom, three toilet, two car park**.
(13)   *In my life, there were **many important person**.
(14)   *I was **a children**.
(15)   *My mother cried for **a long days**.
(16)   ***Every children** will be not go to school.

For concord errors between subjects and subject complements, a singular subject is used with a plural subject complement (e.g. sentence (17)), or a plural subject is used with a singular subject complement (e.g. sentences (18) and (19)).

(17)   ***My important person** is **my girlfriends and my boyfriends**.
(18)   ***My mother and my father** are **the most important person in my life**.
(19)   ***These** are **the reason** why I love Taiwanese.

It should be noted that occasional mismatches in the numbers of subjects and subject complements are found in correct English sentences.

(20)   **Youngsters in this era** arc sometimes **a problem**.
(21)   **Stationery items** are **my priority**.

In sentence (20), the subject complement *a problem* denotes a collective characteristic of the class of *youngsters in this era*, and in sentence (21), the subject complement *my priority* denotes a collective identity to which the class of *stationery items* are assigned. Such collective representations are not present in the erroneous sentences, so the lack of number agreement between the subjects and subject complements in sentences (17–19) are not acceptable in Standard English.

Because most Chinese-Cantonese nouns and verbs are not marked for number, tense or person, a lack of positive transfer from the mother tongue is a probable cause of English concord problems (see Chapter 9 for more details). Another probable cause is learners' inadequate mastery of constituent combinations in L2 phrase or sentence construction (Chan, 2010c).

Confusion Between "Concern" and "Concerned About"

Misuse of the lexical item *concern* is a high-frequency error in Cantonese ESL learners' L2 output (Chan & Li, 2002; Li & Chan, 2001). Learners often misuse *concern* as a verb in a clause where the subject denotes one or more persons who care about or worry about the entity (typically human, but occasionally non-human entities) denoted by the object. For instance, in the respective clauses in sentences (22–24), the subjects *my mother*, *I* and *she* are the persons who worry about the entities denoted by the objects of the respective clauses, namely *me*, *what* and *her health* respectively.

(22) ***My mother concerns** me and my two brothers everytimes.
(23) *What **I concerned** was happiness.
(24) ***She concerns** her health so much that she wake up early in the morning to play sports games including tennis, table tennis and badminton etc.

An additional error associated with the misuse of the verb *concern* is characterized by the co-occurrence of the verb with the preposition *about*, as in sentences (25–27). Like sentences (22–24), the subjects are also the people who care about or are worried about the entities denoted by the noun phrases following the preposition.

(25) *She **concerned about** my schoolwork, meanwhile giving me some extra-curricular activities such as having a picnic hiking.
(26) *I **concerned about** a weight machine with colourful lighting.
(27) *She began to **concerned about** my study, my health, my feeling and my life.

One probable cause of the errors in sentences (22–24) is L1 interference, as word-for-word translation of the sentences often results in acceptable Chinese-Cantonese sentences. The literal Chinese-Cantonese translation of *concern* is 關心 (care about) or 擔心 (worry about), which are transitive verbs typically used with human subjects worrying about the entities denoted by the direct objects.[3] However, the incorrect use of *concern(ed) about* as in sentences (25–27) suggests that L1 interference is not a probable or main source of errors, as the Chinese-Cantonese transitive verbs 關心 and 擔心 do not require a following preposition comparable to the English preposition *about*.

Another probable cause of the errors is learners' unawareness of the structural constraints of the use of the verb *concern* and its related adjective *concerned* (Chan & Li, 2002; Li & Chan, 2001). In idiomatic English, the verb *concern* is used in a clause where the subject denotes the cause of the worry (e.g. *his examination result* and *the high property prices in Hong Kong* in sentences (28) and (29)) and the object denotes the person(s) feeling worried (e.g. *me* and *all of us*).

(28) His examination result **concerns** me.
(29) The high property prices in Hong Kong **concern** all of us.

The adjective *concerned*, on the other hand, is used in a *be + concerned + about* structure with the subject denoting the person(s) feeling worried (e.g. *I* and *all of us* in sentences (30) and (31)) and the prepositional complement of *about* (e.g. *his examination result* and *the high property prices in Hong Kong*) being the cause of the worries.

(30) I **am concerned about** his examination result.
(31) All of us **are concerned about** the high property prices in Hong Kong.

The similar meanings but virtually opposite structural requirements of the two closely related lexical items *concern* (verb) and *concerned* (adjective) often elude many learners, resulting in erroneous language output such as sentences (22–27). While some incorrect structures can arguably be seen as results of direct translation from the L1, the consistent use of subject noun phrases denoting the people feeling worried in both subtypes of errors reflects learners' inadequate understanding of the structural constraints of the two related words.[4]

Inappropriate Case Selection

For this error, an inappropriate case is selected for a target pronoun. For example, the subjective case is inappropriately used in place of the objective case (e.g. sentences (32) and (33)), and the objective case is inappropriately selected for the subjective case (e.g. sentences (34) and (35)).

(32) *I call **he** bear. (cf. call him)
(33) *We can make a home with **she** and we can have a baby too. (cf. with her)
(34) ***Her** and I are very love we. (cf. She and I/We)
(35) *I think **me** maybe had good marks. (I)

Another kind of problem associated with case selection is learners' misuse of a possessive determiner (e.g. *our* in sentences (36) and (37)) in place of a subjective or objective pronoun. Occasionally a target possessive determiner is replaced by a subjective (or, to a lesser extent, objective) pronoun when a possessive meaning is intended (e.g. sentences (38) and (39)).

(36) *When we are sick, she will look after **our**. (cf. look after us)
(37) *She good in cooking, good in shouting me and good in teach **our**. (cf. teaching us)
(38) *But when **I** dictation or test have high marks, my mother will gave me a present or invite me to restaurant. (cf. my dictation)
(39) ***She** face was to appear any wrinkle. (cf. her face)

The inappropriate use of the apostrophe *s* (*'s*) with a pronoun/determiner is also quite common when the noun phrase concerned requires a possessive determiner. There are cases where *'s* and a possessive determiner co-exist (e.g. sentence (40)). There are also cases where *'s* is used with a pronoun in the subjective case (e.g. sentences (41) and (42)).

(40) ***Her's name** is Chan mai yan. (cf. Her name)
(41) *Now, my sister and **I's lives** were very funny. (cf. my sister's and my lives/ our lives)
(42) ***She's food** is very delicious. (cf. Her food)

Inadequate mastery of the distinct forms for the different cases in English and a lack of comparable equivalents in learners' mother tongue are probably the major causes of the problem. Confusion caused by the correct use of *'s* with proper nouns (e.g. *Mary's*) may be a cause of the inappropriate use of the apostrophe *s* in sentences such as (40–42).

Mis-Ordering of Constituents in Indirect Questions

Mis-ordering of constituents in indirect questions is characterized by incorrect application of subject-operator[5] inversion in an indirect question. The ordering of the operator (e.g. *can*, *did* and *will* in sentences (43–45)) and the subject (e.g. *I*, *she* and *Hong Kong*) is the same as that in a direct question.

(43) *At that moment, I don't know what **can I** do. (cf. What can I do?)
(44) *I know how **did she** overcome all the problem. (cf. How did she overcome all the problems?)
(45) *Many people want to know how **will Hong Kong** look like in the year of 2047. (cf. How will Hong Kong look like in the year of 2047?)

Inadequate mastery of the target language norm, that subject-operator inversion is not required in embedded indirect questions, should be a major cause of the problem. The phenomenon of universal processes may also help explain such mis-ordering, as native English children make similar errors in certain stages of their L1 acquisition process (Lightbown & Spada, 2021), suggesting that mis-ordering of constituents in indirect questions is not a unique feature of L2 learning (see Chapter 9).

Misuse of Prepositions

Misuse of prepositions is manifested in different ways. In some cases, an inappropriate preposition is chosen in place of an appropriate one (e.g. sentences (46–48)). In other cases, a superfluous preposition is used when a preposition is not needed (e.g. sentences (49–51)), or when a required preposition is omitted (e.g. sentences (52–54)).

Inappropriate Prepositions

(46) *These are not the reason **of** her place in my heart, but her love. (cf. reason for)
(47) *We also played card games on the bus, although it was crowded **of** people in the morning. (cf. crowded with)
(48) *In the night, my mother come home and buy some fish. (cf. At night)

Superfluous Prepositions

(49)   *We always played **with** together.
(50)   *When I was little, my mother was looking after **for** me very cautiously.
(51)   *But now I go to my new house **for** nine year ago.

Missing Prepositions

(52)   *Because the people is **afraid ^ Hong Kong**, or they do not like the rubbish city. (cf. afraid of Hong Kong)
(53)   *He lived there ^ **more than 10 years** and he can speak Dutch. (cf. for more than 10 years)
(54)   *Although I was **living ^ my uncle and his family members**, they could not love me as my parents. (cf. living with my uncle and his family members)

English preposition use is not easy to generalize, and which preposition to use in a particular context is often lexically determined, context-dependent or idiosyncratic (Chan, 2010c). Learners' inadequate mastery of the use of English prepositions is probably the major cause of most preposition errors.

   For sentences with a missing preposition, L1 interference is arguably at work, as direct translations of some of the erroneous sentences resemble the normative sentence structures in Chinese-Cantonese. For example, the Chinese-Cantonese translations of sentences (52) and (53) do not require a functional equivalent of a preposition before *Hong Kong* and *more than 10 years* respectively, as can be seen in sentences (55) and (56).

(55)   因為   人們   害怕　香港，....。
       because people afraid Hong Kong
       (Because people are afraid of Hong Kong, . . .)
(56)   他　在那裡　住　了　超　　過　十　年，....。
       he in there live ASP more than 10 years
       (He has lived there for more than 10 years . . .)

These erroneous sentences are comparable to calques, where a word-for-word translation from Chinese-Cantonese to English is involved to some extent (see Chapter 4). Given that Chinese-Cantonese does not have a distinct class of prepositions (see Chapter 2), it is not surprising that learners' attempts to employ L1–L2 translation will result in omission of English prepositions. Some instances of preposition omission, however, do not have a clear trace of L1 interference. Examples include sentence (54), the Chinese-Cantonese translation of which also requires the use of a preposition/coverb 跟 (with) before 我的叔父 (*my uncle*). L1 interference, thus, is not apparent in many instances of misuse of prepositions.

Misuse of Relative Clauses

English relative clauses are introduced by a relative pronoun, such as *who, whom, which, that* or *ZERO* (no explicit relative pronoun). When a relative pronoun is used (including *ZERO*), the main verb phrase in the relative clause has to be finite, as in sentences (57) and (58).

(57) Can you see the boy who/that **is hitting** Mary?
(58) I met the boy who/whom/that/ZERO Mary **was dating**.

A finite relative clause with the relative pronoun functioning as subject (e.g. *who is hitting Mary*) can be turned to nonfinite by omitting the subject relative pronoun and the finite verb, resulting in a reduced relative clause, as in sentence (59).

(59) Can you see the boy **hitting Mary**?

English relative clauses are among some of the most difficult sentence structures for Cantonese ESL learners. In forming a finite relative clause, Cantonese ESL learners have a tendency to omit the relative pronoun even when it functions as the subject of the relative clause, as in sentences (60–62).

Omission of Relative Pronouns

(60) *It is the only city ^ **has no sea** in the world.
(61) *At last, water ^ **come out** from the plant is much cleaner.
(62) *Important person may be the one who support you, the one you often talk to and share feeling with, the one ^ **affects you most** or the one you love.

The aforementioned errors resemble, to a certain extent, serial verb constructions or the independent clause as subject/object/complement problem, with a series of finite verbs co-existing in the same sentence or with a finite clause functioning like the subject/object/complement of the whole sentence (see Chapter 4). However, unlike serial verb constructions and the independent clause as subject/object/complement problem, the targeted structures in sentences with a missing relative pronoun are relative clauses which should be introduced by a relative pronoun. It may be argued that L1 interference is at work in learners' production of these errors, but literal L1 translations of such errors do not always resemble canonical Chinese-Cantonese sentences with a target Chinese-Cantonese relative structure.

Omission of relative pronouns sometimes co-exists with *there + be* in existential structures, resulting in a finite clause after *be* (e.g. *a lot of friends stand by me* in sentence (63), *many people go around me* in sentence (64) and *many factors cause stress* in sentence (65)).

(63) *There are a lot of friends ^ **stand** by me.
(64) *Everyday, there are many people ^ **go** around me.
(65) *There are many factors ^ **cause** stress, such as stresses from relationship with colleagues, . . .

Such erroneous sentences have been described as under-generation of participial constructions in Yip (1995), as it is possible to use a reduced relative clause with no relative pronoun but a non-finite participial clause in such structures (e.g. sentences (66–68)).

(66)   There are a lot of friends **standing** by me.
(67)   Every day, there are many people **going** around me.
(68)   There are many factors **causing** stress, such as . . .

Omission of Finite Verbs

Another subtype of errors related to the use of relative clauses is manifested in learners' omission of a finite verb, as if the targeted relative clause is a reduced relative clause but the relative pronoun is incorrectly retained. Some of these errors have the copula omitted, as in sentences (69) and (70). Others omit the verb *be* in a passive structure (e.g. sentences (71) and (72)) or in an *-ing* structure (e.g. sentences (73) and (74)).

(69)   *I think at that time Hong Kong will become a city **which** ^ full of high technology.
(70)   *Now, I am forty years old, working in a secondary school **which** ^ in New Territories.
(71)   *After enjoying our delicious food **which** ^ **cooked** by my mum, we went to school together.
(72)   *But recently, I felt regret that I lost a good chance to join in one famous football club **which** ^ **called** "Happy Valley."
(73)   *They are the last team of person **that** ^ **waiting** for the spaceship which will transfer them to the Mars.
(74)   *In Hong Kong, Social Welfare Department has formed an organization named Child Protective Services Units **which** ^ **providing** a series of service to help the abused children and their families.

Inadequate knowledge of the syntactic requirements of English relative clauses, that a finite relative clause requires the co-occurrence of both a relative pronoun and a finite verb whereas a nonfinite relative clause disallows the presence of a relative pronoun, is probably the major cause of these errors. Learners' failed attempt to produce a reduced relative clause may also be a cause, as the deviant structures less the relative pronouns resemble reduced relative clauses (e.g. sentence (75) and (76)).

(75)   After enjoying our delicious food **cooked by my mum** . . . (cf. sentence (71))
(76)   They are the last team of persons **waiting for the spaceship** . . . (cf. sentence (73))

Use of Inappropriate Relative Pronouns

Another subtype of relative clause errors is concerned with learners' selection of an inappropriate relative pronoun. Examples include the inappropriate use of an objective relative pronoun (e.g. *whom* in sentence (77)) in place of a subjective relative pronoun, a nominal relative pronoun (e.g. *what* in sentence (78)) in place of a subjective or objective relative pronoun, or non-human *which* in place of human *who/whom* (e.g. sentence (79)).

(77) *Moreover, I can get new friend from church **whom** are nice to me. (cf. who are nice)
(78) *Sometimes, he asked me to tell him the story **what** I had read. (cf. which I had read)
(79) *She is my mother **which** is the most important person in my life. (cf. who)

The adverb *where*, which can be used as a relativizer to introduce circumstantial information such as a place (e.g. sentence (80)), is also problematic.

(80) The place **where** I was born is far away from here.

Cantonese ESL learners often substitute *where* for *which* in structures where the target relative pronoun denotes a place (e.g. *H.K.*, *a place* and *countryside* in sentences (81–83)).

(81) *Do you like such kind of H.K., **where** is full of rubbish, buildings?
(82) *He acted as a bad guy, and jumped from a place **where** is 1.5 m height.
(83) *We lived in countryside **where** is close to mainland China.

The most probable cause of errors with an inappropriate relative pronoun is learners' inadequate knowledge of the functions of and the distinctions between different relative pronouns. Misunderstanding that a place/location must be providing circumstantial information and functioning as an adverbial (instead of as subject or object) may also be a cause of the incorrect use of *where*.

Use of Resumptive Pronouns

The use of resumptive pronouns problem is characterized by the co-occurrence of a relative pronoun (*ZERO* inclusive) and a redundant pronoun (e.g. *it*) in a relative structure. The redundant pronoun appears in the original position where the pronoun should be found if the clause in question is not combined with another clause to form a relative structure (Chan, 2004d).

(84) *'Go in for' is a phrasal verb which the meaning of **it** is very different from the literal meaning (Yip & Matthews, 1991: 117).
(85) *There is one thing that I can remember **it** clearly (Chan, 2004d: 54).

(86)   *I denied the fact that I would have entered this band 3 school, which I think **it** is incredible.

The use of a resumptive pronoun is one of the major problems that Cantonese ESL learners have with the use of an English relative clause (Newbrook, 1988). Advanced students, such as university students, tend to use a resumptive pronoun at a position towards the lower end of the accessibility hierarchy (AH),[6] such as those involving genitives (e.g. sentence (84)), whereas students at a lower proficiency level may use a resumptive pronoun even at the direct object or subject positions (e.g. sentences (85) and (86)), the highest end of the AH (Chan, 2004d).

There are a few probable causes of the resumptive pronoun problem. From the perspective of information processing, one probable cause is learners' lax monitoring of their own language output. This is particularly true when the relative clause in question is a long one: In processing a relative clause, learners may have already forgotten their use of a relative pronoun when they reach the original position of the pronoun and thus have a tendency to add a resumptive pronoun in the original position, resulting in expressions such as *that I can remember **it** clearly* (Chan, 2004d).

Another probable cause of the problem is learners' attempt to retain the full structure of a clause. After a resumptive pronoun has been added, the full structure of a phrase/clause (e.g. *the meaning of it, I can remember it, it is incredible* in sentences (84–86)) can be retained, and learners' language information processing may be facilitated (Chan, 2004d).

A third probable cause of the use of a resumptive pronoun is L1 interference. Although it has been argued that there is no straightforward L1 transfer (Gisborne, 2002) in learners' use of a resumptive pronoun due to the different formation of Chinese and English relative structures, some trace of L1 interference can still be seen: In some dialects of Chinese including Cantonese, a resumptive pronoun is often used, or even needed, in contexts where the head noun is an indirect object (example (87)) or where the head noun follows the word 把 (Li & Thompson, 1981), as in example (88).

(87)   我 寄 信 給 **他** 的 那 個 人
      I   send letter to him NOM that CL man
      (the person whom I sent a letter to)

(88)   我 把 **他** 打 了 一 頓 的 那 個 人
      I   BA he hit ASP one CL NOM that CL man
      (the person whom I hit)

There is reason to believe that the acceptability of a resumptive pronoun in such Chinese-Cantonese relative structures may mislead learners into thinking that resumptive pronouns are also allowed in English relative clauses.

It is, however, worth noting that resumptive pronouns are not allowed in Chinese-Cantonese relative clauses where the pronoun is in the subject (example (89)) or direct object positions (example (90)).

(89) *他 打 我 的　 那　 個　 人
     he   hit me NOM that CL man
     (the person who hit me)
(90) *我 打 **他** 的　 那　 個　 人
     I   hit him NOM that CL man
     (the person whom I hit)

Despite the unacceptability of the use of a resumptive pronoun in such Chinese-Cantonese relative structures, Cantonese ESL learners still use a resumptive pronoun in corresponding English relative clauses (see sentences (85) and (86)), suggesting that L1 interference may interact intricately with other factors in this respect. It has been argued that the use of resumptive pronouns may be a universal feature of interlanguage (Gisborne, 2002; Yip & Matthew, 1991), as native speakers of English (whose native language does not allow resumptive pronouns) also have a tendency to use resumptive pronouns when they learn other languages (e.g. Chinese, which allows resumptive pronouns in certain positions). Not only do ESL/EFL learners whose native languages allow resumptive pronouns in certain positions accept English resumptive pronouns in the same positions (Singler, 1988), but native speakers of many languages are also likely to accept English resumptive pronouns in the lower positions of the AH (e.g. genitive, object of comparison) regardless of whether resumptive pronouns are allowed in such positions in their own native languages (Gass, 1979, 1983; Hyltenstam, 1984).

Non-Parallel Structures

Parallelism helps to emphasize related ideas and to provide clarity and rhythm. It can also reinforce grammatically equal elements and facilitate reading (Hodges, Horner, Webb & Miller, 1994). Parallelism is often used when two or more clauses/phrases are joined together by the use of a coordinating conjunction (e.g. *and, or*). If the coordinated elements are of the same level (e.g. both are phrases, or both are clauses) and/or belong to the same grammatical category (e.g. both are verb phrases, or both are noun phrases), then the resultant sentence is regarded as parallel. When two or more clauses are coordinated, they have to be of the same kind (e.g. both are infinitive clauses, both are *wh*-interrogative clauses, or both are -*ing* clauses) (Chan, 2000).

    Cantonese ESL learners often ignore the need for parallelism when they produce L2 input involving coordination. Non-parallel structures can be categorized into different subtypes depending on the kinds of faulty parallelism exhibited.

Coordination of Constituents at Different Levels

One subtype of non-parallel structures can be seen when constituents at different levels are coordinated, such as a phrase conjoined with (part of) a clause, as in sentences (91–93).

(91)   *One day, I **went to the Ocean Park** and **sightseeing**.

(92)   *They should be thoroughly familiar with methods of **data input, file maintenance, handling output** and **troubleshooting** (Chan, 2000: 23).

(93)   *Its main functions are **word processing** and **storing the information of the suppliers and customers** (ibid).

Coordination of Different Kinds of Clauses

Another subtype of non-parallel structures is characterized by the coordination of clauses of different structures, such as a passive clause conjoined with (part of) an active clause (e.g. sentence (94)), or an *-ing* clause conjoined with a *to*-infinitive clause (e.g. sentence (95)).

(94)   *If **the pace of the lesson was lowered** and **added in more explanation**, I think the effect would be much better (Chan, 2000: 24).

(95)   *We have no difficulties in **using** and **to understand our language** because we have been using it since our birth (ibid).

There are also cases in which (part of) a finite clause is conjoined with a nonfinite clause, as in sentences (96) and (97).

(96)   *I could not do anything, just **went to school, did my homework** and **playing**.

(97)   *The company was invited to give a technical proposal for **improving the efficiency of the delivery** and **maximize the company profit** (Chan, 2000: 23).

Coordination of Different Kinds of Phrases

There are cases in which a noun phrase(s) (e.g. *peace* and *love* in sentence (98)) is conjoined with an adjective phrase(s) (e.g. *rich* and *happy*) on a list of phrases.

(98)   *People will live with **peace, love, rich, happy**.

Non-parallelism is also often found in *both . . . and* structures, as in sentence (99), where phrases of different structures (e.g. a prepositional phrase (*in learning German*) and a noun phrase (*English*)) are coordinated.

(99)   *I have confidence both **in learning German** and **English** (Chan, 2000: 24).

It is sometimes difficult to ascertain the intended structure, and thus the intended meaning, of non-parallel sentences. For example, although sentence (99) is normally interpreted as the writer having confidence both in learning German and in learning English (i.e. sentence (100)), it can arguably be interpreted as the writer having confidence in the learning of German and in the

English language in general rather than the learning of the language in particular (i.e. sentence (101)).

(100) I have confidence both **in learning German** and **in learning English**.
(101) I have confidence both **in learning German** and **in English**.

Because of possible indeterminacy in interpretation, faulty parallelism is not simply a stylistic problem but can impact on readers'/listeners' interpretation.

Probable Causes of Faulty Parallelism

Faulty parallelism can be attributed to a number of factors; learners' lack of awareness of structural clarity and cohesion is probably the most important reason. Students may not realize the importance of ensuring cohesion between related ideas by the use of parallel structures. Another reason is that learners may fail to understand the precise structures of the different constituents of a sentence. For example, it may not be obvious to many learners that the conjoined elements on the list in sentence (98) (i.e. *peace, love, rich, happy*) belong to different grammatical categories. Third, a lack of continuity in thought may also lead to inconsistency in writing, especially when one is writing a long or complicated sentence. By the time a learner reaches the end of a long list or has already listed a few items on a list, he/she may have lost track of the syntactic category of the previous constituents and may thus fail to select the same syntactic category for the subsequent constituents. Lastly, a lack of positive transfer in the L1 may also contribute to faulty parallelism, though not significantly. Because Chinese-Cantonese does not make a distinction between, for instance, the nominal and adjectival forms of a word (e.g. *happy* in sentence (98) is 快樂 in Chinese-Cantonese regardless of whether it is used as an adjective or as a noun), learners may be unaware of the need for using distinct forms (i.e. *happy* vs. *happiness*) for different grammatical categories in English, resulting in non-parallel sentences (Chan, 2000).

Punctuation Problems

Errors associated with punctuation can be divided into comma splices and sentence fragments. Comma splices consist of two or more independent clauses separated by a comma instead of a full stop (e.g. examples (102–104)).

Comma Splices

(102) *This change is common especially in factory and office**, most** of the workers and clerks are the favourite jobs of robots.
(103) *I know that he was experiencing his hard time**, the** only thing we could do was spent more time to look after him.
(104) *Every one like imagination**, some** imagine that they will be very rich after a certain period of time**, some** imagine that they will have a happy family.

A comma splice can be corrected by replacing the inappropriate comma with a major punctuation mark, such as a full stop (example (105)), colon (example (106)) or semicolon (example (107)); or by adding an appropriate conjunction, such as *and* or *but* (sentence (108)). For a full-stop and a colon, the first letter of the first word following the punctuation mark should be in capitals.

(105)   This change is common especially in factory and office. **Most** of the workers and clerks are . . .

(106)   This change is common especially in factory and office: **Most** of the workers and clerks are . . .

(107)   I know that he was experiencing his hard time; **the** only thing we could do . . .

(108)   I know that he was experiencing his hard time, **and the** only thing we could do . . .

Sentence Fragments

Sentence fragments, on the other hand, are subordinate clauses used as stand-alone clauses with inappropriate independent status, as in examples (109–111)).

(109)   *Because that was very near the train**. I played with my friend.

(110)   *When I was five years old**. My brother was born.

(111)   *If you always read book**. You think very bored.

A sentence fragment can simply be corrected by replacing the full stop with a comma.

It is sometimes hard to determine whether comma splices and sentence fragments are simply careless mistakes or whether they reflect learners' interlanguage features. Carelessness (or even laziness) may be a probable factor, especially for more advanced students, but inadequate knowledge of the correct use of punctuation and of the status of a clause (e.g. dependent vs. independent, subordinate vs. main) may also be probable causes of the errors.

Verb Form Selection Problems

Verb form mis-selection is characterized by the use of an appropriate verb form. It is common for learners to mis-select an -*ing* participle in place of a target present tense form, a target past tense form, or a target base form (e.g. sentences (112–114) respectively). It is also common for learners to mis-select the past form of a verb in place of a target base form or a target -*ing* participle (e.g. sentences (115) and (116) respectively).

(112)   *My best friend always **running**, and usually is my best friend win. (cf. always runs)

(113) *I'm afraid for taking plane because I never went to other country before, so I never **taking** it. (cf. never took it.)
(114) *Some teenagers think it is "cool" to **smoking**. (cf. to smoke.)
(115) *He gave me much support that made me **felt** very touching. (cf. made me feel)
(116) *We always had some strange idea, such as **found** a secret place and **put** our things in there. (cf. such as finding a secret place and putting)

Some examples of inappropriate verb form selection are arguably errors with the finite form of *be* missing (e.g. sentence (117)), or serial verb constructions (e.g. sentence (118)).

(117) * She ^ **working** in Sheung Shui, and she's work form nine o'clock to six thirty.
(118) *Always **play** games and **watch** television is my favourite. (cf. playing games and watching television)

Chinese-Cantonese verbs do not distinguish between the different forms of a verb, so no L1 interference is traceable, except for the errors which can be interpreted as serial verb constructions (see Chapter 4). For errors such as the one in sentence (117), it is difficult to determine whether the sentence has a missing finite verb or whether it has an inappropriately selected verb form, as both the present tense and the present continuous tense seem plausible in such sentences.

(119) She **is working/works** in Sheung Shui, . . .

Inadequate knowledge of the target language in general and unawareness of the distinction between finite and nonfinite clauses in particular are the most probable causes. Learners have simply failed to sufficiently master the formation of a correct verb phrase/clause in a certain context.

Word Class Confusion

Cantonese ESL learners often have problems distinguishing between different word classes. Many different realizations of word class confusion can be found, including mis-selection of an adjective for a target noun (e.g. sentence (120)), a noun for a target adjective (e.g. sentence (121)), a verb for a target adjective (e.g. sentence (122)), a noun for a target verb (e.g. sentence (123)), an adverb for a target adjective (e.g. sentence (124)) and the like.

(120) *If I feel cold, she will give me **warm**. (cf. warmth)
(121) *My brother don't let me play, because he said that is very **danger**. (cf. dangerous)
(122) *Then Hong Kong will be a **die** city. (cf. dead)
(123) *She will teach me how to **corrections** the wrong things. (cf. correct)

(124)   *But when I was four years old, my family is **sadly**. (cf. sad)

In Chinese-Cantonese, there are often no distinct forms or derivations for different word classes. Learners who have inadequate knowledge of the word-formation processes in English may believe that English words behave in similar ways as Chinese-Cantonese, resulting in word class confusion.

Discoursal Level

At the discoursal level, intralingual errors are less prevalent. Only one type of error has been detected, which is concerned with the misuse of the pronoun *it* as a deictic element in a discourse.

Misuse of It *as Discourse Deixis*

For this error type, the pronoun *it* is inappropriately used as a discourse deictic expression referring to a preceding or following portion of a discourse (e.g. examples (125–127)). The pronoun often does not have a clear referent in the whole discourse.

(125)   *We can be a farmer and a fisherman. **It** will be very free to us.
(126)   *If the quality of graduate is higher, **it** can benefit the economic development.
(127)   *She found a private tutor for me immediately. **It** is so happy for me and I thanked my mum that I don't have worry such problems in my studies.

In English, the pronoun *it* is not normally used to refer to the whole of a preceding or following discourse. Some other pronouns, such as the demonstratives *this* or *that*, are better candidates for achieving the deictic purpose. Therefore, replacing *it* with *that* will be more appropriate, as in example (128).

(128)   We can be a farmer and a fisherman. **That** will be good for us.

Given that *it* does not have a referent in the previous or following portion of the discourse, the pronoun is actually not necessary in the discourse, and the sentence(s) in question can better be rewritten with a completely different structure, such as in examples (129–131)).

(129)   We can be a farmer and a fisherman. **We** will be free. (cf. example (125))
(130)   If the quality of graduates is higher, **the economy will benefit from their qualifications**. (cf. example (126))
(131)   She found a private tutor for me immediately. **I was so happy** and . . . (cf. example (127))

Learners' insufficient mastery of the function of *it*, as well as their unawareness of the use of demonstratives for deictic purposes in a discourse, may be a cause of the problem. It has been argued that because the dummy *it* is often used to fill the subject position of an English sentence which does not have a clear subject (e.g. sentence (132)), or of a sentence with a postponed subject (e.g. sentence (133)), learners may think that the pronoun can simply be used in sentences the subjects of which they find difficult to ascertain (Chan, 2010c), as in example (134).

(132) **It** is cold.
(133) **It** is good that you have made up your mind.
(134) *The heads of the eight universities suggest the government would better to extend the university classes one more year. **It** tends to change the university curriculum from three years to four years.

Because of the misuse of *it* as discourse deixis, the intended subject for a certain sentence/clause is often difficult to identify. It is unclear, for instance, whether the intended subject for the second sentence in example (134) refers to *the suggestion, the government* or *the extension.*

A Taxonomy of Intralingual Errors Made by Cantonese ESL Learners

Table 6.1 summarizes the different kinds of intralingual errors discussed in this chapter.

Conclusion

In this chapter, a taxonomy of common intralingual errors made by Cantonese ESL learners have been established. The probable causes of these problems have

Table 6.1 A taxonomy of intralingual errors

	Morphological Level	*Lexical Level*	*Syntactic Level*	*Discoursal Level*
Error Types	• Inappropriate Selection of affixes • Overuse of affixes	• Synforms	• Concord problems • Confusion between *"concern"* and *"concerned about"* • Inappropriate case selection • Mis-ordering of constituents in indirect questions • Misuse of prepositions • Misuse of relative clauses • Non-parallel structures • Punctuation problems • Verb form selection problems • Word class confusion	• Misuse of *it* as discourse deixis

also been diagnosed. Although the errors are classified as intralingual errors and most of them can be attributed to learners' inadequate mastery of relevant L2 structures and/or their unawareness of target language norms, L1 interference is not totally excluded. Other probable causes, including the lack of positive transfer, discontinuity in thought, lax monitoring and even universal processes, are also evident and may interact intricately with each other in one way or another (see Chapter 9 for more details). There is no attempt here to give an exhaustive error list, so the errors discussed in this chapter, together with those discussed in Chapters 4 and 5, do not represent the totality of morphological, lexical, syntactic or discoursal errors made by Cantonese ESL learners. They are, however, among the most common errors that have been identified in relevant research studies conducted by the author and her colleagues. Not only do Cantonese ESL learners have problems in their acquisition of English grammar, but they also have problems in their acquisition of English phonology. In the next chapter, Cantonese ESL learners' problems with English speech production will be discussed.

Notes

1 The error types *confusion between "concern" and "concerned about"* and *non-parallel structures* are not discussed in Chan (2010c), but the examples used for illustration, unless otherwise stated and acknowledged, also come from unpublished data of the study.
2 Morphs are the different realizations of a morpheme, and the different morphs of the same morpheme are the allomorphs of that morpheme (Yule, 2017).
3 It may be argued that because of possible L1 interference, *confusion between "concern" and "concerned about"* should be classified as an interlingual error type and discussed in Chapter 4. It was decided that this error type be included in this chapter instead, because many tokens and/or subtypes of deviant L2 output associated with the verb *concern* and the related adjective *concerned* cannot be attributed to L1 interference. The same rationale applies to some other errors discussed in this chapter, including *misuse of prepositions* and *use of resumptive pronouns*.
4 Although the errors discussed in this section are associated with the lexical items *concern* and *concerned*, they are classified as syntactic errors instead of lexical errors, because inappropriate use of the words has direct impact on the structures of the clauses/sentences they are in, such as the choice of the subject and of the object.
5 The operator is "the first or only auxiliary verb in the verb phrase" (Nelson & Greenbaum, 2016: 10). It is the constituent that is fronted when an interrogative sentence (e.g. *Is he doing his homework*) is formed from a declarative sentence (e.g. *He is doing his homework*). The negative marker *not* is placed immediately after the operator when a negative sentence (e.g. *He is **not** doing his homework*) is formed from a positive sentence. If a sentence does not have an operator (e.g. *Mary loves John*), then a dummy operator (i.e. *do, does, did*) will be used in forming an interrogative or negative sentence (e.g. ***Does** Mary love John? Mary **does** not love John.*).
6 It has been suggested that the ease with which relative clauses may be formed follows an accessibility hierarchy (Keenan & Comrie, 1977), as follows:

S (subject) > DO (direct object) > IO (indirect object) > OBL (oblique; i.e. object of preposition in English) > GEN (genitive) > OCOMP (object of comparison)
where > means "followed by"

7 Learner Problems in the Acquisition of English Phonology I: Speech Production

In Chapter 3, we explored the major differences between the English and Cantonese phonological systems, including differences in the phonemic inventories of the two systems, the characteristics of the vowel and consonant sounds, the permissible syllable structures, and the rhythmic patterns in the two languages. In this chapter, the production problems that Cantonese ESL learners often encounter and the strategies that they often use to cope with problematic English speech sounds will be discussed. As seen in previous chapters, learners' prior linguistic experiences have significant influences on their learning of L2 grammar. This is also true in learners' acquisition of phonology (Hung, 1993). This chapter presents the argument that many speech production problems encountered by Cantonese ESL learners can be attributed to the differences between the English and Cantonese phonological systems discussed previously; yet L1 interference is, again, not the only probable cause of the problems.

There has been a large, substantial body of empirical and/or descriptive research on Cantonese ESL learners' speech production problems (e.g. earlier studies such as Anderson-Hsieh, 1983; Avery, Ehrlich, Mendelson-Burns & Archibald, 1987; Bolton & Kwok, 1990; Chen, 1976; Forbes, 1993; Han & Koh, 1976; Jones, 1979; Kenworthy, 1986; Lee, 1976; as well as studies in the current millennium, such as Chan, 2006b, 2006c, 2007, 2010a, 2010b, 2014; Chan & Li, 2000; Deterding, Wong & Kirkpatrick, 2008; Peng & Setter, 2000; Stibbard, 2004). The problems included in this chapter and the related arguments are mainly based on the findings of those studies.

The discussions of speech production problems presented in the following sections will begin with problems with consonants, followed by those with consonant clusters, vowels, and suprasegmental features.

Plosives

As discussed in Chapter 3, both English and Cantonese have 6 plosives (/b, d, g, p, t, k/). Although the former three (/b, d, g/) are voiced in English, all Cantonese plosives are voiceless. Unlike English plosives, which are often audibly released in final position, Cantonese final plosives are obligatorily not released. These articulatory differences present difficulties to Cantonese ESL learners, who have

DOI: 10.4324/9781003252498-7

a tendency to devoice English voiced plosives and not release all English final plosives, be they voiced or voiceless (Chan, 2006b, 2010a; Chan & Li, 2000).

Devoicing of English Voiced Plosives

It has often been argued that when producing English voiced plosives /b, d, g/, Cantonese ESL learners tend to substitute the corresponding voiceless counterparts, namely /p, t, k/ for the targets, so words such as *ban* /bæn/ or *den* /den/ may sound like *pan* [pæn] and *ten* [ten][1] respectively. Substitution, as it has often been called, is in effect devoicing, as the "substitute" sounds (e.g. [p] or [t]), though voiceless, are not accompanied by aspiration when they appear in syllable-initial position. That is, there is no emission of a burst of air immediately after oral release. Therefore, rather than describing the speech phenomenon as substitution, it is more appropriate to say that English voiced plosives are often devoiced by Cantonese ESL learners. Not only is devoicing of English syllable-initial voiced plosives common, but devoicing of syllable-final voiced plosives, as /b/ in *robe* /rəʊb/, is also widespread.

Non-Release of English Final Plosives

Non-release of English word-final plosives is another prevalent Cantonese ESL speech phenomenon. That is, for the bilabial plosives /p, b/, the lips remain closed; for the alveolar plosives /t, d/, the tongue tip clings to the alveolar ridge; and for the velar plosives /k, g/, the back of the tongue clings to the velum (Kenworthy, 1986). Words such as *step* or *not* are, therefore, pronounced as [step˺] and [nɒt˺] respectively with unreleased plosives. Non-release of English final plosives often obscures the difference between voiced and voiceless plosives: With the plosives unreleased, minimal pairs, such as *robe* /rəʊb/ and *rope* /rəʊp/ or *maid* /meɪd/ and *mate* /meɪt/, will become indistinguishable. Because of this non-release feature of Cantonese ESL speech, devoicing of final plosives surfaces only when the final plosives are indeed released.

Learner Problems? Casual Speech?

It may be argued that devoicing of English voiced plosives and non-release of English final plosives are not necessarily pronunciation problems, as native speakers of English also exhibit such articulatory habits, especially in fast, causal speech. However, when native speakers do not actualize the voicing contrast between, for example, English /p/ and /b/ in *rope* and *robe* respectively, they lengthen the preceding vowel in the corresponding word with a voiced plosive (i.e. the vowel /əʊ/ in *robe*), so the minimal pair (e.g. *rope* and *robe*) are distinguished by means of vowel length rather than final voicing of plosives, with the vowel in the latter (i.e. *robe*) being longer than the vowel in the former (i.e. *rope*).[2] Many Cantonese ESL learners are not aware of such length differences between minimal pairs with voiced and voiceless plosives. Therefore, while devoicing of voiced plosives or non-release of final plosives alone can arguably be regarded as features of fast speech rather than ESL pronunciation problems, a combination of both articulatory features without any compensation strategies (such as lengthening of the preceding vowel for a target final voiced plosive) will legitimately render the pronunciations non-standard (Chan, 2006b).

Fricatives

As far as fricatives are concerned, there is a big gap between the inventories of English and Cantonese fricatives, with nine fricatives in English (voiced and voiceless) but only three voiceless fricatives in Cantonese (see Chapter 3). The English fricatives without a corresponding Cantonese counterpart create much difficulty for Cantonese ESL learners. Substitution seems to be the most common strategy adopted when learners produce an English fricative non-existent in their native language (Chan, 2006b, 2010a; Chan & Li, 2000).

Voiced Alveolar (/z/) and Voiced Labio-Dental (/v/) Fricatives

Neither the English voiced alveolar nor voiced labio-dental fricatives exist in Cantonese. The most popular substitutes for the former (i.e. /z/) and for the latter (i.e. /v/) may be simply the corresponding voiceless counterpart /s/ and /f/ respectively, which are also found in Cantonese. This is true for /z/: Its voiceless counterpart [s] is the most likely candidate for substitution irrespective of the position (syllable-initial or syllable-final) where the sound appears, so words such as *zip* /zɪp/ or *doze* /dəʊz/ are often pronounced as [sɪp] and [dəʊs] respectively.

On the other hand, for /v/, different substitutes may be used when it appears in different positions. When /v/ appears at the end of a word, the most common substitute is indeed [f], so *five* /faɪv/ will sound like [faɪf]. On the other hand, learners tend to substitute [w] for /v/ when /v/ is in syllable-initial position, so words such as *van* /væn/ or *vine* /vaɪn/ are often pronounced as [wæn] and [waɪn] respectively, though pronunciations such as [fæn] and [faɪn] are also found.

Similar to devoicing of voiced plosives, substitution of /s/ for /z/ or /f/ for /v/ in final position also renders the corresponding voiced fricative voiceless without accompanying lengthening of the preceding vowel (e.g. /uː/ in *lose* /luːz/ is not lengthened when [s] is used to substitute for /z/).

Dental Fricatives (/θ/ and /ð/)

The English dental fricatives /θ/ and /ð/ are very rare in the world's languages (Gamkrelidze, 1978; Maddieson, 1984) and are among the most problematic sounds encountered by Cantonese ESL learners. Substitutions of either [f] (more common)[3] or [t]/[s] (less common) for /θ/ and of either [d] (often in word-initial position) or [f] (often in syllable-final position) for /ð/ are found. Words such as *thin* /θɪn/ or *teeth* /tiːθ/ are often pronounced as [fɪn] and [tiːf] respectively, and words such as *they* /ðeɪ/ or *with* /wɪð/ are often pronounced as [deɪ] and [wɪf] respectively.

Palato-Alveolar Fricatives (/ʃ/ and /ʒ/)

Cantonese does not have palato-alveolar fricatives, so both the English voiceless palato-alveolar fricative /ʃ/ and the voiced palato-alveolar fricative /ʒ/ present difficulties to Cantonese learners of English. [s] is the most common substitute for /ʃ/, so words such as *shave* /ʃeɪv/ or *ship* /ʃɪp/ are often pronounced like *save* [seɪv] and *sip* [sɪp] respectively without the required lip rounding for the English target.[4] /ʒ/, which has a defective distribution in English in that it rarely occurs in word-initial position[5] and is seldom found in word-final position, is often replaced by either [s] or [ʃ] in word-medial position, so words such as *measure* /ˈmeʒə/ or *pleasure* /ˈpleʒə/ are often pronounced as [ˈmeʃə] and [ˈpleʃə], or [ˈmesə] and [ˈplesə] respectively.

Affricates

Although Cantonese does have affricates in its phonemic inventory, the affricates in Cantonese are alveolar /ts/ and /dz/ and do not require lip-rounding like what is required of the two English palato-alveolar affricates /tʃ/ and /dʒ/. Cantonese ESL learners may treat English affricates as the same as their Cantonese counterparts, so the affricates in words such as *China* /ˈtʃaɪnə/ or *George* /dʒɔːdʒ/ are often pronounced without lip-rounding (i.e. [ˈtsaɪnə] and [dzɔːdz] respectively), resulting in the English affricates pronounced like the corresponding Cantonese counterparts (Chan & Li, 2000).

Nasals and Liquids[6]

English nasals /m, n, ŋ/ and liquids /l, r/ are also among some of the most problematic English consonants for Cantonese ESL learners. Different problems have been attested.

Neutralization of /l/ and /n/ in Initial Position

In syllable-initial position, Cantonese learners of English tend to substitute English [l] for /n/, so words such as *nine* /naɪn/ or *night* /naɪt/ are often pronounced as [laɪn] and [laɪt] respectively, resembling the words *line* and *light*. Interestingly, initial /l/ is, to a lesser extent, sometimes pronounced with some "n" quality, giving the impression of a nasalized /l/ sound, viz. [l̃], so words such as *love* /lʌv/ will be pronounced as [l̃ʌv] or [nʌv]. Such reciprocal substitutions, in effect, neutralize the differences between the two English sounds.

Neutralization of Cantonese /l/ and /n/ in word-initial position is very common (see Chapter 3) and does not normally give rise to communication problems because the intended meaning may usually be disambiguated by the context. On the other hand, neutralization of initial /l/ and /n/ in English may cause misunderstanding. More importantly, substitution of English [l] for English /n/, or vice versa, is not acceptable in Standard English (Chan, 2006c; Chan & Li, 2000).

Vocalization and Deletion of Final /l/

In RP English, final /l/ is often realized as a dark [ɫ] with a secondary articulation of the raising of the back of the tongue towards the velum. This second articulation occurs concurrently with the primary articulation characteristic of an alveolar lateral (i.e. the tip of the tongue touching the alveolar ridge and air escaping through the sides of the tongue) (Abercrombie, 1967; Gimson & Ramsaran, 1989; Roach, 2009). Cantonese ESL learners often replace the dark [ɫ] with a [u]-like sound (which also necessitates the raising of the back of the tongue towards the velum) without actualizing the primary articulation characteristic of a lateral, thus resulting in vocalization of final /l/. As [u] is typically produced with lip rounding, words containing a dark [ɫ] but no rounded vowels, such as *Bill* /bɪl/ or *kill* /kɪl/, are also often pronounced with unnecessary lip-rounding (i.e. [bɪu] and [kɪu] respectively).

Vocalization is not the only strategy adopted by Cantonese ESL learners in their production of English final /l/. Deletion is also common. In words such as *goal* /gəʊl/, *bull* /buːl/ or *ball* /bɔːl/, the final /l/ is often deleted, resulting in pronunciations such as [gəʊ], [buː] and [bɔː] respectively.

The linguistic environments where the English final /l/ appears have an impact on Cantonese ESL learners' production of the sound (Chan, 2006b): Deletion is more common in words consisting of a round and/or back vowel (e.g. *goal* /gəʊl/, *bull* /buːl/ or *ball* /bɔːl/), whereas vocalization is more typical in words with a close, front vowel (e.g. *Bill* /bɪl/ or *kill* /kɪl/). As both the dark [ɫ] and a preceding round, back vowel (e.g. /uː/ in *bull*) require the raising of the back of the tongue, the two sounds may be regarded by learners as equivalent and thus produced as if they were just one single sound, resulting in the dark [ɫ] completely deleted. On the other hand, as the dark [ɫ] and a preceding close, front vowel (e.g. /ɪ/ in *Bill*) are often perceived by learners as dissimilar[7] but the secondary articulation of the dark [ɫ] is often perceived as equivalent to an [u] sound, vocalization by means of substitution by [u], rather than deletion of the sound altogether, is more commonly adopted. What makes the dark [ɫ] difficult is, therefore, not the secondary articulation of raising the back of the tongue itself but the co-articulation requirement of this feature together with the primary articulation of the lateral (i.e. alveolar contact and lateral release) (Chan, 2006b).

Deletion of Final /n/ After a Diphthong

The English /n/ in final position of words containing a diphthong, especially /aɪ/, such as *mine* /maɪn/ or *line* /laɪn/, is often deleted, resulting in open syllables [maɪ] and [laɪ] respectively. This phenomenon is very likely due to mother tongue interference, as Cantonese diphthongs are allowed only in open syllables (Bauer & Benedict, 1997; Chan & Li, 2000). It is, however, difficult to understand why deletion of /n/ following other diphthongs (e.g. /aʊ/) and deletion of /m/ after diphthongs are not widespread. The influence of the preceding vowel on a final nasal seems to be rather idiosyncratic (Chan, 2006b).

Table 7.1 Most common strategies adopted by Cantonese ESL learners in their production
of English consonants

Sound Categories	Sounds	Most Common Strategies Adopted
Plosives	/p, t, k, b, d, g/ in final position	Not released
	/b, d, g/	Devoiced
Fricatives	/v/	Substitution of [w] for target sound in initial position Substitution of [f] for target sound in final position
	/z/	Substitution of [s] for target sound
	/θ, ð/	Substitution of [f] for /θ/ Substitution of [d] for /ð/ in initial position Substitution of [f] for /ð/ in final position
	/ʃ, ʒ/	Substitution of [s] for /ʃ/ Substitution of [s] or [ʃ] for /ʒ/
Affricates	/tʃ, dʒ/	Substitution of Cantonese affricates [ts] and [dz] respectively for target sounds
Liquids and nasals	/l/ and /n/ in initial position	Neutralized
	/l/ in final position	Deleted or vocalized
	/n/ in final position	Deleted after a diphthong, especially /aɪ/
	/n/ and /ŋ/	Reciprocal substitution
	/ŋ/	Audible release
	/r/	Substitution of [w] or [l] for target sound

Other Problems

Other production problems related to English nasals include reciprocal substitution of /n/ and /ŋ/ in final position. For words such as *hang* /hæŋ/ or *tongue* /tʌŋ/, Cantonese ESL learners may substitute [n] for /ŋ/, resulting in pronunciations such as [hæn] and [tʌn] respectively. For words such as *Don* /dɒn/ or *gone* /gɒn/, substitutions of [ŋ] for target /n/ are sometimes found. In terms of frequency, substitution of [n] for /ŋ/ is more common than substitution of [ŋ] for /n/. Non-standard audible release of final /ŋ/, in words such as *king* or *long*, is also occasionally found, resulting in pronunciations such as [kɪŋg] and [lɒŋg] respectively (Chan, 2010a).

As for /r/, the most common problem is substitution of [l] or [w] for the target, so words such as *ride* /raɪd/ or *road* /rəʊd/ are often pronounced as [laɪd] and *load* [ləʊd], or [waɪd] and [wəʊd] respectively. Although both kinds of substitution are found, substitution by [w] is more common than substitution by [l] (Chan, 2010a).

Table 7.1 gives a summary of the major problems that Cantonese ESL learners encounter and the strategies they employ in their production of English consonants.[8]

Consonant Clusters

In the discussion of Cantonese ESL learners' coping strategies for English consonants, one aspect which cannot be ignored is the ways English consonant clusters are handled. Unlike English, which allows a maximum of three pre-vocalic consonants and a maximum of four post-vocalic consonants in a syllable, Cantonese has no consonant clusters (see Chapter 3). To simplify English consonant clusters, learners tend to adopt either deletion or vowel epenthesis. Deletion, which is commonly found in both syllable-initial and syllable-final positions, reduces the number of consonants occurring together (e.g. from three consonants to two or one consonant(s), or from two consonants to one consonant), thus reducing the clusters to singleton consonants or rendering the clusters less complex. Epenthesis, which is more common in initial position or across word boundaries, breaks up a consonant cluster by the insertion of an unwanted vowel, thus creating an extra syllable with a singleton consonant at the onset[9] (Hung, 1993). Other than deletion and vowel epenthesis, substitution is also observed (Chan, 2006c). The following sections will be devoted to discussions of these strategies.

Deletion

Deletion of one or more consonants is often employed when Cantonese ESL learners tackle a complex English consonant cluster. The consonants which are most prone to deletion are the alveolar plosives /t, d/ and the lateral /l/, which is also alveolar. For example, the word *bold* /bəʊld/ is often pronounced as [bəʊd] or [bəʊ], with only the lateral deleted in the former and both the lateral and the alveolar plosive deleted in the latter, resulting in an open syllable for the latter. Consonant clusters comprising the final consonant(s) of a stem word and a past tense marker, such as /t/ or /d/, are also prone to deletion. For example, past tense verbs such as *booked* /bʊkt/ or *begged* /begd/ are often pronounced as [bʊk] and [beg] respectively, resulting in confusion between the base forms (i.e. *book* and *beg*) and the past forms. Given that English verbs are obligatorily marked for tense and the subject must also agree with the verb in number, if a sentence consisting of a regular past tense verb is pronounced with deletion of the past tense marker (e.g. *He touched it* being pronounced as [hɪ tʌtʃ ɪt]), the sentence would be perceived as ungrammatical due to a lack of agreement between the subject (*he*) and the verb (pronounced as *touch* [tʌtʃ]) (Chan & Li, 2000).

Not only is deletion found in final position, but it is also very commonly used to simplify syllable-initial consonant clusters. For example, when /r/ follows a plosive, it tends to be deleted, so words such as *prolong* /prəˈlɒːŋ/ or *free* /friː/ may sound like [pəˈlɒːŋ] and [fiː] respectively, with /r/ deleted. Although liquids and alveolar plosives are the most likely candidates for deletion, other plosives are also sometimes deleted. Examples include /k/ in *screen* /skriːn/, which is sometimes pronounced as [sriːn] (Chan, 2006c).

Vowel Epenthesis

Apart from deletion, vowel epenthesis is also a common strategy used by Cantonese ESL learners to overcome English consonant clusters. For instance, the word *film* /fɪlm/ may have an extra vowel (often the schwa /ə/ or other short vowels in English or in Cantonese) added between the two consonants /l/ and /m/ of the final consonant cluster, resulting in pronunciations such as [ˈfɪləm]. Words with an initial consonant cluster, such as *clutch* /klʌtʃ/, and more typically words with an initial consonant cluster beginning with /s/, such as *spoon* /spuːn/, are also often subject to vowel epenthesis, resulting in pronunciations such as [keˈlʌtʃ] or even [kaˈlʌtʃ] for the former, and [sɪˈpuːn] for the latter.

Deletion or Vowel Epenthesis: What Is the Choice?

Given that both deletion and vowel epenthesis result in the simplification of a complex consonant cluster and both strategies are found in learners' pronunciation of an English consonant cluster, there comes the question of which strategy is preferred and why. For learners at a higher proficiency level, a strategy which preserves the original number of syllables in a word is favoured. Retaining the total number of syllables in a word may avoid re-syllabification and result in less perceptual distortion, which may in turn lead to a less negative impression of the speaker's English proficiency and thus a less strong feeling of disapproval by the listener (Chan, 2006c). Deletion, therefore, significantly outnumbers epenthesis in advanced learners' actual speech production. Vowel epenthesis, if adopted, is more typical of learners at lower proficiency levels.

Substitution

Instead of adopting deletion or vowel epenthesis, some Cantonese ESL learners tend to adopt the strategy of substitution in coping with an English consonant cluster, replacing a sound segment in a cluster with another sound. Of these substitutions, the most common is the substitution of [l] or [w] for /r/. For instance, the word *produce* /prəˈdjuːs/ may sound like [pləˈdjuːs], and the word *Fred* /fred/ may be pronounced as [fwed]. This kind of substitution resembles the strategies that learners use when corresponding problematic consonants appear in singletons instead of in a cluster (see the previous section, "Nasals and Liquids"). The use of [w] to replace /l/ in a consonant cluster, though to a lesser extent, is also found, so words such as *English* /ˈɪŋglɪʃ/ may be pronounced as [ˈɪŋgwɪʃ] with [w] replacing /l/ in the second syllable.

Another common kind of substitution is the use of an English or Cantonese affricate to replace a plosive + liquid cluster (e.g. /d/ + /r/), so words such as *drum* /drʌm/ or *tree* /triː/ are often pronounced as [dʒʌm] or [dzʌm] and [tʃiː] or [tsiː] respectively, with the English affricate [dʒ] or the Cantonese affricate [dz] replacing the whole of the cluster /dr/ in *drum*, and the English affricate [tʃ] or the Cantonese affricate [ts] replacing the whole of the cluster /tr/ in *tree*.

Interestingly, reciprocal substitutions are also found in consonant clusters, so substitutions of [l] for /r/ in words such as *freeze* (/friːz/ being pronounced as [fliːz]) and substitutions of [r] for /l/ in words such as *problem* (/ˈprɒbləm/ being pronounced as [ˈprɒbrəm] or even [ˈplɒbrəm]) are both found. As the same sound, namely [w], is used to replace both /l/ and /r/ in a consonant cluster (see the previous paragraph) and reciprocal substitutions between /l/ and /r/ are observed, it has been argued that in the interlanguages of Cantonese ESL learners, there is a phonological rule which neutralizes liquids in a consonant cluster (Chan, 2006c).

It should be noted that substitution of a certain sound segment(s) in a cluster may occur simultaneously with deletion of another sound segment in the same cluster. Chan (2006c), for example, has noted the pronunciation of [ʃiːt] for the word *street* /striːt/ by advanced Cantonese ESL learners. When that happens, it is difficult to determine which sound in a certain consonant cluster exhibits deletion or substitution, or both. For instance, it is not clear whether the incorrect pronunciation [ʃiːt] for the word *street* is the result of substitution of [ʃ] for /s/ and simultaneous deletion of both /t/ and /r/, or the result of substitution of [ʃ] for /st/ and simultaneous deletion of /r/, or other processes in combination.

Unnecessary Aspiration of Plosives After /s/

Another common phenomenon associated with Cantonese ESL learners' production of English consonant clusters is concerned with the aspiration feature of plosives after the consonant /s/. As is well known, (voiceless) plosives occurring after /s/ are unaspirated.[10] However, many Cantonese ESL learners tend to unnecessarily aspirate the plosive after /s/, preserving the characteristic feature of the sound in initial position without a preceding /s/. Words such as *spoon* /spuːn/ or *star* /staː/ are, therefore, often pronounced as [spʰuːn] and [stʰaː] respectively. Such a strategy can be seen as an indication of learners' incomplete grasp of the production of English plosives and their inappropriate generalization of a phonetic property to other contexts (Chan, 2006c). Learners' tendency to adopt a safe way to handle the same speech sounds in different phonological environments is apparent. From a second language learning perspective, such a strategy may also be seen as a kind of avoidance behaviour, with learners' avoiding making changes to some well-known properties (i.e. aspiration) which are characteristic of a certain group of sounds (i.e. voiceless plosives).

Table 7.2 summarizes the major strategies that Cantonese ESL learners employ in their production of English consonant clusters.

Segment Composition of Clusters

One question about the production of English consonant clusters concerns the kinds of clusters which present more difficulties to Cantonese ESL learners. While it is commonly assumed that more complex clusters (e.g. four-consonant clusters or three-consonant clusters) should be more difficult than less complex clusters (e.g. three-consonant clusters or two-consonant clusters), are consonant clusters with the same complexity equally difficult? In line with what has been put forward in the literature (e.g. Stockman & Pluut, 1992), that the presence of a certain segment in a syllable is the most significant factor affecting error distribution, it has been argued that the segment composition of a consonant cluster is important in determining its overall difficulty level (Chan, 2006c). Some sounds often create more problems

Table 7.2 Most common strategies adopted by Cantonese ESL learners in their production of English consonant clusters

Strategies	Sounds Affected	Examples
Deletion	Liquids (+ Plosives)	e.g. *bold* /bəʊld/ pronounced as [bəʊd] or [bəʊ]
		e.g. *prolong* /prəˈlɒːŋ/ pronounced as [pəˈlɒːŋ]
	Plosives	e.g. *booked* /bʊkt/ pronounced as [bʊk] e.g. *screen* /skriːn/ pronounced as [sriːn]
Vowel epenthesis	/ə/ or a short vowel	e.g. *film* /fɪlm/ pronounced as [ˈfɪləm])
		e.g. *spoon* /spuːn/ pronounced as [sɪˈpuːn]
Substitution	/r/	Substitution of /l/ for /r/ e.g. *produce* /prəˈdjuːs/ pronounced as [pləˈdjuːs]
		Substitution of /w/ for /r/ e.g. *Fred* /fred/ pronounced as [fwed]
	/l/	Substitution of /w/ for /l/ e.g. *English* /ˈɪŋglɪʃ/ pronounced as [ˈɪŋgwɪʃ]
		Substitution of /r/ for /l/ e.g. *problem* /ˈprɒbləm/ pronounced as [ˈprɒbrəm]
	Plosives + Liquids (e.g. /d/ + /r/)	Substitution of English or Cantonese affricate for target sound e.g. *drum* /drʌm/ pronounced as [dʒʌm] or [dzʌm]
Unnecessary aspiration of plosives after /s/	Voiceless plosives	e.g. spoon /spuːn/ pronounced as [spʰuːn]

than other sounds. For example, liquids (/r/ in particular) and certain fricatives, namely /ʃ/ and /θ/, often create more problems to Cantonese ESL learners than plosives and other "easier" fricatives, such as /f/ and /s/, even when they occur as singleton consonants (see earlier in the "Consonant Clusters" section). The former are also more difficult than the latter when appearing in a consonant cluster, regardless of which other sounds they co-occur with in the cluster. Consonant clusters consisting of one or more "difficult" sound segment(s), thus, exhibit many more cases of deletion and substitution than consonant clusters which do not comprise a difficult sound segment. These inherent properties of a certain sound segment in a cluster determine the level of difficulty of the whole cluster. To Cantonese ESL learners, thus, English consonant clusters that comprise sounds all of which have comparable equivalents in Cantonese will be easier than consonant clusters that comprise sounds some of which do not have comparable equivalents in Cantonese.

The segment composition of a consonant cluster also helps to explain learners' more frequent use of deletion than vowel epenthesis. When a sound is deleted, learners can avoid producing that sound, and if the sound that undergoes deletion is a difficult one (which is often the case), then learners will be relieved of the trouble to produce it. On the other hand, vowel epenthesis only creates a drastic change to the internal structure of a word by turning a consonant cluster to a syllable with fewer consonants. The epenthetic vowel cannot help to relieve learners of the need to pronounce the difficult sound segments that are originally in the cluster. For example, in a word such as *freeze* /fri:z/, where /r/ itself is a problematic sound to Cantonese ESL learners, adding an epenthetic vowel between /f/ and /r/ cannot ease learners' difficulties in pronouncing /r/. On the contrary, it necessitates the use of two coping strategies, one to add an epenthetic vowel (e.g. [ɪ]) and the other to use an "easier" sound to substitute for the difficult sound (/r/), thus resulting in compounded difficulties (Chan, 2006c).

Pure Vowels

In the foregoing sections, the most common strategies used by Cantonese ESL learners in coping with English consonants and consonant clusters have been presented. In the following sections, learners' problems with English vowels and their coping strategies will be discussed, including difficulties in distinguishing between long and short vowels and between /æ/ and /e/, as well as the addition of a consonantal glide before /i:/ and /ɪ/. Learners' problems with diphthongs will also be diagnosed.

Indistinguishable Long and Short Vowel Pairs

Cantonese ESL learners often have difficulties actualizing the differences between English long and short vowel pairs, namely /i:/ and /ɪ/, /u:/ and /ʊ/, and /ɔ:/ and /ɒ/. Short vowels tend to be unnecessarily lengthened, whereas long vowels tend to be inappropriately shortened. Sometimes a sound which is somewhere between the long and short vowels may be produced for either target. As such, the distinction between the corresponding long and short vowels in each pair is often under-differentiated. For instance, /i:/ and /ɪ/ as in *cheap* /tʃi:p/ and *chip* /tʃɪp/, /u:/ and /ʊ/ as in *suit* /su:t/ and *soot* /sʊt/, /ɔ:/ and /ɒ/ as in *caught* /kɔ:t/ and *cot* /kɒt/, are often indistinguishable in learners' L2 speech production (Chan & Li. 2000).

It should be noted that although phonemically, Cantonese has only three corresponding short vowels, namely /i/, /u/ and /ɔ/ for the English long and short vowel pairs in question, all three Cantonese vowels have long and short allophones realized in different phonological environments (see Chapter 3). The length differences of the allophones of a Cantonese short vowel phoneme are not distinctive, meaning that a change in the length of a vowel will not change lexical meanings and will not result in a different word as is the case in English. Durational distinctions between English long and short vowel phonemes, thus, surface in Cantonese as allophonic variations in different phonological environments. The allophonic, non-distinctive features of the Cantonese vowels may help explain learners' difficulties in distinguishing long and short vowel contrasts in English: The English long and short vowels (e.g. /u:/ and /ʊ/) are very similar[11] to the long and short allophones of the corresponding Cantonese vowels (e.g. /u/). Learners find it hard to discriminate between the distinctive length feature of the English vowel phonemes and tend to confuse them in production, producing a sound which is somewhere in between for both targets or under-differentiating the length differences between them (Chan, 2010a).

/æ/ *and* /e/

Many Cantonese learners of English are unaware that English /æ/ is pronounced with more open lips than English /e/. Reciprocal substitutions have been observed, though substitution of [e] for /æ/ is much more common than [æ] for /e/ (Chan, 2010a). This can probably be explained by the inventory of Cantonese vowels, which only has the less open /e/. As such, words such as *man* /mæn/ and *men* /men/ and *sat* /sæt/ and *set* /set/ may become indistinguishable.

Insertion of Consonantal Glide Before /iː/ *and* /ɪ/

When English /iː/ or /ɪ/ occurs in initial position, Cantonese ESL learners tend to insert the semi-vowel /j/ before the vowel. For example, words such as *ease* /iːz/ and *index* /ˈɪndeks/ are often pronounced as [ˈjiːz] and [ˈjɪndeks] respectively. This strategy will obscure the pronunciation difference between pairs of words as *east* /iːst/ and *yeast* /jiːst/, the difference between which lies only in the existence of /j/ before /iː/ in the latter. As Cantonese /i/ in word-initial position is consistently preceded by the consonantal glide[12] /j/ (e.g. 醫 'medical' /jiː/), the redundant insertion of /j/ to English words beginning with /iː/ or /ɪ/ may be seen as an example of transfer from Cantonese to English (Chan & Li, 2000).

/ɜː/ *and* /ə/

The central vowel /ɜː/ as in *bird* /bɜːd/ and *fur* /fɜː/ is often pronounced with unnecessary lip-rounding, resembling the Cantonese similar-sounding vowel /œ/ (Chan & Li, 2000). Another central vowel, namely the schwa /ə/, which is a reduced vowel often found in unstressed syllables of polysyllabic words, is often given full vowel quality (Peng & Setter, 2000), so a word such as *accept* is often pronounced as [ekˈsept] or [ækˈsept] instead of /əkˈsept/.

Diphthongs

Cantonese ESL learners also have problems with the pronunciations of English diphthongs. Some common problems include the diphthong /ɔɪ/ occurring before a nasal, which tends to be replaced by a similar pure short vowel, such as [ɒ], in words such as *point* (i.e. /pɔɪnt/ pronounced as [pɒnt]). The diphthong /eɪ/ is often replaced by the vowel [e], resulting in pronunciations such as [klem] for the word *claim* /kleɪm/ and [men] for the word *main* /meɪn/. Centring diphthongs (i.e. /eə, ʊə, ɪə/) are also often pronounced as a combination of two discrete vowels separated by a glottal stop. For instance, the word *poor* /pʊə/ may be pronounced as [pʊʔa], with a glottal stop [ʔ] separating the first element (i.e.

Table 7.3 Most common strategies adopted by Cantonese ESL learners in their production
of English vowels

Sound Categories	Sounds Affected	Most Common Strategies Adopted
Pure vowels	/iː/ and /ɪ/ /uː/ and /ʊ/ /ɔː/ and /ɒ/	Long and short vowels in each pair are often indistinguishable
	/ æ/ and /e /	Indistinguishable
	/iː/ and /ɪ/	Addition of a consonantal glide before targets in initial position
	/ɜː/	Unnecessary lip-rounding
	/ə/ in polysyllabic words	Given full vowel quality
Diphthongs	/ɔɪ/	Substitution of [ɒ] for target
	/eɪ/	Substitution of [e] for target
	/eə, ʊə, ɪə/ (Centring diphthongs)	Two discrete vowels separated by a glottal stop
	/eə/	Substitution of [e] or [æ] for target

/ʊ/) of the diphthong and the second element of the diphthong (i.e. /ə/) replaced by a stronger vowel (e.g. [a]). Deletion of the second element of the diphthong (i.e. /ə/) is also common for centring diphthongs, especially /eə/, which may be replaced by the short vowels [e] or [æ] and result in pronunciations such as [pe] or [pæ] for words such as *pair* /peə/ (Chan & Li, 2000).

Table 7.3 gives a summary of the major problems Cantonese ESL learners encounter and strategies they employ in their production of English vowels.

Words in Connected Speech

As mentioned in Chapter 3, English function words (e.g. *can, do, of*) are often reduced to their weak forms in connected speech. This phenomenon has no parallel in Cantonese. Cantonese learners of English tend to pronounce English function words in their strong forms in connected speech irrespective of whether the intended meanings of the function words are emphatic or not. For example, for a sentence such as *I can make it*, while a native speaker of English will reduce the auxiliary verb *can* /kæn/ to its weak form [kən] and say [aɪ kən meɪkɪt], Cantonese ESL learners often give full vowel quality to the vowel in *can* and say [aɪ kæn meɪk ɪt], resulting in an unnatural and foreign-sounding impression (Chan & Li, 2000).

The phenomena related to linkage are also often ignored by Cantonese ESL learners. Instead of linking two vowels which occur next to each other across word boundaries in the same tone group using a linking [r], or instead of carrying a final consonant of a word forward to the vowel in the next word in the same tone group, Cantonese ESL learners tend to separate the words through the use of pauses. For example, the expression *far away* [faːrəweɪ] is often spoken without the use of a linking [r] between *far* and *away* (i.e. [faː əweɪ]). The expression *pick it up* [pɪkɪtʌp] is also often pronounced with a pause across word boundaries (i.e. [pɪk ɪt ʌp]) instead of having the final consonant [k] of *pick* carried forward to the initial vowel [ɪ] of *it* and the final consonant [t] of *it* carried forward to the initial vowel [ʌ] of *up*. The resultant speech, thus, has a very staccato rhythm (Chan & Li. 2000).

Rhythm

Cantonese ESL learners also have problems in learning English rhythm. For example, in the Chinese-Cantonese noun phrase 國際機場 /gʷɔk dzai gei tsœŋ/ and the sentence 約翰以前學過法文 /jœk hɔn ji tsin hɔk gʷɔ faːt man/, each of the syllables is given more or less the same amount of time in Cantonese speech (cf. syllable-timed rhythm; see Chapter 3). In contrast, the English equivalents, *inter<u>na</u>tional <u>air</u>port* and *<u>John</u> has <u>learnt</u> <u>French</u> be<u>fore</u> respectively, are usually spoken only with the underlined syllables stressed. The syllables that are not underlined are normally spoken with a much faster rhythm and a weaker intensity, resulting in a more or less equal interval between the stressed syllables (cf. stress-timed rhythm; see Chapter 3). Cantonese learners of English often transfer the Cantonese syllable-timed rhythm into English, giving the same amount of stress and time to each and every syllable of the corresponding expressions (i.e. *in-ter-na-tion-al air-port; John-has-learnt-French-be-fore*). Such L2 speech phenomena are sometimes perceived as "flat and boring" by native speakers of English (Chan & Li, 2000; Forbes, 1993).

Sentence Stress

Cantonese ESL learners also tend to put the tonic stress, i.e. the syllable which receives the strongest stress in an intonation unit (Demirezen, 2016), at the end of an utterance irrespective of whether there is another word which should become the focus of information in the utterance. There is also an absence of de-accenting, i.e. reduced emphasis, for repeated and predictable information (Bolton & Kwok, 1990). Therefore, for utterances such as (1), where the word *city* and the second occurrence of *first* and of *London* should normally be de-accented because of their being repeated or predictable, Cantonese ESL learners tend to give unnecessary tonic stress or substantial emphasis to the highlighted syllables.

(1)   That was my first time to London . . . was the **first** time I went to England . . . so my stay in **Lon**don was the first experience I had of the **city** (Deterding, Wong & Kirkpatrick, 2008: 170, details omitted),

Pronouns and determiners, irrespective of their positions in an utterance, also receive unexpected emphasis (Deterding, Wong & Kirkpatrick, 2008). For instance, the personal pronoun *we* in sentence (2), the possessive determiner *my* in sentence (3), and the demonstrative determiner *this* in sentence (4) are often unexpectedly stressed even when they are not being contrasted with other words.[13]

(2)   **We** enjoyed that a lot. (Deterding, Wong & Kirkpatrick, 2008: 170)
(3)   I will tell you about **my** summer holiday. (ibid)
(4)   I enjoyed **this** job very much. (ibid)

Conclusion

In this chapter, we have examined the different kinds of speech production problems encountered by Cantonese ESL learners and the most common strategies
they adopt in coping with the problematic sounds/sound sequences. At the segmental level, substitution of an inappropriate sound for the target, devoicing of
voiced obstruents[14] (especially in final position), neutralization of initial /l/ and
/n/ in singletons and of /l/ and /r/ in consonant clusters, and deletion of singleton
final consonants and of one or two consonants in a consonant cluster (initial or
final), are also common. Vowel epenthesis is sometimes adopted for coping with
consonant clusters, whereby an unnecessary vowel is added between the consonants to create an extra syllable. For vowels, long and short vowel pairs, as well as
/æ/ and /e/, are often indistinguishable. Suprasegmentally, Cantonese ESL learners also tend to stress most syllables of an English word, resulting in an unnatural
foreigner accent. Inappropriate tonic stress given to syllables which should be
de-accented is also observed.

Many of the speech phenomena discussed in this chapter need to be addressed.
For instance, substitution of a non-target sound for a target sound often obscures
the difference between minimal pairs (e.g. *wide* and *ride* may sound the same
because of substitution of [w] for /r/ in *ride*, and *set* and *sat* may sound the
same because of substitution of [e] for /æ/ in *sat*) and may result in miscommunication, which may or may not be easily disambiguated by the context.
Remedial instructional efforts are therefore needed to help learners tackle such
common pronunciation problems (see Chapter 11 for some pedagogical suggestions). In the next chapter, Cantonese ESL learners' speech perception problems
will be explored.

Notes

1   In addition to the target English sounds which are being discussed (e.g. plosives in the
current paragraph), other English sounds not under discussion may also be mispronounced by Cantonese ESL learners. The phonetic transcriptions given in this chapter (enclosed in []) only reflect the mispronounced sounds currently under discussion.
Other mispronunciations not under discussion are not simultaneously presented. For
instance, although the vowel /æ/ in the word *ban* /bæn/ may also be mispronounced,
the phonetic transcription [pæn] given in the current paragraph shows only the mispronounced plosive, not the mispronounced vowel.

2   The length difference between vowels preceding voiced and voiceless plosives has
been widely documented in the literature (e.g. Roach, 2009). Not only are the vowels
before voiced plosives longer than those before voiceless plosives, but they are also
longer before voiced fricatives and affricates than before corresponding voiceless ones
(see the following sections covering pronunciation problems about English fricatives
and affricates).

3 Substitutions of [f] for /θ/ is regarded as TH-fronting in the literature (Hansen Edwards, 2019).

4 Despite common substitutions of [s] for /ʃ/, when /s/ co-occurs with a rounded vowel, such as /uː/ in words such as *soup* /suːp/, [ʃ] is sometimes used to substitute for target /s/ instead, resulting in mispronunciations such as [ʃuːp].

5 Many English words beginning or ending with /ʒ/ are borrowings from other languages, e.g. *rouge* /ruːʒ/ is a word borrowed from French.

6 English /l/ and /r/ are often collectively referred to as liquids in the literature (Gussenhoven & Jacobs, 2017).

7 See Chapter 8 for a more detailed discussion about similarity, dissimilarity and equivalence.

8 It is difficult to give a very precise summary of all the strategies adopted by Cantonese ESL learners in coping with problematic sounds, as different sounds may be used to substitute for the same target sound, with some substitutions being more common and others less common. Different strategies may also be adopted for the same sound in different positions. The strategies listed in Tables 7.1–7.3 are only the most common problems and corresponding strategies.

9 The consonantal element(s) before the vocalic element of a syllable is collectively known as the *onset* of the syllable (Yule, 2017).

10 The phonotactics of English do not allow voiced plosives /b, d, g/ to co-occur with /s/ in initial position, so all plosives after /s/ are voiceless.

11 See note 7. A more detailed discussion about similarity, dissimilarity and equivalence will be given in Chapter 8.

12 Semi-vowels /j/ and /w/ are also known as glides (Roach, 2009). In terms of classification, they are classified as consonants instead of vowels (see Chapter 3).

13 It should be noted that the production problems discussed in this chapter are not mutually exclusive, as different learners may exhibit different problems. For example, while some Cantonese ESL learners, especially elementary learners, may say an English sentence with equal stress on each and every syllable (as discussed in the section "Rhythm"), other learners may place inappropriate stress on certain syllables (as discussed in the current section).

14 The sound categories plosives, fricatives and affricates are collectively known as obstruents, as in the production of these consonants, there is airflow obstruction somewhere in the vocal tract (Zsiga, 2013).

8 Learner Problems in the Acquisition of English Phonology II: Speech Perception

In the previous chapter, the most common speech production problems that Cantonese ESL learners encounter, as well as the strategies that they often adopt to tackle their problems, were discussed. This chapter focuses on learners' speech perception problems. The importance of understanding speech perception will be discussed, and the concepts of similarity and dissimilarity will be explored. A detailed discussion of Cantonese ESL learners' perception of English speech sounds and their perceived similarity between English and Cantonese sounds will also be given.

Importance of Understanding Speech Perception

Cantonese ESL learners' speech production problems, as can be seen from Chapter 7, have been the subject of wide research. Though essential, speech production is not the only area which can enhance our understanding of L2 phonology. Speech perception is another major area of speech learning that deserves attention. It has often been argued that learners' perception of a speech sound has important effects on their accuracy in producing the sound (Flege, 1995; Munro & Derwing, 1995b; Rochet, 1995; Schmid & Yeni-Komshian, 1999), as accurate perceptual targets can guide the sensorimotor learning of target L2 speech sounds, without which speech production will not be accurate (Flege, 1995). Speech perception, thus, informs speech production in learners' learning of L2 pronunciations (Best, 1994; Flege, 1995).

It is important to understand learners' speech perception problems. Although speech perception problems per se normally do not cause serious communication problems, especially when contextual cues are available for disambiguation, there are occasions on which correct word identification is important, such as note-taking during meetings, or identification of isolated words over the phone. Misperception of isolated sounds will result in misidentification of words and/ or phrases, which may in turn cause misunderstanding (Chan, 2010c) and even embarrassment or frustration. Given the intimate relation between speech perception and speech production, a good understanding of speech perception problems will not only enhance our understanding of speech production but also inform pronunciation pedagogy. If it is found that a certain speech production problem stems

DOI: 10.4324/9781003252498-8

from certain perception problems, pedagogical attention can target both areas of learning. On the other hand, if some production problems are independent of learners' perception of relevant sounds, or if a certain perception problem is solely perceptually related, pedagogical efforts can be invested accordingly. Speech perception is, therefore, an indispensable component of discussion in studies of L2 phonology.

Similarity, Dissimilarity and Equivalence

A lot of research has been devoted to speech perception and/or the interaction between speech perception and speech production. Many research studies are concerned with the perception of English by speakers of other languages, including Dutch, Japanese, Korean, Italian, Malay, Polish, Portuguese and Vietnamese learners (e.g. Balas, 2018; Flege & Mackay, 2004; Goriot, McQueen, Unsworth, Hout & Broersma, 2020; Guion, Flege, Akahane-Yamada & Pruitt, 2000; Ingram & Park, 1997; Ingvalson, McClelland & Holt, 2011; Pilus, 2003; Proctor, 2004; Rato & Carlet, 2020), as well as by Cantonese/Chinese learners (e.g. Chan, 2009a, 2011, 2012, 2013, 2014; C. Chan, 2001; Lai, 2010; Sun & van Heuven, 2007). The perception of target languages other than English has also been researched into, such as Larson-Hall (2004), who examined the perceptual difficulties of Russian segments by Japanese learners, and Pater (2003), who investigated the perceptual acquisition of Thai phonology by English speakers.

In the debate about speech perception, the concepts of similarity, dissimilarity and equivalence are important objects of discussion. Recall that in previous chapters on speech production and also on grammar, differences between Cantonese and English have been seen as the sources of many learner problems. In the study of speech perception, the "differences resulting in difficulties" formula is not taken for granted. Instead, the similarity between the native and target languages is often argued to have a stronger adverse effect on second language speech learning. A number of theories/models which have been proposed to explain speech perception, including the Speech Learning Model (SLM) (Flege, 1995), the Perceptual Assimilation Model (PAM) (Best, 1994), the Native Language Magnet Model (NLM)[1] (Kuhl & Iverson, 1995), and the like, all advocate the adverse effects of similarity on speech perception.

According to the SLM, the greater the perceived phonetic dissimilarity between an L2 sound and the closest L1 sound, the more likely it is for a learner to be able to discern the phonetic differences between the sounds and to produce the L2 sound more accurately. This is because if a learner can perceive some of the phonetic differences between the L1 sounds and an L2 sound, a phonetic category for that L2 sound can be established, and the learner's production of the L2 sound will correspond to the properties represented in the phonetic category. If the perceived phonetic dissimilarity between a pair of L1 and L2 sounds increases, the chance that cross-language phonetic differences will be discerned is higher (Flege, 1995). On the other hand, when a pair of L1 and L2 sounds are judged to be equivalent, the cognitive mechanism of "equivalence classification", which "permits humans to perceive constant categories in the face of inherent sensory variability found in the many physical exemplars which may instantiate a category" (Flege, 1987b: 49), may lead L2 learners to merge the phonetic properties of the two sounds and develop an incorrect perceptual target for the L2 sound (Flege, 1987a). As a result, the two sounds will resemble each another in production, and learners' production of the L2 sound will not be accurate.

In a similar fashion, the PAM argues that non-native contrasts are perceived in terms of their phonetic similarities/dissimilarities to the phonological categories present in a listener's L1 (Best, 1994; Best, Goldstein, Tyler & Nam, 2009; Harnsberger, 2001). In this model, four assimilation patterns are identified, namely two-category assimilation, single-category assimilation, category goodness and non-assimilable. Two-category assimilation occurs when the members of a non-native contrast are perceived as acceptable exemplars of two different native phonemes. Single-category assimilation occurs when two non-native sounds assimilate equally well or equally poorly to the same native phoneme. Category goodness describes an assimilation pattern where both members of the non-native contrast are assimilated to a single native phoneme, but one is more similar to the native phoneme than the other. A non-assimilable pattern is when both non-native sounds are so discrepant from the general properties of any native phoneme that the sounds are not perceived as speech sounds at all (Best, 1994; Best & Tyler, 2007). If a non-native sound is perceived as very similar to an L1 phoneme category, then the discrepancies between the native and non-native phonemes will not be detected.

Other than the SLM and PAM, the NLM also proposes that the nearer a foreign language unit is to an L1 magnet,[2] the more the unit will be assimilated to the L1 sound category, and the foreign-language unit will become indistinguishable from the L1 sound (Kuhl & Iverson, 1995). Notwithstanding the differences in the theoretical orientations and the details of the proposals, it is evident that the similarity between the L1 and L2 sounds is vital in the discussion of speech perception, and that L2 sounds that are perceived as similar to some L1 sounds are often seen as more difficult to produce than dissimilar sounds.[3] In the following sections, the perception of English speech sounds by Cantonese ESL learners will be examined, and the effects of L1–L2 similarity on their perception of English speech sounds will also be discussed.

Cantonese ESL Learners' Perception of English Speech Sounds

Unlike our discussions on speech production problems, which often explore learners' difficulties on individual sounds by focusing on the common production strategies or substitutes adopted to realize a certain target, research on speech perception often includes confusable sound pairs for investigation. For example, instead of directly requiring learners to say out what a particular phone they have heard (e.g. [v]) is, many research studies investigate how learners perceive either or both members of a confusable sound pair, such as a voiced and voiceless obstruent pair, a long and short vowel pair, an "easy" and "problematic" sound pair,[4] and the like.

Two general kinds of perception tasks are involved, namely discrimination tasks and identification tasks (including word identification and picture identification tasks). In a sound discrimination task, learners are often presented with trios of isolated phones consisting of two instances of one phoneme (e.g. /v/) and one instance of another confusable phoneme (e.g. /f/). Learners need to determine which other phone in the trio is the same as a certain phone in the same trio. For example, in the trio [v, **v**, f], learners need to determine whether the middle phone is the same as the first phone or the third phone.[5]

In a word identification task, learners are often presented with words spoken in isolation and asked to identify which of a pair of written words the spoken word represents. For instance, when presented with [væn], learners need to identify whether the spoken word is *fan* /fæn/ or *van* /væn/. In a picture identification task, learners are often required to do the same as in a word identification task, but the response alternatives provided are picture pairs showing the target words for identification, such as a picture showing a fan and another picture showing a van, instead of word pairs in spelling form.[6]

Findings on speech perception also often differ from those on speech production, in that the relative degrees of difficulty levels in learners' perception of different speech sounds, rather than the popular substitutes used for replacing individual sounds, are reported. The following sections about Cantonese ESL learners' perception problems, which are based on empirical data and insights obtained from Chan (2009a, 2011, 2012, 2013, 2014),[7] will also focus on the relative degrees of difficulties of different confusable sound pairs. Reference will also be made to individual sounds when necessary.

Obstruents

For Cantonese ESL learners, many English obstruents (plosives, fricatives, affricates) are difficult to perceive, but the relative degrees of perception difficulties posed by different obstruent pairs vary. The obstruent pair which creates most confusion is /θ, f/ (e.g. in words such as *thirst* and *first*, and *Ruth* and *roof*), which is also the obstruent pair many native speakers themselves find confusing (Tabain, 1998). /z, s/ (e.g. in words such as *zinc* and *sink*, and *buzz* and *bus*) and /v, f/ (e.g. in words such as *vat* and *fat*, and *save* and *safe*) have also been found to present a lot of problems, whereas other obstruent pairs such as /v, w/ (e.g. in words such as *verse* and *worse*),[8] /ð, d/ (e.g. in words such as *though* and *dough*, and *bathe* and *bayed*), and /ʃ, s/ (e.g. in words such as *shell* and *sell*, and *mash* and *mass*) are less problematic perceptually, although /ð/ and /ʃ/ are problematic for many Cantonese ESL learners in production and /d/ and /s/ are their popular production substitutes respectively (see Chapter 7).

The position of a word in which an obstruent is found seems to be an important factor affecting learners' differentiation of obstruent pairs differing in voicing, with the word-final position creating greater confusion and resulting in more perception difficulties than the word-initial position. This is true for /v, f/, which are better differentiated in initial position than when they are in final position; and

Table 8.1 Cantonese ESL learners' perception of English obstruents

Degrees of Perceptual Difficulties	Positions of Voiced and Voiceless Obstruent Pairs	Other Confusable Obstruent Pairs	Individual Obstruents
More difficulties	Final position	/θ, f/; /z, s/; /v, f/	/θ/; /z/; /v/
Fewer difficulties	Initial position	/v, w/; /ð, d/; /ʃ, s/	/ʃ/; /ð/

/dʒ, tʃ/, which are also more accurately differentiated when they appear in initial position (in words such as *joke* /dʒəʊk/ and *choke* /tʃəʊk/) than when they are in final position (in words such as *George* /dʒɔːdʒ/ and *church* /tʃɔːtʃ/), whereas positional effects for the differentiation of /z, s/ do not seem to be significant. Other obstruent pairs which do not differ in voicing, such as /ʃ, s/, /ð, d/ and /θ, f/, do not trigger significant perceptual differences irrespective of which position of a word they appear in: /ʃ, s/ and /ð, d/ are perceived well in both initial and final positions, but /θ, f/ are perceived poorly in both initial and final positions.

When individual obstruents are taken in consideration, /θ/ is the most difficult to perceive, followed by /z/. /v/ also presents some difficulties, but not as much as /θ/ and /z/. On the other hand, /ʃ/ is the easiest to perceive, followed by /ð/. Table 8.1 shows a summary of Cantonese ESL learners' perception of English obstruents (Chan, 2011).

Sonorant Consonants

Sonorant consonants (nasals, liquids, semi-vowels) are among the sound categories which are least prone to misperception. The sound pairs most difficult to discriminate is /l, uː/[9] in word-final position (e.g. in words such as *fill* /fɪl/ and *few* /fjuː/, and *dill* /dɪl/ and *due* /djuː/),[10] mostly with /uː/ being misperceived as [l]. The pair /ŋ, n/ (in words such as *rang* and *ran*) is also problematic in perception, but not as seriously as /l, uː/. Though [w] and [l] are often used as production substitutes for /r/, the sound pairs /r, w/ and /r, l/ (e.g. in words such as *right* and *white*, and *ray* and *lay*) do not cause much perceptual difficulty to Cantonese ESL learners. /n, l/ in initial position (e.g. in words such as *no* and *low*), though often neutralized in production, does not create much perceptual difficulty, either.

As far as individual sonorant consonants are concerned, /l/ in final position presents the most perception difficulty, followed by /ŋ/. The position of a sonorant consonant, thus, also has an effect on perception, with sonorant consonants appearing in final position also more problematic than those appearing in initial position (e.g. /r/, initial /l/). It should be noted, however, that some sonorant consonants can appear only in initial position (e.g. /r/ and /w/ in RP English), and other sonorant consonants can appear only in final position (e.g. /ŋ/). Such distributional differences may obscure the effects of positions, but when a certain consonant is permissible both word-finally and word-initially (e.g. /l/), the final

Table 8.2 Cantonese ESL learners' perception of English sonorant consonants

Degrees of Perceptual Difficulties	Sonorant Consonant Pairs	Individual Sonorant Consonants
More difficulties	/l, uː/ (only contrasted in final position) /ŋ, n/ (only contrasted in final position)	Final /l/ /ŋ/ (only appearing in final position)
Fewer difficulties	/r, w/ (only contrasted in initial position) /r, l/ (only contrasted in initial position) /n, l/ (only contrasted in initial position)	/r/ (only appearing in initial position) Initial /l/

position (e.g. [ɫ]) is less easily perceptible than the initial position. It is, therefore, evident that final sonorant consonants present more perception problems to Cantonese ESL learners than initial sonorant consonants, a phenomenon which is shared by obstruents (Chan, 2011). Table 8.2 shows a summary of Cantonese ESL learners' perception of English sonorant consonants.

Vowels

Cantonese ESL learners' perception of vowels is the poorest among the three categories of obstruents, sonorant consonants and vowels. All the English long and short vowel pairs, including /iː, ɪ/ (in words such as *eat* and *it*), /uː, ʊ/ (in words such as *fool* and *full*), and /ɔː, ɒ/ (in words such as *walk* and *wok*), present a lot of perception problems to Cantonese ESL learners, of which /ɔː, ɒ/ is the most difficult pair to differentiate. Short vowels (i.e. /ɪ/ and /ʊ/) are more easily perceived than the corresponding long vowels (i.e. /iː/ and /uː/), except for /ɒ/, which is the least accurate sound in perception. The open and close vowel pair, namely /æ, e/ (e.g. in words such as *bag* and *beg*), is also very confusable. Other vowel pairs, on the other hand, such as /aɪ, ɑː/ (e.g. in words such as *life* and *laugh*) and /aɪ, æ/ (e.g. in words such as *die* and *dad*), practically create no perceptual difficulty to Cantonese ESL learners.

As for the perceptual difficulties of individual vowel sounds, /ɒ/ is the most difficult to perceive, whereas /ɪ/ is best perceived. Table 8.3 summarizes Cantonese ESL learners' perception of English vowels.

Relationship Between Speech Perception and Speech Production

There has been supporting evidence in earlier studies, such as C. Chan (2001), that a positive correlation existed between Cantonese ESL learners' perception and production of English word-initial consonants, in that word-initial consonants which were poorly perceived were also poorly produced, and word-initial

Table 8.3 Cantonese ESL learners' perception of English vowels

Degrees of Perceptual Difficulties	Vowel Pairs	Individual Vowels
More difficulties	/iː, ɪ/ /uː, ʊ/ /ɔː, ɒ/ /æ, e/	/ɒ/
Fewer difficulties	/aɪ, ɑː/ /aɪ, æ/	/ɪ/

consonants which were well perceived were also well produced. More recent and comprehensive studies, however, show that perception and production by Cantonese ESL learners are not in a strict one-to-one relationship (Chan, 2011, 2012, 2014). Some instances of positive correlation between perception and production are observed. For example, for the long and short vowel pair /iː, ɪ/, the short member (i.e. /ɪ/) is both better perceived and more accurately produced. However, many English speech sounds that have been documented as problematic in speech production for Cantonese ESL learners, such as /ʃ/ and /ð/, do not pose serious perceptual problems when they are contrasted with their popular production substitutes, namely /s/ and /d/ respectively. Sounds which are "easy" to produce, such as /e/, are still problematic in perception, and more importantly, learners' perception of "difficult-to-produce" English speech sounds (e.g. word-initial /r/) is not much worse than their perception of "easy-to-produce" sounds (e.g. initial /l/). "Easy-to-produce" sounds occasionally create even more perception problems than sounds which are difficult to produce. For example, learners' perception of /f/ is even worse than their perception of /v/, and when contrasted with /r/, /w/ presents more perception difficulties than /r/. All these show that the relations between speech perception and speech production are inconsistent (Chan, 2011, 2014).

Factors Affecting Speech Perception

A number of factors affect learners' perception of speech sounds, including the effects of previous word knowledge, interaction of positional and voicing effects, frequency of occurrence of a target sound, and effects of L1–L2 phonetic similarity. Some of these factors can also explain the inconsistent relations between speech perception and speech production.

Effects of Previous Word Knowledge

The interference of learners' pre-determined pronunciation of a word is a factor affecting speech perception. When learners are presented with contrasting phones in isolation, such as [v, ʋ, f], category determination involves only the discrimination of the acoustic features of the input sounds, which are received in the form of semi-continuous acoustic signals (Fromkin, Rodman & Hyams, 2017).

On the other hand, when learners are presented with contrasting phones embedded in words (e.g. [uː] and [ʊ] as in *fool* /fuːl/ and *full* /fʊl/ respectively), category determination involves not just the detection of sensory information but also the use of higher-level linguistic information (Miller & Eimas, 1995), including learners' knowledge of word structure and their previous knowledge of the pronunciations of the words. Such previous knowledge may override the detected acoustic differences between two sounds and result in word misidentification. For instance, a learner who has constantly confused the pronunciations of the words *fool* /fuːl/ and *full* /fʊl/ may regard the acoustic signals that they have heard for *fool*, namely [fuːl], as representing *full*, or vice versa, despite the fact that the acoustic differences between [uː] and [ʊ] may be detected by ear. In a sense, a learner's mental representation for perception has been mediated by pre-determined word pronunciations. Input acoustic signals are often converted to "forms which fit his or her shifted mental representation, resulting in incorrect perceptual judgements" (Chan, 2011: 737).

Interaction of Positional and Voicing Effects

The concept of perceptual salience can possibly explain the positional effects on learners' perception of obstruents and sonorant consonants: Final consonants are less salient than initial consonants, so the former are less perceptible than the latter (Redford & Diehl, 1996), giving rise to learners' greater difficulties in the perception of final consonants than initial consonants. Positional effects, however, often "work in tandem with voicing effects" (Chan, 2011: 736–737) in learners' speech perception. Recall that terminal devoicing of voiced obstruents is a very common production strategy adopted by Cantonese ESL learners and that differences between minimal pairs differing in final voicing, such as *save* /seɪv/ and *safe* /seɪf/, are often not actualized in production (see Chapter 7). When encountering corresponding sound stimuli, learners may tend to identify whichever stimulus as either word irrespective of whether the actual stimulus contains a final voiced obstruent (i.e. [seɪv]) or a final voiceless obstruent (i.e. [seɪf]), or whether the voicing feature of the final consonant sound can be detected from the input signals by ear. The higher degree of perceptual difficulties that learners have with final obstruents than with initial obstruents may be the result of the interaction of positional and voicing effects.[11]

Frequency of Occurrence of Target Sound

Another plausible factor affecting speech perception concerns the frequency of occurrence of a target sound. Some sounds are inherently more difficult than others simply because of their rare occurrence. A case in point is the English dental fricatives /θ, ð/. They are exceptionally rare sounds in the world's languages (Gamkrelidze, 1978; Maddieson, 1984) and are also found to be difficult for production by speakers in many parts of the world, including those of Southeast Asian languages (Deterding & Kirkpatrick, 2006). Cantonese ESL learners' difficulties in perceiving /θ/ is possibly due to the enhanced difficulty of the sound as a result of its universally rare occurrence. It is unclear why the voiced counterpart /ð/ does not pose comparable perception difficulties, though.

Effects of L1–L2 Phonetic Similarity

Learners' native language also has an effect on their perception of English speech sounds, albeit in a different fashion from their production. Production difficulties have often been explained by the differences between the native and target languages, in that the more different a target sound is from a native sound, the more difficult it is to produce the target. Contrastive differences, however, cannot adequately explain learners' speech perception. An English sound pair with one or both members of the pair non-existent in Cantonese (e.g. English /aɪ, æ/ and /r, l/) may still be well discriminated, so inventory gaps do not categorically cause perception difficulties. Instead, perception difficulties can better be explained by the phonetic similarities between Cantonese and English speech sounds. Consider English /θ, f/. Though learners' perception problems can be explained by the absence of /θ/ in Cantonese, there is no doubt that /θ/ shares a number of articulatory and acoustic similarities between itself and /f/, a sound found in both English and Cantonese: In terms of articulation, both /θ/ and /f/ are voiceless fricatives, the only difference being in the place of articulation, where the former is dental and the latter is labio-dental. In terms of acoustic properties, both /θ/ and /f/ have relatively low intensity (Gimson & Ramsaran, 1989), and they both have the main noise energy in the high-frequency band from about 6,000 to 8,000 Hz (Fry, 1979). Cantonese ESL learners' difficulties in distinguishing between English /θ/ and English /f/ can, thus, be due to the similarities between English /θ/ and the /f/ sound, which is a sound also found in Cantonese. In a similar fashion, although it may be argued that learners' difficulties in discriminating between the long and short members of the English vowel pairs /iː, ɪ/, /uː, ʊ/ and /ɔː, ɒ/ are caused by inventory gaps (that Cantonese only has corresponding short vowel phonemes, namely /i, u, ɔ/), the long and short allophones of the Cantonese short vowels may be so similar to the corresponding English long and short vowel phonemes phonetically that learners fail to discern the differences between the non-native contrasts.

Perceived Similarity (and Dissimilarity)

Similarities between the L1 and the L2, as recognized in the previous section, refer to observable and/or measurable phonetic similarities, including acoustic and articulatory similarities. It is, however, difficult to determine what constitutes similar or dissimilar (Major & Kim, 1999), or which sound is more similar or dissimilar to a certain sound. For example, should a certain L2 sound non-existent in the L1 (e.g. English /θ/) be classified as a new and *dissimilar* sound, or as a sound *similar* to an existing L1 sound (e.g. Cantonese /f/)? Without a clear definition of similarity/dissimilarity, it is difficult to ascertain its effects on learners' speech perception (and production). As a learner's perceptual acquisition of a second language is largely shaped by his/her experience in his/her native language (van Leussen & Escudero, 2015), in the discussions about similarity and dissimilarity, learners' perceived (dis)similarity is more important than phonetic (dis)similarity (see the earlier section "Similarity, Dissimilarity and Equivalence" in this chapter). The distance between a pair of English sounds or between a pair of English and Cantonese sounds can be perceived differently by different learners, or by the same learner at different stages of proficiency as a result of some phonological and phonetic restructuring[12] (Chan, 2012). How ESL learners' perceived L1–L2 (dis)similarity impacts on their L2 speech perception has been another significant area of inquiry. Cantonese ESL learners' perceived similarity between English and Cantonese sounds will, thus, be the focus of the following sections.

Learners' Perceived Similarity Between English and Cantonese Sounds

Learners' perceived L1–L2 similarity has been the object of much research, especially after the introduction of the SLM (e.g. Aoyama, Flege, Guion, Akahane-Yamada & Yamada, 2004; Baker, Trofimovich, Mack & Flege, 2002; Chan, 2012; Guion, Flege, Akahane-Yamada & Pruitt, 2000). In an attempt to understand Cantonese ESL learners' degrees of perceived similarity between different English and Cantonese speech sounds, Chan (2012) conducted a number of perception tasks where participants were given some English words containing a target English sound (e.g. English /iː/ as in *bean* /biːn/) and some Cantonese words containing "similar"[13] Cantonese sounds (e.g. Cantonese /i/ as in 邊 (edge) /bin/) and asked to rate the degree of similarity between the two L1–L2 sounds using a scale from 1 (very different) to 5 (very similar). The following sections are based on the research findings and insights from Chan (2012).

Perceived Degrees of Similarity Between English and Cantonese Consonants

Cantonese ESL learners' perceived degrees of similarity between confusable English and Cantonese consonants, including English /ð/ and Cantonese /d/; English /r/ and Cantonese /w/; English /v/ and Cantonese /w/; and English /r/ and Cantonese /l/ are, on the whole, quite low,[14] with the perceived similarity between English /r/ and Cantonese /l/ being the lowest. These show that despite widespread documentation of substitution of the Cantonese sounds for the target English sounds in Cantonese ESL learners' speech production, these confusable sound pairs are perceived by learners as rather or very dissimilar to each other.

Some L1–L2 consonant pairs are perceived as slightly more similar to each other than other L1–L2 consonant pairs. These include English /θ/ and Cantonese /f/; English /v/ and Cantonese /f/; English /ʃ/ and Cantonese /s/; and English /z/ and Cantonese /s/. However, when different English consonants are contrasted with the same Cantonese consonant, there are no significant differences between their perceived degrees of similarity. For example, English /θ/ and English /v/ are perceived as more or less equally similar to Cantonese /f/, and English /ʃ/ and English /z/ are perceived as more or less equally similar to Cantonese /s/.

Voicing difference seems to be most difficult to detect: Learners' perceived degree of similarity between two English and Cantonese consonants which only differ in voicing (e.g. the English *voiced* alveolar fricative /z/ and the Cantonese *voiceless* alveolar fricative /s/) is the greatest. On the other hand, consonant pairs which differ in two or more articulatory features, such as in both place of articulation and manner of articulation (e.g. English /r/ (voiced *post-alveolar approximant*) and Cantonese /l/ (voiced *alveolar lateral*)), seem not to trigger lower perceived degrees of similarity than consonant pairs which differ only in one articulatory feature, such as in either place of articulation or manner of articulation (e.g. English /ʃ/ (voiceless *palato-alveolar* fricative) and Cantonese /s/ (voiceless *alveolar* fricative)). These show that articulatory features other than voicing do not have much impact on learners' perceived degrees of similarity.

Perceived Degrees of Similarity Between English and Cantonese Vowels

English vowels and "similar" Cantonese vowels are generally perceived as more similar to each other than English and Cantonese consonants are.[15] All the English long and short vowel pairs, namely /iː/ and /ɪ/, /uː/ and /ʊ/, and /ɔː/ and /ɒ/, are perceived as quite similar to their nearest Cantonese correlates, namely Cantonese /i/, Cantonese /u/, and Cantonese /ɔ/ respectively. This is not surprising given the phonetic similarities between the English long and short vowel pairs and the corresponding Cantonese short vowels. Interestingly, despite the phonetic similarities between English /e/ and Cantonese /e/, English open /æ/ is perceived as more similar than English /e/ to Cantonese /e/.

Phonological environments often have a noticeable impact on learners' perceived degrees of similarity between English and Cantonese vowels. Before velars, the long members of English /iː, ɪ/ and /uː, ʊ/ are seen as least similar to Cantonese /i/ and /u/ respectively, whereas the short members are seen as very similar to the corresponding Cantonese vowels when occurring in this phonological environment. For instance, in words such as *beak* /biːk/ and *Luke* /luːk/, English /iː/ and /uː/ are not regarded as quite similar to the corresponding Cantonese vowel /i/ and /u/. On the other hand, in words such as *tick* /tɪk/ and *took* /tʊk/, English /ɪ/ and /ʊ/ are regarded as quite similar to Cantonese /i/ and /u/ respectively. Such a perceived similarity pattern, however, is not observed for English /ɔː, ɒ/.

As for other phonological environments, before alveolars (e.g. in words such as *teen* /tiːn/ and *bin* /bɪn/, and *food* /fuːd/ and *foot* /fʊt/), there are no significant differences in learner's degrees of perceived degrees of similarity between the English long and short vowel pairs and the corresponding Chinese short vowels. Before labials (e.g. in words such as *leap* /liːp/ and *lip* /lɪp/), English /iː/ is significantly regarded as more similar than English /ɪ/ to Cantonese /i/.

Interestingly, when phonological environments are not factored in, neither of English /iː/ or /ɪ/ and neither of English /uː/ or /ʊ/ is significantly perceived

Table 8.4 Perceived degrees of similarity between L1–L2 vowel pairs in different phonological environments

Degrees of Perceived Similarity	Before Velars	Before Alveolars	Before Labials
Higher perceived Similarity	English /ɪ/ to Cantonese /i/ English /ʊ/ to Cantonese /u/	No significant differences	English /iː/ to Cantonese /i/
Lower perceived Similarity	English /iː/ to Cantonese /i/ English /uː/ to Cantonese /u/	No significant differences	English /ɪ/ to Cantonese /i/

as more similar than the other member to the corresponding Cantonese counterparts. Only English /ɒ/ is significantly perceived as more similar than English /ɔː/ to Cantonese /ɔ/. Table 8.4 shows a summary of the effects of phonological environments.

Recall that the short allophones of Cantonese /i/ and of Cantonese /u/ also occur before velars, and the long allophone of Cantonese /i/ occurs before labials (see Chapter 3). Cantonese ESL learners' perceived similarity between English /iː, ɪ/ and the closest Cantonese correlate /i/ and their perceived similarity between English /uː, ʊ/ and the closest Cantonese correlate /u/ are consistent with the allophonic variations of Cantonese vowels. Thus, there is reason to believe that for Cantonese ESL learners, English and Cantonese vowels are related "perceptually to one another at a position-dependent allophonic level instead of at a phonemically-based level" (Chan, 2014: 59), though the relations are not categorical across all vowels and all allophones.

According to Tobin (2005), whether a phone is classified as a separate phoneme or as an allophone of a phoneme depends on a number of factors. The contribution of the phone to communication is one important factor: Phonemes are the smallest units of sound which can distinguish between two words, whereas allophones are not distinctive. Another factor concerns the kinds of distinctive and nondistinctive acoustic and articulatory features that speakers must learn. The third factor is relative predictability: While the distribution of phonemes in minimal pairs is unpredictable, the complementary distribution of allophones is predictable. From a phonological point of view, the long and short allophones of Cantonese /i/ and /u/ are accorded allophonic status, but the corresponding English long and short vowels are accorded phonemic status as a result of the aforementioned factors. However, a certain allophone of a phoneme (e.g. the short allophone [ɪ] of Cantonese /i/) can be acoustically and articulatorily very "different" from another allophone of the same phoneme (e.g. the long allophone [iː]) to an extent which is comparable to the articulatory and acoustic differences between two phonemes of another language (e.g. English phonemes /iː/ and /ɪ/). Therefore, from a perception point of view, it is inevitable that learners' degrees of perceived L1–L2 vowel similarity match the allophonic variations in Cantonese (Chan, 2012).

Relationship Between L1–L2 Perceived Similarity and L2 Perception

An inversely proportional relationship between Cantonese ESL learners' perceived similarity between English and Cantonese sounds and their perception of English sounds can be observed from the previous discussion: The greater the perceived similarity is between an English sound and a Cantonese sound, the more difficult it is to perceive the English sound. On the other hand, differences between the two languages as a result of inventory gaps fall short of satisfactory explanations for speech perception. Such observations are consistent with the proposals of perception models which advocate the adverse effects of similarity, such as the SLM, PAM and NLM.

There are exceptions to these observations, though. Although there are pairs/groups of L2 consonants which are perceived as more or less equally similar to the same L1 consonant, the L2 consonants concerned are not categorically perceived with equal accuracy. For instance, although both English /ʃ/ and English /z/ are perceived as equally similar to Cantonese /s/, English /ʃ/ does not present a lot of perception problems to Cantonese ESL learners while English /z/ does (see Table 8.1). In a similar fashion, although both English /θ/ and English /v/ are perceived as more or less equally similar to Cantonese /f/, English /θ/ is much more difficult to perceive than English /v/. Perceived similarity is, thus not an absolute indicator of speech perception. As argued previously, other factors may also play a role in determining learners' perception of a target sound, including interaction between positional effects and voicing effects, learners' previous word knowledge, and the like. The question of how exactly these different linguistic, sociolinguistic, psycholinguistic or even extra-linguistic factors interact with perceived similarity to impact on learners' speech perception should be subject to further research.

Relationship Between L1–L2 Perceived Similarity and L2 Production

Not only is learners' perceived L1–L2 similarity inversely related to speech perception, but it has also been argued to have a negative impact on speech production (e.g. Bohn & Flege, 1992; Flege, 1995). However, as with speech perception, the adverse effects of perceived L1–L2 similarity on L2 speech production are not absolute for Cantonese ESL learners. Although there are some "difficult-to-produce" English sounds (e.g. English /æ/) which are perceived as rather similar to the nearest Cantonese correlates, many other "difficult-to-produce" English sounds (e.g. English /ð/, /v/, /r/) are not regarded as very similar to their closest Cantonese counterparts. In a similar fashion, learners also have more difficulties in producing certain English long vowels (e.g. English /iː/ and /uː/) than the corresponding short ones (e.g. English /ɪ/ and /ʊ/), although both the long and short members of the vowel pairs are on the whole perceived as more or less equally similar to the corresponding Cantonese counterparts (Chan, 2014). What contributes to these discrepant relations in perceived degrees of similarity and speech production is not clear, but there is reason to believe that, again, other phonological factors and/or predominant acquisitional difficulties, such as devoicing of voiced obstruents, may also override the effects of perceived similarity on speech production.

Conclusion

In this chapter, we have examined Cantonese ESL learners' perception of English speech sounds, the factors which affect learners' perception, their perceived degrees of similarity between different pairs of English and Cantonese speech sounds, as well as the relationships between L1–L2 perceived similarity and L2 speech perception/production. Although there is an intimate relation between speech perception and speech production and many production errors have a perceptual basis, for Cantonese ESL learners, the two areas of learning do not seem to bear a one-to-one relationship. L2 speech sounds that cause perception problems may not necessarily cause speech production problems, whereas L2 speech sounds that are easy to perceive may still cause production problems.

Perceived similarity is not the only indicator of a learner's L2 perception ability. Other factors, such as the frequency of occurrence of a target sound, the position of a target sound in a word, and other sociolinguistic, psycholinguistic or even extra-linguistic factors, may also affect L2 perception. The boundary between what constitutes similar and what constitutes dissimilar is often fuzzy. A pair of L1 and L2 sounds regarded as similar by a certain learner may be regarded as dissimilar by another learner. What is more, learners' perceived similarity can change over time. The same pair of L1 and L2 sounds can be regarded as similar by the same speaker at one point of time but as dissimilar at another point of time because of some phonological and/or phonetic restructuring. Therefore, the use of the terms *similar* and *dissimilar* needs to be qualified in cross-linguistic perception studies. In the next chapter, a more detailed discussion about different factors affecting L2 phonological acquisition, as well as factors affecting L2 grammatical acquisition, will be scrutinized.

Notes

1 A revised version of the SLM, namely the SLM-r (Flege & Bohn, 2021), and an expanded version of the NLM, namely the NLM-e (Kuhl, Conboy, Coffey-Corina, Padden, Rivera-Gaxiola & Nelson, 2008), have been developed recently.

2 According to Kuhl (2000: 11853), once a sound category exists in memory, "it functions like a magnet for other sounds".

3 Theories which go in different ways from the SLM, PAM and NLM also exist, such as the Second Language Linguistic Perception (L2LP) Model, which argues that although similar sounds do pose a challenge, learners will adjust their L1 perception to become optimal L2 listeners. As a result, L2 sounds that are similar to some L1 sounds are easier to master than "new" sounds which do not exist in the learners' L1 (Escudero, 2005, 2009).

4 In this chapter, sounds which are seldom documented in the literature as problematic to Cantonese ESL learners in production are regarded as "easy" sounds, whereas those which have often been documented as posing problems for production are regarded as "problematic" sounds (see Chapter 7).

5 Such a kind of discrimination task is often known as a categorial AXB discrimination task in the literature (Best, McRoberts & Goodell, 2001; Tyler, Best, Faber & Levitt, 2014).

6 Many variations of discrimination and identification tasks have been used in L2 perception studies (Strange & Shafer, 2008). The descriptions given in this section only represent exemplars of the tasks used by the author in her studies.

7 RP English was adopted as the English accent used in all the perception tasks in the studies, and Hong Kong Cantonese was adopted as the Chinese accent.

8 /w/ is not an obstruent, but because it is often found to be used as a production substitute for the obstruent /v/ (see Chapter 7), the two sounds have been regarded as a pair of confusable sounds in the investigation of Cantonese ESL learners' perception of /v/ (e.g. Chan, 2011, 2012, 2013, 2014).

9 /uː/ is a vowel, not a sonorant consonant, but because it is a popular production substitute for final /l/ (see Chapter 7), the two sounds have also been used as a pair of confusable sounds in the investigation of Cantonese ESL learners' perception of sonorant consonants (e.g. Chan, 2011, 2012, 2013, 2014).

10 The word pairs *fill* and *few*, *dill* and *due* are not minimal pairs, as they consist of different vowels (i.e. /ɪ/ in the former and /uː/ in the latter) and the second word in each pair also has a preceding glide /j/. However, Cantonese ESL learners often pronounce the [ɫ] in the former (e.g. *fill, dill*) with vocalization, resulting in indistinguishable pronunciations between the two words in the same pair (see Chapter 7). These word pairs have been included in relevant studies for investigating learners' perception of /l/ (e.g. Chan, 2011, 2012, 2013, 2014).

11 All English sonorant consonants are voiced, so voicing effects do not play a role in learners' perception of sonorant consonants.

12 According to Corder (1978), L2 learning is viewed as a restructuring continuum. L2 acquisition starts with learners' L1, but learners constantly and progressively replace their L1 by their L2, thus restructuring their interlanguage.

13 In this chapter, the word "similar", when enclosed in double quotation marks, refers to the common interpretation of similarity. That is, the English and Cantonese sounds in question have often been regarded as similar in the literature, and the Cantonese sounds are often used as substitutes for the target English sounds.

14 All these pairs of English and Cantonese consonants received a similarity rating of around or less than 2 in a scale of 5 in Chan's (2012) study.

15 Many pairs of L1–L2 vowels received a similarity rating of over 3.5 in a scale of 5 in Chan's (2012) study.

9 Cantonese ESL Learners' Acquisition of Grammar and Phonology: L1 Influence?

In the previous chapters, we have explored the problems that Cantonese ESL learners often encounter in their learning of English grammar and phonology, including interlingual and intralingual errors, as well as speech perception and speech production problems. In this chapter, the extent of L1 influence on Cantonese ESL learners' acquisition of grammar and phonology will be examined. Other probable non-L1-related causes of learner problems will also be explored. It will be argued that learner errors are seldom attributed to one single source. Many non-L1-related factors are also at work, and there are often intricate interactions between L1- and non-L1-related factors.

Cantonese ESL Learners' Acquisition of English Grammar

Extent of L1 Transfer

It is evident that L1 transfer is an important source of learner errors in Cantonese ESL learners' acquisition of English grammar. A significant proportion of errors identified in this book, including all the errors discussed in Chapter 4 and some of the errors discussed in Chapter 6, are reminiscent of the normative sentence structures in Chinese-Cantonese. L1 interference can be seen at all the lexical, syntactical and discoursal levels, and the units affected range from individual words/phrases to whole sentences with verbatim word-for-word translation. At the morphological level, not much evidence shows the effects of L1 transfer. As Cantonese words are typically mono-morphemic not analysable into component morphemes,[1] it is hard to envisage L1 transfer in learners' application of English affixation. At the lexical, syntactic and discoursal levels, there is reason to believe that in producing an English expression, many Cantonese ESL learners, elementary to advanced learners inclusive, tend to think in their L1 and convert their mental output into the target language. There are learners who process their mental output directly in the target language, English, but when encountering difficulties or when dealing with unfamiliar concepts, they may also resort to their L1 repertoire and rely more heavily on their L1 than on their developing L2. Variations in learners' reliance of L1 exist, depending on learners' proficiency levels, the degree of complexity of the language structure being constructed, as well

DOI: 10.4324/9781003252498-9

as the amount of time available for mental processing. While L1 transfer from Chinese-Cantonese to English is more widespread among students at lower proficiency levels, advanced students sometimes also produce strings that strongly resemble the structures of their L1. When a target L2 structure is considered more difficult or unfamiliar, calling upon their L1 is a common compensation strategy among learners (Chan, 2004c).

L1 interference may be exacerbated when learning is situated in a context where the L1 is readily available as input, such as the use of the mother tongue as the medium of instruction or the use of translation in L2 teaching (Newson, 1998).[2] An English–Chinese bilingualized dictionary,[3] which provides definitions and examples in both English and Chinese, also induces some form of L1 interference: In constructing a sentence using a target English lexical item with the use of a bilingualized dictionary, Cantonese ESL learners tend to model their English sentence construction on the syntactic structure of an English definition or example based on the Chinese translations of that English definition or example given in the dictionary (Chan, 2017a, 2019a). L1 interference, thus, is triggered or even aggravated by the presence of L1 input facing an ESL learner.

Lack of Positive Transfer

Other than negative transfer from the L1 to the L2, learner difficulty may also be the result of a lack of comparable equivalents in the L1. As argued in Odlin (1989), positive transfer, which results from the similarities between learners' L1 and the target language, has facilitating influence on second language learners' acquisition of different aspects, such as grammar, reading and writing. However, there is a lack of positive transfer from Chinese-Cantonese to English in many aspects of L2 grammar. For instance, Chinese-Cantonese does not have articles; it does not require explicit marking for subject-verb agreement; it lacks distinct forms for a verb, for singular and plural nouns or for different cases of a pronoun; and it does not have relative pronouns. The absence of such comparable structures in the L1 may have resulted in a lack of facilitation from the L1 in learners' use of respective structures. The common errors in, for instance, learners' use of English articles, their dismissal of determiner-head noun agreement or subject-subject complement agreement, their failure to select the correct form of a verb or the correct case for a pronoun, and the like (see Chapters 5 and 6), all demonstrate a low level of positive transfer from Chinese-Cantonese to English because of a lack of comparable equivalents in the L1 (Chan, 2010c).

Possible "Positive" Transfer?

There exists some correct English usage by Cantonese ESL learners which can be seen as the result of influence from the L1 but which cannot be classified as manifestations of positive transfer.[4] An illuminating example concerns some correct use of the English definite article. As discussed in Chapter 5, a "translation and comparison" strategy in Cantonese ESL learners' use of the English definite article has been observed. Given the absence of comparable structural equivalents of English articles in Chinese-Cantonese, direct translation from Chinese-Cantonese to English is impossible. Instead, learners are influenced by transfer from related categories in the L1, such as demonstratives (Ionin, Baek, Kim, Ko & Wexler, 2012), in that they tend to seek confirmation for the use of the definite article *the* based on the presence or absence of a Chinese-Cantonese demonstrative (e.g. 那個, 嗰個 (*that*) or 那些, 嗰啲 (*those*)) in the L1-translated version of a target L2 sentence (see Chapter 5 for detailed examples). In the selection of an English article for use in a certain context, "Cantonese ESL learners tend to formulate their thoughts in their native language, translate their thoughts to the target language and compare the structures of the two languages in their minds" (Chan, 2019a: 108). Such a strategy is presumably rooted in learners' misconceptions about the two language systems: They have mistakenly equated a Chinese-Cantonese demonstrative with an English article, probably because of the shared function of the two categories in showing definiteness.

L1 influence, thus, is manifested in learners' simulated reproduction of structures based on presumed but false equivalence postulated for the two languages. Unlike the interlingual errors discussed in Chapter 4, such L1 influence does not necessarily result in erroneous structures. On the contrary, it may give rise to correct usage, yet the correctness is grounded on undesirable comparisons between similar but distinct items in the two languages, apparently due to learners' unawareness of the subtle differences between the two language systems. The resultant correct output is by no means evidence of positive transfer. Instead, it can be seen as the result of an undesirable strategy learners adopt to compensate for the lack of comparable equivalents in the native language while attempting to seek confirmation of L2 language use from their formulation of thoughts in their L1.

Non-L1-Related Factors

L1 interference alone is not adequate in accounting for the formation of all the error types discussed so far. There is often an intricate relation between L1-related and non-L1-related factors. Some probable causes other than L1 interference can be identified, including lack of awareness of L2 norms, confusion between similar L2 structures, misapplication of L2 rules or overgeneralization, selectional mishits, universal processes, and avoidance behaviour. In this section, these non-L1-related factors will be discussed in detail with relevant error examples reproduced from Chapters 4–6 where necessary.

Lack of Awareness/Inadequate Mastery of Target L2 Norms

A lack of awareness of or inadequate mastery of target language norms is inevitably the most significant non-L1-related factor contributing to many learner errors. The errors which have been discussed in the previous section as the results of a low level of positive transfer from the L1 (see the section "Lack of Positive Transfer") may result from an intricate interaction between the lack of positive transfer and learners' inadequate mastery of the target language. Learners' problems in English article use are also illustrative examples. Their misconceptions about the default mapping between a certain article (e.g. *the*) and a certain reference representation (e.g. definite) and about the equivalence between the English definite article and Chinese-Cantonese demonstratives are clear exemplars of their inadequate knowledge of the English article system. Other than article use, the majority of non-L1-related errors discussed in Chapter 6 can also be seen as resulting from learners' lack of awareness and/or inadequate mastery of target L2 norms. For example, the pseudo-passive structure (e.g. sentence (1)) is very likely the result of learners' failed acquisition, and thus, unawareness of English passive morphology (Simargool, 2008). By the same token, learners' failure to acquire English verb finiteness and their lack of awareness of the requirement of a non-finite participial structure with no explicit relative pronoun post-modifying the existent in an existential sentence are probably the major causes of their under-generation of participial structures (e.g. sentence (2)).

(1)   *But the sea in Hong Kong, and KLN, will not be there again. Because in 2020 **the people numbers can't control** (cf. can't be controlled)
(2)   *There are a lot of friends ^ **stand** by me.

Confusion Caused by "Similar" L2 Structures

Other L2-related factors, when coupled with learners' lack of awareness of L2 norms, may aggravate learners' production of certain error types. One such factor is confusion caused by "similar"[5] L2 structures. Some acceptable L2 structures seemingly look so "similar" to learners' erroneous output that those sentences may be mistakenly regarded by learners as positive evidence[6] affirming their own interlanguage hypotheses. Errors such as the *very* + V problem, the pseudo-tough movement structure, the *there* + *have* structures, and the like, are some examples. The following sections will scrutinize the confusing "similarities" between some acceptable and corresponding unacceptable structures.

Use of Adverbials Before Verbs

It is acceptable in English to have a degree adverbial (e.g. *very much*) placed before the verb where the verb is followed by a *that*-clause or *to*-infinitive clause (e.g. sentences (3) and (4)).

(3)   I **very much hope** that I can pass the test.
(4)   They **very much want** to leave now.

Learners' misplacement of an adverb immediately before a verb (e.g. *very love*) for the *incorrect order of adverbs* error (e.g. sentence (5)) can be explained by the superficially "similar" structure between the acceptable and unacceptable sentences. Learners may simply model their use of adverbs (e.g. *very*) on the position of degree adverbials in the acceptable sentences without being aware that *very* cannot be used as an adverbial on a par with *very much*.

(5) *I **very love** the food.

Their inadequate knowledge of the contexts which allow a fronted degree adverbial (e.g. *very much* is used with a verb followed by a *that*-clause or a *to*-clause) may apparently add to the confusion (Chan, Li & Kwan, 2003). The acceptability of sentences with an adverb (e.g. *finally, really*) functioning as an adverbial immediately before the verb (e.g. sentences (6) and (7)) may also be probable sources of confusion, misleading learners into believing that all adverbs have the same syntactic behaviour.

(6) She **finally finished** her homework.
(7) I **really love** you.

Tough Movement Structures

The tough movement structure, such as sentences (8) and (9), is often mistakenly taken as positive evidence affirming learners' use of the pseudo-tough movement structure (e.g. sentence (10)).

(8) Mary is **easy to convince**.
(9) Peter is **difficult to work with**.
(10) *This stage is **very easy to receive bad things**.

The major difference between the acceptable tough movement structure and the unacceptable pseudo-tough movement structure lies in the *to* + *V* clause embedded in the adjective phrase. For a tough movement structure, the subject of the main clause (e.g. *Mary, Peter*) can be interpreted as the underlying object or prepositional object of the *to* + *V* clause (i.e. *to convince **Mary**; to work with **Peter***). On the other hand, the subject of the main clause in a pseudo-tough movement structure (e.g. *this stage*) cannot be understood as the object or prepositional object of the *to* + *V* clause, as there already exists an explicit object (e.g. *bad things*) or prepositional object in the clause.

In other words, the tough movement structure is the result of moving or raising the object or prepositional object of the embedded *to* + *V* clause in an anticipatory-*it* sentence[7] (e.g. sentences (11) and (12)) to the subject position.

(11) It is easy to **convince Mary**.
(12) It is difficult to **work with Peter**.

Learners who are unaware of the constraints for tough movement may simply model their construction on such "similar" structures and produce sentences where the subject of the main clause cannot be interpreted as the object or prepositional object of the embedded *to* + *V* clause (Chan & Li, 2002).

Existential Structures in the Perfect Tense

For learners who have not adequately grasped the distinction between the possessive verb *have* and the present perfect forms of the verb *be*, existential structures with the main verb in the present perfect tense (e.g. *has been* and *have been* in sentences (13) and (14)) may mislead learners into thinking that the *there + have* structure is correct (e.g. sentence (15)) (Chan, Kwan & Li, 2002a).

(13) There **has been** a cat lying there since yesterday.
(14) There **have been** a lot of discussions about this topic.
(15) *There **will not have** any paper.

A Chain of Verbs in English Sentences

To some Cantonese ESL learners, some acceptable English constructions (e.g. sentences (16) and (17)) may seem to consist of a chain of verbs juxtaposed as if they were serial verbs in serial verb constructions.

(16) The explanations given by the teacher **helped clarify** John's misunderstanding.
(17) They **let** us **go**.

Sentences (16) and (17) are acceptable because the second verbs (e.g. *clarify*, *go*) are nonfinite verbs whereas the first verb (e.g. *helped*, *let*) are finite. Without being aware of the finiteness distinction between the different verbs in the different clauses of the same sentence, Cantonese ESL learners may be misled into accepting serial verb constructions, such as sentence (18).

(18) *I remember I broke a vase and **play balls broke the windows**.

Acceptable "Somewhere Has Something" Sentences

There are many grammatical English sentences with the verb *have* and a subject noun phrase which seemingly denotes a place or a location (e.g. sentences (19) and (20)). These acceptable sentences may be a probable cause of the unacceptable *somewhere has something* problem (e.g. sentence (21)).

(19) This house **has** a garden.
(20) This table only **has** three legs.
(21) ***The table has** a lot of books.

Careful scrutiny of the acceptable sentences shows that the subject noun phrases (e.g. *this house*, *this table*) do not denote places or locations. Instead, they denote entities which can be seen as possessors, possessing the entities denoted by the complements (e.g. *a garden*, *three legs*) (Halliday, 2004; Lock, 1996). The possessed entities are also inherent parts of the possessors (Chan, Kwan & Li, 2002b).

On the other hand, in the unacceptable *somewhere has something* structures, there isn't such a relationship, thus disallowing a possessive interpretation but inviting an existential interpretation.

While the learner errors discussed earlier are syntactically anonymous, the *somewhere has something problem* is more semantic in nature. The sentences do not violate any syntactic rules as other errors do.[8] Instead, the anomaly lies in the incompatibility between the subject and the verb of possession (i.e. *have*) at the semantic level. Such subtle constraints may further obscure the distinctions between the acceptable and unacceptable sentences, thus triggering greater indeterminacy in learner use.

All the analyses presented in this section suggest that there often exist some acceptable L2 structures which apparently provide false positive evidence to learners during their acquisition of English grammar, confirming their interlanguage hypotheses and reinforcing their production of their interlanguage output. Structures affected range from the use and/or placement of individual constituents (e.g. use of *very much* vs. *very*) and the finiteness of verbs across different clauses (e.g. serial verb constructions) to the semantic compatibility of the subject and the verb (e.g. the *somewhere has something* problem). For learners who are only in the process of approximating target language norms, confusion caused by such false positive evidence may present added learner difficulty.

Misapplication of L2 Rules/Overgeneralization

Misapplication of L2 rules may also be a major cause of learner errors. Examples can be found at all the morphological, lexical and syntactic levels.

In English word formation, certain forms of regularity are often displayed, such as the addition of the suffix *-ly* in the formation of adverbs from adjectives (e.g. *happy* + *-ly* → *happily*) and the addition of *-ness* in the formation of nouns from adjectives (e.g. *happy* + *-ness* → *happiness*). Learners who overgeneralize these regularities to inappropriate contexts will make errors, such as mis-formation of L2 comparative and superlative structures (e.g. the use of *more* + *-er* in sentence (22)) and overuse of affixes (e.g. the use of *-ly* in the formation of adverbs or adjectives as in sentence (23)).

(22)   *I think that dog is **more better** than dinosaurs.

(23)   *When I got into the church, I felt peace and pleasant, I probably think it was the place where I can find my answers and so I **oftenly** go there.

The pseudo-tough movement structure is another good exemplar of overgeneralization. Under the influence of acceptable sentences with tough movement, learners may overgeneralize the movement of the object or prepositional object of the embedded *to* + *V* clause to all contexts where tough adjectives (e.g. *easy, difficult*) are used.

Recall that the pseudo-tough movement structure has been argued as an exemplar of confusion caused by "similar" L2 structures (see the previous section).

Confusion caused by "similar" L2 structures often interacts intricately with mis-application of L2 rules or overgeneralization, with the former inducing the latter. However, not all kinds of misapplication of L2 rules/overgeneralization are the results of confusion caused by "similar" L2 structures. Overuse of affixes as demonstrated in sentence (23), for example, should not be induced by any kinds of confusion caused by "similar" L2 structures, as it is hard to envisage the existence of lexical items "similar" to *oftenly* in the L2. Learners have simply overused the affix in question due to a lack of understanding of different word classes and inadequate mastery of the word class of a target lexical item (*often* is already an adverb and does not need to undergo any affixation). There seems to be no trace of any false positive evidence that may have misled learners into believing that their output is accurate.

Selectional Mishits

Selectional mishits can be understood as learners' mis-selection of a word that is very close to a target word in sound and/or spelling. The use of synforms (see Chapter 6) is a clear exemplar of selectional mishits, where learners make errors in the selection of a target word during their process of accessing their mental lexicons.

There have been arguments that words in the mental lexicon are often tied to each other by meaning, form, sound and also sight (Nattinger, 1988), and that meaning-based links are the most important (Sharifi, Sabet & Tahriri, 2018). Selectional mishits in Cantonese ESL learners' written output, however, do not display strong semantic motivations. On the other hand, the mishits seem to be oriented from sight, where the target words and the mishits are similar in appearance (i.e. spelling).[9]

Universal Processes and Developmental Errors

As is well known, learner language includes universal developmental sequences, which are predictable, and individual learner variation, which is not precisely predictable (Lenzing, 2015). A number of errors made by Cantonese ESL learners can be explained by universal processes. For example, Cantonese ESL learners' mis-ordering of constituents in indirect questions (e.g. sentence (24)), which demonstrates overgeneralization of subject-verb inversion to embedded questions (Larsen-Freeman & Long, 1991), can be explained by the phenomenon of universal processes, as the same kind of overgeneralization (e.g. sentence (25)) is common even in first language acquisition by native English children (Bloom, 1991).

(24) *At that moment, I don't know **what can I do**.
(25) *Ask him **why can't he go out** (Lightbown & Spada, 2021: 12).

The omission of the copula problem typical of more elementary Cantonese ESL learners (e.g. sentence (26)) is also often found in the speech of native English children (e.g. sentence (27)) (Becker, 2002; Brown, 1973; Eisenberg, Guo & Germezia, 2012).

(26) *If I ^ **sick**, they **will** ^ **very nervous**.
(27) *I ^ **in the kitchen** (Becker, 2002: 37).

Cantonese ESL learners' difficulties with English relative clauses can also be seen as resulting from developmental sequences as guided by the Accessibility Hierarchy (AH). According to the AH, the subject position is the most accessible position, followed by the direct object position, which in turn is more accessible than the indirect object position, and so on, with the object of comparison position being the least accessible (Keenan & Comrie, 1977). As such, relative clauses in which the relative pronoun is in the subject position should be acquired earlier than relative clauses in which the relative pronoun is in the direct object position, and so on. Resumptive pronouns, which are more often found in relative clauses in which the relative pronoun is the direct object or other less accessible functions (e.g. sentence (28)), may be manifestations of such universal processes (Chan, 2010c).

(28) *There is one thing **that I can remember it** clearly (Chan, 2004d: 54).

Avoidance Behaviour

Avoidance behaviour, which can be defined as learners' choice to use one language feature instead of another in order to avoid making an error (Kleinmann, 1977; Schachter, 1974; Tarone, Cohen & Dumas, 1976) and which is regarded as a symptom of transfer (Kleinmann, 1977), may explain some ESL learners' language output. Learners tend to adopt avoidance behaviour when a target L2 structure is non-existent in their native language or when it is different from comparable structures in their native language. Examples of errors which are likely the results of Cantonese ESL learners' avoidance behaviour include calques (e.g. sentences (29) and (30)), where direct word-for-word translation is used in favour of a more desirable but unfamiliar structure, such as the relative structure.

(29) *Here was **my job/doing/work the place** (Chan, 2004c: 64). (cf. Here is the place where I work.)
(30) *She was **see me's people** in the yesterday (Chan, 2004c: 64). (cf. She was the person who saw me yesterday.)

It has already been documented in the literature that Chinese students tend to avoid using English relative clauses (Yip & Matthews, 1991). Examples of calques, as demonstrated earlier, probably result from Cantonese ESL learners' attempts to avoid producing relative clauses which they are not confident of producing (Chan, 2004c).

Errors in the use of English articles, such as the incorrect use of bare singular noun phrases (e.g. sentence (31)), may also be seen as learners' avoidance to use an article because of their tendency to avoid making errors in article selection (Chan, 2022).

(31)　*In some extend, ^ **law** can prohibit anyone to cause child abuse (Chan, 2022: 213).

Avoidance behaviour is not directly observable (Kleinmann, 1977), as it is accompanied by absence of analysable interlanguage output due to non-use of a target structure. Therefore, it is difficult to ascertain whether certain learner output is indeed the result of avoidance behaviour. What is more, other undesirable inaccuracies may still come to light during learners' use of a certain structure (e.g. sentences (29) and (30)) in an attempt to avoid a structure that they are not competent to produce (e.g. relative clause), so avoidance, in effect, cannot prevent learners from making errors.

Interaction Between L1- and Non-L1-Related Factors

As can be seen from the preceding discussions, a learner error is seldom attributed to one single source. There is often an intricate interaction between different L1- and non-L1-related factors. The pseudo-tough movement structure, for example, is not solely the outcome of L1 transfer but is best seen as the result of a complex interplay among L1 transfer, overgeneralization (where the tough movement structure is overgeneralized in an inappropriate context), lack of awareness of L2 norms, and confusion caused by "similar" L2 structures. By the same token, pseudo-passives, which have been argued earlier as cases of under-generation where learners fail to generate the target passive, can be seen as manifesting the typological characteristic of topic-prominence in Chinese-Cantonese (Chan, 2010c; Han, 2000; Yip, 1995; Yip & Matthews, 1995), where the subjects of the pseudo-passives coincide with the topic of corresponding Chinese-Cantonese sentences. For lower-proficiency learners, though direct translation from Chinese-Cantonese to English suggests a fairly strong case for L1 transfer, calquing can also arguably be seen as a strategy that they adopt to compensate for their avoidance of using unfamiliar structures, such as relative structures. In a similar fashion, learners' production of anomalous structures such as the wrong placement of adverbs before verbs and the erroneous *there + have* structure cannot solely be attributable to the existence of false positive evidence in the L2 input. L1 transfer cannot be ruled out, given that learners' exposure to the "confusing" positive evidence is often relatively less frequent than to the target structures (Chan, 2004c).

　　L2 development is not a product (Lowie & Verspoor, 2015). It is a process. In this complex process, different mechanisms are often at work (Ortega, 2009). Learners' incomplete knowledge of the target language may trigger L1 transfer, so the use of a target L2 item may reflect the fact that it has been processed receptively with the aid of knowledge of items from the L1 (Chan, 2004c; Singleton, 1987). However, L1 transfer alone cannot radically alter the route of L2 acquisition. It often works in tandem with other factors, such as the psychological factors governing developmental sequences. Learners' perception of the distance between the L1 and the target language, their knowledge of the target language, the psychological structure of their L1, and so on also work together to control the use of transfer (Chan, 2004c; Kellerman, 1979).

Cantonese ESL Learners' Acquisition of English Phonology

The previous sections discuss the extent of L1 influence and the effects of non-L1-related factors on Cantonese ESL learners' acquisition of grammar. The following sections focus on learners' acquisition of phonology, including their perception and production of English speech sounds. Probable factors that may influence learners' perception and/or production of English will be discussed.

Extent of L1 Transfer

L1 transfer has also been argued as one important source of difficulties for L2 phonology (Guion, Harada & Clark, 2004). Consonant to arguments about L1 transfer in grammar, phonology research which relies on a contrastive analysis has often argued that speech sounds not present in the learners' L1 are more diffi-cult to acquire than items which are present both in the L1 and the L2 as a result of a lack of positive transfer (Chan & Li, 2000; Hansen Edwards, 2001, 2004, 2006). Many of the Cantonese ESL learners' production problems discussed in Chapter 7 (as well as some perception problems discussed in Chapter 8) are associated with English speech sounds non-existent in Cantonese (e.g. /r/, /ʃ/, /æ/), and the popular production substitutes for these L2 sounds are typically sounds which are also found in the learners' L1, Cantonese (e.g. /w/, /s/, /e/). Learners' difficulties in acquiring English rhythm are also explained from a negative transfer perspec-tive, as fundamental differences exist between English and Cantonese rhythms: English is stress-timed, whereas Cantonese is non-stress-timed. Again, the use of L1 non-stress-timed rhythm in the production of English utterances is very com-mon (Chan & Li, 2000; also see Chapter 7).

The extent of L1 transfer on Cantonese ESL learners' production of consonant clusters, however, warrants special attention. As discussed in Chapters 3 and 7, there are no consonant clusters in Cantonese, so many Cantonese ESL learners encounter difficulties in pronouncing English consonant clusters. Despite the non-existence of consonant clusters in Cantonese, the individual sound segments (e.g. /l, p, r/) that make up an English consonant cluster (e.g. /pl/, /pr/) may or may not have comparable equivalents in Cantonese. When Cantonese ESL learners encounter a cluster comprising consonants which have comparable equivalents in the native language (e.g. /pl/), positive transfer operates at the segmental level, and so learners can pronounce the clusters correctly. When learners encounter a cluster comprising (some or all) consonants which do not have comparable equiv-alents in the native language (e.g. /pr/ or /ʃr/), positive transfer could not operate (fully) at the segmental level, and the clusters become more difficult because of the inherent difficulty of its constituting members (Chan, 2010b).[10]

Notwithstanding the prevalence of L1 transfer, the "differences resulting in difficulties" formula that has often been put forward in the literature is not sufficient or appropriate in the debate about the role of L1 transfer in L2 phonology acquisition. Other factors need to be considered, the most important of which include typological markedness[11] and similarity.

Typological Markedness

The construct typological markedness/universal markedness[12] deserves attention as far as NL-TL differences are concerned. It says that a phenomenon A in some language is more marked than another phenomenon B if, cross-linguistically, the presence of A (which is known as the *implicans*; Eckman, 1984), necessarily implies the presence of B (which is known as the *implicatum*; Eckman, 1984), but the presence of B does *not* necessarily imply the presence of A (Eckman, 1981a, 1981b). Markedness, thus, refers to "the relative frequency or generality of a given structure across the world's languages" (Eckman, 1996: 198). It is an "independently motivated, empirical construct" (Eckman, 1996: 201) rather than a matter of judgement or conjecture and is often interpreted based on documented implicational universals, such as those in Greenberg (1978).

Of relevance to the construct of typological markedness are the Markedness Differential Hypothesis (MDH) and the Structural Conformity Hypothesis (SCH; also known as the Interlanguage Structural Conformity Hypothesis (ISCH)). The MDH attempts to explain difficulties in L2 acquisition based on cross-linguistic data. It proposes that the relative degree of difficulty of the areas of the target language corresponds to the relative degree of markedness, so within the areas of difference between the target language and the native language, structures which are marked are more difficult than the corresponding structures which are unmarked. On the other hand, those areas of the target language which are different from the native language but which are not more marked than the native language will not be difficult (Eckman, 1977, 2008). It may be argued that because the MDH is grounded on NL-TL differences, it is directly linked to L1 transfer, but the hypothesis contends that NL-TL differences do not inevitably lead to learner difficulties.

The SCH, on the other hand, argues that "the universal generalizations that hold for primary languages hold also for interlanguages" (Eckman, 1991: 24). Therefore, even if there are no NL-TL differences, so long as a learner performs a less marked structure better than a more marked structure, then the SCH can explain the acquisitional pattern. In this sense, typological markedness is independent of L1 influence. Based on the major premises of the MDH and SCH, the "differences resulting in difficulties" formula as has often been asserted does not hold strictly.

The relative degree of markedness of different speech sounds/sound categories has been proposed in the literature, and the concept of universal markedness has been widely used to explain L2 difficulties (e.g. Bhatia, 1995; Edge, 1991; Major & Faudree, 1996; Stockman & Pluut, 1992). Of relevance to Cantonese ESL learners' L2 phonology acquisition is the markedness relationship between voiceless obstruents, voiced obstruents and sonorant consonants: Word-final voiced obstruents are more marked than word-final voiceless obstruents, which are in turn more marked than word-final sonorant consonants (Eckman, 1984).[13] As noted in Chapter 7, Cantonese ESL learners find English voiced obstruents more difficult than English voiceless obstruents, and devoicing of voiced obstruents, especially those in final position, is commonly observed. This pattern of learner difficulty is, thus, compatible with the relative degree of markedness between the two sound categories.

Another area of markedness concerns the dental fricatives. Dental fricatives are rare cross-linguistically (Gamkrelidze, 1978; Maddieson, 1984), so English /θ/ and /ð/, which are dental fricatives, can be considered universally marked. Both of these two consonants present a lot of production difficulties to many ESL learners, including Cantonese ESL learners, and the former also presents a lot of perception problems (see Chapters 7 and 8).

The lengths of a syllable are also in some form of markedness relationship: Longer syllables with complex onsets and/or codas, such as three-member clusters (e.g. /spr/) and two-member clusters (e.g. /bl/), are more marked than shorter syllables, such as two-member clusters (e.g. /pr/) and singleton consonants (e.g. /l/) (Greenberg, 1978).[14] Longer syllables are also more difficult to acquire (Carlisle, 1998). The relative degrees of difficulty of English voiceless and voiced obstruents and those of consonant clusters and singleton consonants, as well as the notorious difficulties of the English dental fricatives for Cantonese ESL learners, provide evidence for the effects of typological markedness, that typological markedness plays a significant role in explaining facts about L2 phonology (Eckman, 2008).

There exists, however, empirical evidence countering the claims about the effects of universal markedness, and thus the predictions of the MDH and SCH, on L2 phonology acquisition. One example concerns Cantonese ESL learners' relatively higher degree of difficulties in the production of final /l/, which is a sonorant consonant, than in their production of English word-final voiceless obstruents, despite the fact that word-final sonorant consonants are universally less marked than word-final voiced and voiceless obstruents. Allophonic variations can help explain such counter evidence to the MDH: In generalizing universal statements regarding different sounds or sound sequences, linguists often use phonemes, rather than allophones, as the basis. Frequency counts are also made on the basis of phoneme occurrences. However, a certain allophone of a phoneme may be more frequent than (an)other allophone(s) of the same phoneme. The less frequent allophone(s) is non-basic and possesses a marked feature (Greenberg, 1966). The English lateral /l/ has two allophones, the clear [l] and the dark [ɫ], with the former occurring more frequently than the latter across languages (Maddieson, 1984). The infrequent distribution of dark [ɫ], coupled with the velarization feature that is required in production, obfuscates the relative markedness, and thus the relative degrees of difficulty between word-final English sonorant consonants and word-final voiceless obstruents for Cantonese ESL learners (Chan, 2007). Given that predictions based on markedness are made on patterns that are supposed to be universal (Hume, 2004), yet allophonic variations may be specific to a certain language (e.g. the two allophones of English /l/), it is debatable whether universal markedness alone should be used to predict acquisitional difficulties (Major, 2001). Although markedness has been claimed to be an empirical and scientific construct (Eckman, 1996), its precise effects on second language learning still remain elusive. Other factors, such as allophonic variations and frequency effects, are not to be ignored (Chan, 2007).

Similarity

In the discussions of L1 influence on phonology acquisition, not only are NL-TL differences important, but the similarity between the native and target languages is also significant, especially in the arena of speech perception. As observed in Chapter 8, many speech perception problems encountered by Cantonese ESL learners do not stem from NL-TL differences. Absence of an equivalent speech sound in a learner's mother tongue may not categorically lead to L2 perception problems, whereas a target L2 sound also present in the native language may still cause perception problems and does not necessarily facilitate perception. Native language repertoire, thus, does not form the basis of perceptual abilities, and inventory gaps as a result of NL-TL differences should not be taken as the principal source of speech perception problems. Mother tongue influence, thus, "does not surface as a coefficient of inventory gaps" (Chan, 2011: 735–736) as far as speech perception is concerned. On the other hand, the adverse effects of similarity on L2 phonology are evident, in that the greater the perceived similarity between an L2 sound and the closest L1 sound, the less likely it is for a learner to be able to discern the phonetic differences between the two sounds. Not only is NL-TL similarity a significant factor affecting speech perception, but it can also explain L2 speech production, as speech perception informs speech production: If a learner can perceive some of the phonetic differences between two L1–L2 sounds, his/her production of that L2 sound will be more accurate (Flege, 1995) (see Chapter 8).

Similarity is, however, a difficult construct to establish, and the kind of similarity advocated in relevant theories, such as the SLM, is perceived phonetic similarity rather than articulatory and/or acoustic similarity. Whether it is perceived similarity or actual phonetic similarity that affects L2 phonological acquisition is difficult to determine. While the boundary between phonetic similarity and dissimilarity is often fuzzy, perceived similarity is not constant and may vary with people and time. Learners' perceived similarity between phonetically "similar" L1–L2 sounds may also be affected by allophonic variations in different phonological environments (e.g. the long and short allophones of Cantonese short vowels before different consonants) (see Chapter 8). Therefore, explanations of L2 phonology acquisition from the perspectives of NL-TL similarity also fall short of explanatory precision.

Relations Between L1 Transfer, Similarity and Typological Markedness

It is sometimes difficult to determine whether L1 influence (be it the result of NL-TL similarity or NL-TL dissimilarity/difference), universal markedness or a combination of different factors can best explain certain speech phenomena. The devoicing of voiced obstruents phenomenon that we have frequently called upon in our previous discussions is one good example. The phenomenon is common not only in L2 speech but also in native speakers' speech (Hansen Edwards, 2014). For Cantonese ESL learners, L1 transfer is presumably at work, given the non-existence of voiced obstruents in Cantonese, but universal markedness (that word-final voiced obstruents are relatively marked) should also be a significant factor. On the other hand, the differences between "similar" English and Cantonese sounds can sometimes be too small to detect. For example, the differences between a certain English speech sound with no comparable equivalents in Cantonese (e.g. English /æ/ and /θ/) and their closest L1 correlates (e.g. Cantonese /e/ and /f/, respectively) can be very small. Such minimal differences between "similar" sounds often go unnoticed, resulting in non-learning of the target sounds. As such, transfer persists (Major, 2008).

There are often intricate relations between L1 transfer, similarity and typological markedness. For similar and marked phenomena, the relative importance of L1 transfer and universals differs from that for normal phenomena: For marked phenomena, the role of universals is much more important than the role of L1 transfer (when compared to less marked phenomena). In contrast, for phenomena similar in the L1 and L2, the role of universals is relatively smaller than the role of L1 transfer (when compared to normal or marked phenomena) (Major, 2001, 2008). Attempts to apply typological markedness to predict patterns of L2 phonology are constrained by the relationships implicated by relevant universal generalizations, so such attempts cannot go beyond the implicational relationships. Where no implicational relationship exists between two sounds or sound categories, typological markedness cannot be determined, so the inherent difficulty of a sound resulting from the phonotactics of the L1 remains the most important factor for determining learner difficulty (Chan, 2010b).

Other Considerations

In the understanding of Cantonese ESL learners' L2 speech, other factors should not go unnoticed. One phenomenon which deserves attention is neutralization. As seen in Chapter 7, English long and short vowel pairs are often pronounced indistinguishably by Cantonese ESL learners. There are also reciprocal substitutions[15] between liquids (i.e. /l/ and /r/) in initial consonant clusters. These two-way substitutions can be seen as manifestations of neutralization. While neutralization of English long and short vowel pairs can be explained by the allophonic feature of the corresponding Cantonese short phonemes (which have comparable long and short allophones; see Chapter 3), L1 transfer does not seem to operate for neutralization of /l/ and /r/ in onset clusters. Given that initial /l/ is found in both languages whereas /r/ is non-existent in Cantonese, a simple transfer account will predict substitution of /l/ for /r/, but not vice versa. There is, thus, reason to believe that, in the interlanguage of Cantonese ESL learners, there is a phonological rule which neutralizes liquids in onset clusters, resulting in a higher difficulty level for English /l/ than what a simple transfer account will predict (Chan, 2010a, 2010b).

Another phenomenon which deserves attention is developmental processes. Substitution of [f] for /θ/ may be a developmental phenomenon in Hong Kong English as a result of misperception effects, given that [f] is a common realization of /θ/ in early stages of acquisition and that learners of advanced proficiency are more likely to pronounce the sound accurately (Hansen Edwards, 2019).

Other factors have also been observed in the literature to have effects on L2 phonology for learners of different native languages, such as grammatical conditioning[16] (e.g. Hansen Edwards, 2016a, 2016b; Hazen, 2011; Walker, 2012) and linguistic environments[17] (e.g. Carlisle, 1997; Hansen Edwards, 2011). Whether these factors are applicable to Cantonese ESL learners' L2 phonological acquisition is yet to be ascertained, but it is evident that L1 transfer alone is not a sufficient account of Cantonese ESL learners' L2 phonology, although it "has always been, and still is, a factor in explaining L2 pronunciation" (Eckman, 2004: 543).

Conclusion

In this chapter, we have examined the various factors which may help explain Cantonese ESL learners' acquisition of English grammar and phonology. Though L1 interference is the major source of problems, many of the errors or problems cannot be explained from a simple contrastive perspective. Many errors/problems are also due to different non-L1-related factors. As far as grammar acquisition is concerned, overgeneralization, misapplication of L2 rules, avoidance behaviour and the like are some probable causes. As for phonology acquisition, issues such as universal markedness, NL-TL similarity, developmental processes may also be contributing factors. There are also intricate and complex interactions between various factors, be they L1-related or non-L1-related. Therefore, L1 transfer alone is not sufficient in accounting for all learner problems, but it remains one most important contributing factor.[18]

Notes

1 Although Chinese has been regarded as an isolating language with very little inflection and every syllable is a morpheme (Sapir, 1921), there are complex words in Chinese-Cantonese formed by reduplication, affixation or compounding (Matthews & Yip, 2011).

2 Counterarguments also exist about the use of the L1 in L2 teaching, that the use of translation exercises following grammar instruction can eliminate L1 interference (e.g. Pan & Pan, 2010). As the purpose of this chapter is not to ascertain the best medium of L2 instruction, the details of those arguments will not be pursued.

3 A bilingualized dictionary (e.g. *Oxford Advanced Learner's English–Chinese Dictionary*) is a dictionary with definitions and examples which have been translated in full or in part into the target language (e.g. Chinese), but there are also definitions and examples in the source language (e.g. English) (Hartmann, 1994; James, 1994; Marello, 1998).

4 As the focus of this book and particularly of this chapter is on the problems that Cantonese ESL learners often encounter, the precise effects of positive transfer and relevant discussions will not be pursued.

5 In this section, the words "similar" and "similarities" are both enclosed in double quotation marks, as the structures under discussion (acceptable structures and corresponding unacceptable ones) just look similar on the surface, yet they may not bear any genuine relationships or display any legitimate similarities.

6 Positive evidence is evidence that a particular utterance is grammatical (or possible) in the language which a learner is learning (Richards & Schmidt, 2010).

7 In an anticipatory-*it* sentence, the subject is usually postponed to the end of the sentence, and its position is taken by the dummy *it*, which is known as the anticipatory subject (Nelson & Greenbaum, 2016).

8 Like most other error types discussed in this book, some sentences with the unacceptable *somewhere has something* structure may contain other grammatical anomalies, such as subject-verb agreement (e.g. *The table **have** four legs*) or determiner-noun agreement (e.g. *The table has **four leg** *). These anomalies, however, do not invalidate the claim that the *somewhere has something* problem is more semantic in nature.

9 The current discussion about selectional mishits is based on Cantonese ESL learners' written output. No attempt is made to generalize the discussions to learners' spoken output.

10 Chan (2010b) focuses on Cantonese ESL learners' acquisition of initial consonant clusters. It is not clear whether the argument discussed in this paragraph about individual segments in a cluster is applicable to final consonant clusters.

11 Typological markedness is used not only to describe phonology acquisition. It has also been used to explain aspects of grammar, such as relative clauses, where the subject position (the most accessible item in the AH) is the least marked item and the object of comparison position (the least accessible item in the hierarchy) is the most marked item (e.g. Eckman, Bell & Nelson, 1988). In this chapter, only markedness relationships related to phonology are discussed.

12 Typological markedness is understood as markedness relationships that exist cross-linguistically. The term "universal markedness" is also used in the literature. In this chapter, these two terms will be used interchangeably to refer to the same concept.

13 This markedness relationship is based on the universal generalization that if there are voiced obstruents word-finally, then there are voiceless obstruents word-finally, and if there are voiceless obstruents word-finally, then there are sonorant consonants word-finally (Eckman, 1984).

14 This markedness relationship about consonant clusters is based on Greenberg's (1978: 250) Resolvability Principle, which says that "every initial or final sequence of length m contains at least one continuous subsequence of length m − 1".

15 In Chapters 7 and 8, the term "substitution" has consistently been used to describe learners' production of another sound to replace a certain target sound. The use of the term "assumes that the learners' underlying representation for the L2 target is identical to the L2 target, and that the substituted sound is therefore a phonetic variant of this underlying representation. This, however, may not be the case" (Zampini, 2008: 231), so the term "substitution" is not an entirely accurate term in describing learner productions.

16 Examples of grammatical conditioning are evidenced in learners' more frequent deletion of /t, d/ in consonant clusters when the alveolar plosives appear in bimorphemic forms (e.g. as past tense markers) than when they appear in monomorphemic forms, or vice versa.

17 The effects of linguistic environments have been attested in different studies. For example, in Carlisle (1997), it was found that epenthesis in sC and sCC onsets by Spanish learners of English occurred significantly more frequently after the consonantal

environment than after the vocalic environment. In Hansen Edwards (2011), it was found that a preceding nasal had the strongest effect on /t, d/ deletion by Mandarin Chinese ESL learners.

18 Although the major causes of grammar problems and those of phonology problems are discussed separately in this chapter, some factors, such as the effects of universal/developmental processes, or even typological markedness (see note 11), can help explain both aspects of L2 learning.

10 The Teaching of Grammar to Cantonese ESL Learners

In Chapters 4–6, we examined various types and subtypes of grammatical errors made by Cantonese ESL learners, including interlingual and intralingual errors. Special attention was also paid to errors associated with English articles, some of the most common function words in English. In this chapter, pedagogical suggestions for the teaching of grammar to Cantonese ESL learners will be given. It will be argued that explicit grammar teaching is needed for alerting learners' awareness of target language norms and enhancing their knowledge of various grammatical structures.

Importance of Explicit Grammar Teaching and Explicit Error Correction

With the development of the Communicative Language Teaching (CLT) approach in the last century, which advocated that language was mainly acquired through communication (Howatt, 1984), the importance of explicit grammar teaching and error correction was once disregarded. Under the advocacy of CLT, second language was acquired through a naturalistic environment, in much the same way as a child acquiring his/her native language (Krashen, 1982, 1985). The goal of learning was communicative competence, and communication of meaning was seen as of paramount importance (Richards & Rodgers, 1986). Successful language learning, thus, involved learners' knowledge of the functions and purposes of a language in different communicative settings rather than their knowledge of the grammatical forms in isolation (Lightbown & Spada, 2021). Language production was also seen as important, as it provided one with the opportunity for "meaningful practice of one's linguistic resources permitting the development of automaticity in their use" (Swain, 1993: 159).

Notwithstanding the claims of CLT and its disregard of explicit grammar teaching, there has also been a lot of research advocating explicit teaching of grammar and/or error correction (e.g. Doughty, 1991; Doughty & Varela, 1998; Spada & Tomita, 2010; White, 1991; White, Spada, Lightbown & Ranta, 1991). Empirical evidence supporting the use of explicit grammar teaching is abundant. For example, Doughty (1991) shows that acquisition of interlanguage grammar can be promoted by alerting learners' attention to language forms through the use of

DOI: 10.4324/9781003252498-10

detailed analysis of a structure or through highlighting a certain target structure in context. Lando (1998) notes that when explicit, intensive form-focused instruction is combined with continuous meaning-focused practice, a more accurate use of language features that are closely related to the target language items will result. Ellis (2002) argues for the contribution of form-focused instruction to the acquisition of implicit knowledge. And Ellis (2002) and Mohamed (2004) show evidence of learners themselves viewing explicit grammar teaching as useful to second language acquisition.

As far as error correction is concerned, it has been argued that learners' noticing their errors is important in contributing to their success in error correction. However, learners may or may not notice their own errors (cf. the Noticing Hypothesis; Schmidt, 1990, 1992). Even if they can notice their errors, they may not be competent enough to correct the errors by themselves. Therefore, explicit intervention is needed to help learners "progress to fully mature linguistic competence" (Tomasello & Herron, 1988: 237) and to prevent learner errors from becoming fossilized. Research supporting the use of explicit error correction in the learning of a second language is also abundant. Bell (1992), for example, argues that it is useful to give explicit error correction in meaning contexts targeting errors that hamper understanding. Carroll, Swain and Roberge (1992) and Carroll and Swain (1993) found positive evidence supporting the role of negative feedback on the learning of French suffixation and dative alternation, respectively. In both studies, learners receiving explicit negative feedback outperformed those who did not.

Explicit error correction is useful not only in an exclusively form-focused context but also in a communicative context. Studies investigating the use of form-focused corrective feedback in communicative programmes also yield positive results. For example, Lightbown and Spada (1990) have found that the use of timely form-focused instructive and corrective feedback in communicative teaching contexts facilitates learners' development of L2 accuracy, fluency and overall communication skills.

It has been argued that for form-focused instruction to be effective, the structures targeted must be processable, and thus learnable at the time when instruction is given (Long, 1996). Related to this is the concept of teachability and the Teachability Hypothesis (Pienemann, 1984, 1985), later understood as a subset of the Processability Theory (Pienemann, 1998). The Processability Theory argues that a number of interrelated stages are involved in learners' acquisition of a target form. During the learning process, learners progress from one developmental stage to another, with each stage containing processing pre-requisites required at the next stage. When a learner has not reached a certain stage, it is difficult for him/her to acquire related linguistic structures even after extensive or intensive teaching, as he/she is not cognitively ready to benefit from the instruction. A learner cannot skip a natural stage of development, because skipping stages implies that a gap will exist in the processing procedure (Pienemann, 1998). Despite some empirical support, the Teachability Hypothesis is argued to affect only a subset of grammar (Rutherford & Sharwood Smith, 1988). Given that "the presence of all processing procedures does not guarantee that the structure will emerge at that point" (Pienemann, 1998: 252), formal instruction can help learners to apply stage-appropriate rules and improve their accuracy within the developmental stages they are in (Lightbown & Spada, 1990).

Explicit second language instruction is, thus, conducive to second language acquisition of target language norms (Ellis, 1995). In a city where English is not normally used other than formal domains such as government, business, law and education, such as Hong Kong (Li, 1999) and other similar ESL or EFL contexts, form-focused instruction and error correction on processable and learnable structures is not only necessary but also essential (Chan & Li, 2002).

An Algorithmic Approach to Error Correction

In the literature on explicit grammar and/or error correction intervention, a difference is made between Focus on Form (FonF) and Focus on Forms (FonFs) (Long, 1991). The former refers to brief attention devoted to linguistic forms during meaning-focused interaction, with a primary focus on meaning. The latter, on the other hand, focuses primarily on the presentation of linguistic structures as discrete grammar rules or other metalinguistic information, with learners' attention directed at linguistic forms rather than meaning (Shintani, 2013). It is the latter (FonFs) which the previous section about explicit instruction has been discussing. The teaching approach that will form the focus of the current section, an algorithmic approach to error correction, is also aligned with the FonFs approach.

An algorithmic approach to error correction is one example of a consciousness-raising approach aiming at helping students overcome persistent errors. In line with the contention that language items to be learnt need to be processable and learnable, it is characterized by an algorithmic operation, with explanations broken down algorithmically into a number of small, proceduralized, cognitively manageable steps or stages which are easy and highly structured (Chan, 2006a). The proceduralized steps consist of very simple questions requiring short answers or simple instructions. These questions/instructions will ensure that the cognitive load required of learners is minimal when they make intermediate decisions, thus facilitating their progress from one step to another. A subsequent question or instruction builds on and often extends the answers/information revealed from the previous question(s), thus facilitating learners' acquisition of the target structure step-by-step. The questions to be asked or instructions to be given are not isolated or unrelated. They are all intertwined and work together like building blocks, leading learners to progress to the target language norms. In some of the proceduralized steps, where appropriate, there will be instructive examples showing how the targeted error can be corrected and/or explicit rules spelling out the appropriate use of the target items, so that learners will be guided to arrive at the target structure (see Figure 10.1). Reinforcement exercises are also provided to help reinforce learners' understanding where appropriate (Chan, 2006a; Li & Chan, 2000).

Given the nature of an algorithmic approach, not all kinds of errors are suitable for implementation. Morpho-syntactically well-defined lexico-grammatical anomalies, the corrections of which are amenable to the design of small

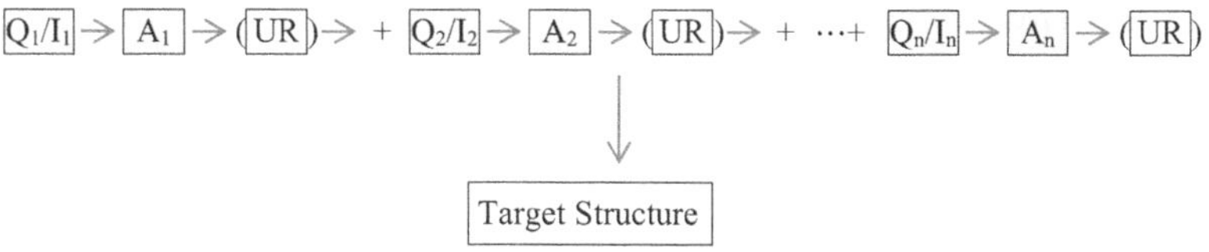

$$Q_1/I_1 \rightarrow A_1 \rightarrow (UR) \rightarrow + \; Q_2/I_2 \rightarrow A_2 \rightarrow (UR) \rightarrow + \cdots + \; Q_n/I_n \rightarrow A_n \rightarrow (UR)$$

Target Structure

where Q/I = Question/Instruction; A = Answer; () denotes an optional step; and

UR   =   Usage Rules and/or Instructive Examples

Figure 10.1 A diagrammatic representation of an algorithmic approach

instructional steps, are more prone to the kinds of proceduralized teaching steps characterized by an algorithmic approach (Li & Chan, 2000), whereas more abstract concepts such as the use of English articles or the use of prepositions may not be suitable items for implementation.

Applications of an Algorithmic Approach

Remedial instructional materials/guidelines using an algorithmic approach have been developed for many of the errors discussed in Chapters 4 and 6. These include confusion between *concern* and *concerned about* (Chan & Li, 2002; Li & Chan, 2001); incorrect order of adverbs (Chan, Li & Kwan, 2003); misuse of *on the contrary* (Chan & Li, 2002; Li & Chan, 2001); misuse of *until and till* (Chan, 2003); periphrastic-topic constructions (Kwan, Chan & Li, 2003); the independent clause as subject or object/complement problem (Chan, Kwan & Li, 2003); the missing relative pronoun problem (Chan, Kwan & Li, 2002a); the pseudo-tough movement structure (Chan & Li, 2002; Li & Chan, 2001); the resumptive pronoun problem (Chan, 2004d); the *somewhere has something* problem (Chan, Kwan & Li, 2002b); the *there + have* existential structure (Chan, Kwan & Li, 2002a); and the *too + adj + to VP* structure (Li & Chan, 2000). Other common lexico-grammatical errors which are not discussed in Chapters 4 and 6 but which are amenable to correction using an algorithmic approach have also been the target of instruction, including confusion between *-ed* and *-ing* participles[1] (Li & Chan, 2000) and the dangling modifier problem[2] (Chan, Kwan & Li, 2002a).

An Example: Pseudo-Tough Movement

In this section, the correction procedure for the pseudo-tough movement structure proposed in Chan and Li (2002) and Li and Chan (2001) will be used to illustrate the operation of an algorithmic approach. As discussed in Chapters 4 and 9, pseudo-tough movement is characterized by the use of a tough adjective, such as *easy* or *inconvenient*, in an inappropriate context (e.g. sentences (1) and (2)), where, unlike the correct tough movement structure (e.g. sentence (3)), the subject of the main clause cannot be interpreted as the object/prepositional object of the embedded *to* + *V* clause.

(1)   *You **are easy** to do the homework.
(2)   *She **is inconvenient** to talk to you now.
(3)   The question is **difficult to answer**.

Correction Procedure

The correction procedure targets the core of the problem and the confusion caused by the correct tough movement structure. It consists of seven phases.

PHASE 1

Because it is important that learners notice the error before they can correct it, the first phase of remedial instruction using an algorithmic approach is devoted to helping learners notice the error by showing a few examples with the pseudo-tough movement structure, such as in sentences (1) and (2).

PHASE 2

In the second phase, short questions requiring short answers are used to guide learners through the error correction procedure, as in the following:

- Can you identify and circle the adjectives in sentences (1) and (2)?
- They are: _____ (easy, inconvenient)[3]
- Let's look at sentence (1):
  - You are easy to do the homework.
- Can you work out **what** is easy?
- (a)_____ is easy   (to do the homework)
- Now, can you work out **for whom XXX is easy**?
- for (b) _____.   (you)
- Okay, can you put (a) and (b) together and say what is easy, and for whom?
- (c) _____ is easy.   (for you to do the homework)
- (c) is correct; can you identify the subject?
- _____ is easy.   (for you to do the homework)
- But English sentences with long subjects are not preferred. They are usually avoided. How can this be improved?
- To improve (c), move the subject to the right, after the adjective, resulting in (d), i.e.
- _____(for you to do the homework) __ | is   easy ↓
- (d) _____ is easy for you to do the homework.
- Put the word "It" in the subject position, resulting in (e):
- (e) _____ is easy for you to do the homework. (It)
  (adapted from Li & Chan, 2001: 23–24; example modified)

As can be seen from the preceding steps, the answers to the short questions are all easily retrievable from the given sentences. Learners first identify the adjective (i.e. *easy*) used in the erroneous sentence, then identify the action which is easy (i.e. *to do the homework*), and then identify the entity for which the action is easy (i.e. *for you to do the homework*). After learners have identified the intended sentence structure, the subsequent steps show how the intended sentence structure could be realized in normative English sentences (i.e. *It is easy for you to do the homework*).

PHASE 3

In the third phrase, the correction procedure is repeated with a similar error, such as sentence (2), using similar sets of questions for consolidation purposes (details omitted).

PHASE 4

In the fourth phase, a summary of the correction procedure is presented:

- Step 1: Identify the ADJ.
- Step 2: WHAT is ADJ?
- Step 3: for WHOM?
- Step 4: Put the answers to Step 2 and Step 3 together.
- Step 5: Move the subject to the right, after the VERB and ADJ.
- Step 6: Put "It" at the beginning of the sentence.

(adapted from Li & Chan, 2001: 25; details modified)

PHASES 5 AND 6

In the fifth and sixth phases, supplementary information about other adjectives with similar syntactic behaviour and reinforcement exercises are given to consolidate learners' understanding. It is expected that by this time students will be able to grasp the correct structure for expressing the intended meaning.

PHASE 7

There still exists learners' confusion between the erroneous structure and the tough movement structure. The last phase is devoted to the explanation of the circumstances under which the tough movement structure is appropriate. Focus is put on the structures of sentences with correct tough movement (e.g. sentences (4) and (5)).

(4)   The question is **difficult to answer**.
(5)   Amy is **easy to please**.

The following questions and/or instructions are used to help students understand the correct usage:

- Sentences with verbs such as "answer" and "please" require an Object to complete them, i.e. ***answer something*** and ***please somebody***.
- What is the object of "answer" in sentence (4)?   (the question)
- What is the subject of sentence (4)?   (the question)
- What is the object of "please" in sentence (5)?   (Amy)
- What is the subject of sentence (5)?   (Amy)
- What is the relationship between the objects of these verbs and the subjects of the sentences?   (They are the same)
- A useful rule of thumb is:

> If missing Object of Verb = Subject, then
> *Subject + is/are + ADJ + to + Verb* is acceptable
> (Li & Chan, 2001: 26; examples modified)

As can be seen from the preceding steps, in identifying the answers to the short questions, students are guided step-by-step to see the relationship between the missing objects of the verbs and the subjects of the sentences. Such proceduralized steps go in line with the consciousness-raising approach, raising learners' consciousness of the circumstances under which the tough movement structure is correctly used and of the subtle differences between the correct and erroneous structures.

Summary of Correction Procedure

Table 10.1 summarizes the different phases involved in the correction of the pseudo-tough movement structure using the algorithmic approach as demonstrated in this section.

Table 10.1 The correction procedure for the pseudo-tough movement structure

Phase	Activity
1	Help learners notice the error.
2	Go through the error correction procedure using Q-A (Question-Answer).
3	Consolidate learners' understanding by repeating the correction procedure with other examples.
4	Summarize the correction procedure.
5	Give supplementary information about the error where appropriate.
6	Consolidate learners' understanding through reinforcement exercises.
7	Explain the circumstances under which sentences with a similar structure are grammatical.

Merits of an Algorithmic Approach

An algorithmic approach to error correction has been tried out with different errors (Chan, 2006a; Chan & Li, 2002). Empirical evidence shows that the approach is effective in (i) advancing knowledge construction, (ii) facilitating internalization of correct sentence structures and (iii) promoting self-learning (Chan, 2006a).

The very nature of an algorithmic approach makes it possible for students to continuously construct knowledge and reinforce the knowledge constructed. As various intermediate decisions (e.g. identifying the underlying object of the embedded *to + V* clause in a sentence with the tough movement structure; identifying the subject of that sentence) have to be made when learners follow the small, proceduralized steps, initial (partial) knowledge about the correct usage of a target item (e.g. that the missing object of the embedded *to + V* clause is the same as the subject of the sentence) will be constructed (cf. merit (i)).

The constructed knowledge is tested/reinforced in a subsequent step (e.g. answering similar questions about different sentences with the same structure). When learners do so, further knowledge will be constructed, tested and reinforced. With such construction and testing/reinforcement of knowledge, "learners will be empowered to manipulate the language within definable limits. Their understanding of the language will gradually increase, and their misconceptions will slowly vanish" (Chan, 2006a: 143). Such continuous knowledge construction and reinforcement operations facilitate learners' internalization of the correct sentence structures and accelerate their acquisition of the target language models (cf. merit (ii)).

What is more, because the proceduralized steps are user-friendly and require minimal cognitive efforts, learners, especially those of higher English proficiency, can accomplish the tasks even without teacher intervention. The remedial instructional materials can be used as self-learning aids for promoting self-learning, where learners reactivate their memory of the correction procedure to internalize the target language norms (cf. merit (iii)) (Chan, 2006a).

Other Consciousness-Raising Teaching Techniques

An algorithmic approach is by no means the only effective approach to explicit grammar intervention. Discovery-based consciousness-raising strategies, which help learners to discover the distinctive functions of different structures, should also be useful in the teaching of English grammar. The following consciousness-raising activities from Chan (2008) on the teaching of English ergative verbs is one example.

Ergative Verbs

Ergative verbs, such as *increase, decrease, change, drop, move* and the like, are verbs which can be used not just in the active (e.g. sentence (6)) and passive voices (e.g. sentence (7)) but also in the middle voice (e.g. sentence (8)) (Lock, 1996). When the middle voice is used, the object (e.g. *the prices of the products*) of the transitive, active use of the verb has become the subject of the intransitive use of the verb (e.g. sentence (8)).

(6)   The seller increased **the prices of the products**. (Transitive; Active Voice)
(7)   The prices of the products were increased (by the seller). (Transitive; Passive Voice)
(8)   **The prices of the products** increased. (Intransitive; Middle Voice)

From a structural perspective, clauses/sentences in the middle voice are distinguished from those in the active and passive voices in that the verb is used intransitively in the middle voice clauses but transitively in the active and passive voice clauses. However, ergative verbs are different from other verbs which can be used transitively or intransitively, such as *drive*, *drink*, or *eat*. For these non-ergative verbs, the same subject (e.g. *we*) can be used in both the intransitive and transitive clauses (e.g. sentences (9) and (10)). Although a passive clause can be formed for its transitive use (e.g. sentence (11)), the object of the transitive, active clause (e.g. *the red car* in sentence (10)) cannot be used as the subject of the corresponding intransitive clause without changing the meaning or affecting the grammaticality of the clause (e.g. sentence (12)).

(9)   We drove yesterday. (Intransitive)
(10)   We drove **the red car** yesterday. (Transitive; Active Voice)
(11)   The red car was driven (by us) yesterday. (Transitive; Passive Voice)
(12)   ***The red car** drove yesterday. (Intransitive; Unacceptable Middle Voice)

The unacceptability of *the red car* as the subject of sentence (12) illustrates the major meaning and functional differences between ergative verbs and non-ergative verbs: The event/action denoted by an ergative verb in the middle voice happens more or less spontaneously instead of being done by a doer intentionally or deliberately. Therefore, the middle voice clause does not necessarily require a doer for the action or a causer for the event concerned. The constituent involved (e.g. *the prices of the products*) is still the constituent being affected by the action/event denoted by the verb, although it has become the subject of the middle voice clause. In contrast, the action denoted by a non-ergative verb such as *drive* has to be done by a doer (e.g. *we*). This action cannot happen spontaneously, and so the middle voice is not acceptable.

Teaching the Use of Ergative Verbs Using a Discovery-Based Consciousness-Raising Approach

To help ESL learners notice the correct use of ergative verbs, it is important to arouse their awareness of the differences in the meanings of the corresponding sentences in the three voices of active, passive and middle. Explicit comparisons with different texts or written examples and related grammatical information using dictionaries should of course be useful (Lock, 1995), but it is more cost-effective if students can discover the major differences themselves. The following is a suggested activity adapted from Chan (2008), where students are guided to give different responses authentically and spontaneously and to discover the appropriate contexts for using ergative verbs in different voices.

i First, Teacher drops a rubber (or a small object) onto the floor and asks "What did I do?" Students will not hesitate to answer *You dropped the rubber*;

ii Teacher continues by asking "What happened to the rubber?" Students will say something like *The rubber was dropped by you*;

iii Teacher puts the rubber on the edge of a desk, continues to say something to engage the students, walks to the back of the desk and suddenly bumps into the desk hard (as if he/she could not balance himself/herself) so that the rubber drops by itself;

iv Then, Teacher asks "Oh, what happened to the rubber?" Some students may keep saying *The rubber was dropped* (*by you*), but a couple of them may answer *The rubber dropped*;

v Teacher invites students to repeat their answers, asking them to pay attention to the differences between the structure of their answers (i.e. The former is in the passive voice and the latter is not);

vi Teacher introduces the use of the active, passive and middle voices by stating the difference between the first incident (i.e. *The teacher dropped the rubber/The rubber was dropped by the teacher*) and the second incident (i.e. *The rubber dropped by itself*) (Chan, 2008: http://iteslj.org/Techniques/Chan-ErgativeVerbs.html; examples modified).

As can be seen from the preceding activity, the questions asked by the teacher in the two scenarios help to alert learners to the distinction between the different voices: For the first scenario, the first question (i.e. *What did I do?*) is about the teacher's deliberate action and invites an answer in the active voice (i.e. *You dropped the rubber*). The second question (i.e. *What happened to the rubber*), which immediately follows an answer in the active voice, invites a response in the passive voice (i.e. *The rubber was dropped by you*). For the second scenario, although the question (i.e. *Oh, what happened to the rubber?*) shares the same structure as the previous question, it does not follow any utterances which may imply a doer and helps to focus learners on the absence of a doer, thus inviting an answer in the middle voice.

Consolidating exercises can be introduced requiring students to decide whether an action/event denoted by the verb in a certain context should be better represented as implying a doer or not. Students can also discuss the effects of the use of different voices on the interpretation of a text and try to formulate a rule about the occasions on which the passive voice is preferably used and those on which the middle voice is preferably used (Jones, 1995).

Merits of Discovery-Based Consciousness-Raising Strategies

Unlike an algorithmic approach, which has a structured instructional pattern with heavily controlled steps, the discovery-based consciousness-raising technique for teaching ergative verbs described earlier is much less controlled and more spontaneous. The activity is heavily dependent on students' spontaneous reactions to teachers' questions. Students' answers may vary, and there is no guarantee that an "expected" answer will come up from every student. However, students are placed in an authentic situation where they themselves discover the need for using different structures to describe different scenarios. Many learners, especially advanced learners, may not find middle voice sentences exotic. They may have come across such sentences many times and might have used them subconsciously in their own language output without realizing the actual meanings conveyed. Explicit grammar teaching using discovery-based consciousness-raising techniques can help alert learners' awareness of the occasion on which the middle voice is preferable to other voices. As such, their language production will be grounded on deepened metalinguistic awareness.

Use of Metalinguistic Explanations in the Teaching of Grammar

In our previous discussions on an algorithmic approach to error correction, it has been pointed out that such an approach is most suitable for errors of which the correction process can be broken down into a sequence of cognitively manageable steps requiring minimal efforts on the part of the learner. Some errors, such as the wrong use of articles, are not amenable to correction using an algorithmic approach (Li & Chan, 2001). For these errors, the use of metalinguistic explanations should be useful for enhancing learners' knowledge of the English article system, eradicating their misconceptions and heightening their awareness of the correct use of English articles (Chan, 2021).[4]

Merits of Metalinguistic Explanations and Empirical Evidence

As argued earlier, a learner has to notice a language feature before he/she can learn it (Schmidt, 1990). Some language features are easier to notice than others, and English articles belong to the latter: They are non-salient features not easily noticed at the input stage (VanPatten, 1996). Therefore, explicit intervention is particularly necessary. Early explicit interventions on the use of English articles put more focus on performance and suggested using "canonical information structure as a preliminary guess" (Master, 2002: 340) or "providing interactional modifications" and leading "learners to produce modified output within a problem-solving task" (Muranoi, 2000: 617). However, because metalinguistic explanations direct learners to pay attention to specific linguistic forms (Oyama, 2017), explicit instruction in the form of metalinguistic explanations targeting learners' explicit knowledge of the English article system should be more useful for helping them better analyse article errors (Akakura, 2012).

Explicit instruction using metalinguistic explanations to teach English article use has been experimented with in the literature. Relevant studies have largely been found to be successful. For example, Snape, Umeda, Wiltshier and Yusa (2016) found that L2 learners benefited from explicit instruction on generics; and Umeda, Snape, Yusa and Wiltshier (2019) found short-term positive effects for learners who had received explicit instruction on genericity. Akakura's (2012) study, which explained form-function mappings of English articles, found that explicit instruction could benefit not only implicit knowledge but also explicit knowledge. By the same token, although learners from Snape and Yusa's (2013) study on definiteness, specificity and genericity using Krifka, Pelletier, Carlson, ter Meulen, Link and Chierchia's (1995) framework did not benefit greatly from explicit instruction as far as article choices were concerned, learners did show improvements in their perception of sentences with articles. As such, explicit instruction targeting the enhancement of learners' metalinguistic awareness and advancement of their explicit knowledge is useful in the teaching of English articles. Given the diverse kinds of problems learners have and their misconceptions about the English article system and reference representations, teaching focuses should target the eradication of such misconceptions. Explicit teaching of English articles should involve not just instructions by teachers but also learners' verbalization of relevant linguistic concepts.

Teaching of English Articles Using Metalinguistic Explanations

In the teaching of English articles, variations in article use among the standard and non-standard varieties of native speakers (known as the inner circle; Bolton, 2012), as well as variations among users of English as a second language (known as the outer circle; Bolton, 2012) or as a foreign or international language (known as the expanding circle; Bolton, 2012), should not be neglected. However, for advanced ESL learners who aim to attain mastery of "correct," standard use of articles, the following teaching suggestions are worth implementing.

Unveiling Shadowy Effects of Correct Article Use

Because there are only three articles in English (*the*, *a/an*, and *ZERO*), it is more than expected that some form of guessing is involved. Thus, learners' correct uses of English articles can be deceptive. In the teaching of English articles, teachers should be aware of the shadowy problems underlying correct article uses (Chan, 2017b). In order to understand the root of learners' problems and to ensure that article use is guided by learners' explicit knowledge instead of ungrounded intuitions (Chan, 2016), teachers can set aside some time for activities that can probe into learners' thinking processes during article selection, such as asking learners to voice the reasons underlying their article choices and to verbalize the references of the chosen articles in an authentic text. Teachers can also ask learners to substitute another article for a target article and discuss the possible changes to the interpretation of the sentence/text after substitution (Lock, 1996) and/or to explore the possibility of variations of article use in different varieties of English. Learners' ability to analyse the intended reference of a noun phrase in a certain context is but one of the most important teaching focuses as far as English articles are concerned.

Using Learners' Dictionaries, Concordances and Corpuses for Countability and Article Use

The differences between the countable, uncountable and singular uses of an English noun are often too subtle for learners to discern, resulting in indeterminacy in deciding on the acceptability of using *a/an* or *ZERO* or pluralization in a certain context (see Chapter 5). Teachers can encourage learners to consult reliable self-learning resources such as learners' dictionaries. It is well known that countability information is one important piece of information about nouns in a learner's dictionary, with a number of definitions and/or examples showing relevant usages. However, dictionary information may sometimes be misleading or difficult to interpret. Teachers can design dictionary consultation tasks highlighting the variability of noun countability and the importance of context in determining countability and related article use. Awareness-raising activities akin to the noun countability task used in Chan (2017a) should be useful in this respect. For example, learners can be given a few sentence contexts that trigger varied article choices with a certain target English noun and be required to determine, with the use of a learner's dictionary, the countability of the target noun and its correct usage in the different contexts, as shown in examples (13) and (14).

(13) The police have _____ to believe that he is guilty. C/U (reason)

    a.   reason
    b.   reasons
    c.   a reason

(Chan, 2017a: 209)

(14) Their goal is simply to cause terror without _____. C/U (a justified reason)

    a.   justified reason
    b.   justified reasons
    c.   a justified reason

(ibid)

With the help of suitable software tools, learners can also access reliable online concordances and/or corpus files and extract sentence contexts that trigger a certain structure. For example, to determine the correct expression in (15), teachers can ask students to use a reliable concordance such as the British National Corpus (https://www.english-corpora.org/bnc/) and type in the three options to find the most acceptable form of the target word *assessment*. The corpus will show that *a fair assessment* is the most commonly used expression, as in (16) and (17).

(15) Would you say that this is _____ of the current situation? (a fair assessment)

    a. fair assessment
    b. fair assessments
    c. a fair assessment

(16) Would you think that was **a fair assessment**?
(17) I think that's **a very fair assessment** of him.

Learners can then engage in deeper discussions about the most desirable choice of articles with a target word as evidenced in people's authentic language production in different contexts.

Tackling Confusion Between Definiteness and Specificity

Given the widespread misconception that definiteness is equated with specificity (see Chapter 5), teachers need to diagnose learners' understanding of the two concepts so as to detect gaps in their knowledge. Learners need to be made aware of and given clear contexts for the distinction between definite and specific noun phrases. Although most definite noun phrases are specific, such as *the boy with long hair* in sentence (18), a specific noun phrase is not necessarily definite, such as *a boy* in sentence (19), nor is a definite noun phrase necessarily specific, such as *the winner* in sentence (20), which is definite but not specific.

(18) **The boy with long hair** is my boyfriend.
(19) **A boy** is coming.
(20) Joan wants to present the prize to **the winner** – so she'll have to wait around until the race finishes (Lopez, 2019: 202).

An example using metalinguistic explanations to teach definiteness and specificity can be seen from Lopez (2019), who experimented with a simplified, pedagogical version of definitions for definiteness and specificity based on Ionin, Ko and Wexler's (2004) definitions. Definiteness was explained as knowledge shared by both the speaker and the listener, in that both parties should be able to identify the person or object being referred to. Specificity was explained as the speaker's intention to refer to one particular individual. There was also explicit mention that the concept "*the* = specific and *a* = non-specific" was false. Practice exercises requiring learners to discuss the difference in meaning between different noun phrases were also provided. These exercises consisted of pairs of noun phrases that were both definite (or both indefinite), but one noun phrase was specific whereas the other was non-specific, as in sentences (21–24).

(21) Where did you leave **the cake which you bought for dessert**? (Lopez, 2019: 210)

(22) When you go shopping, please buy **the cake with the most chocolate** (ibid).

(23) That shop has closed; maybe **a new café** will open there instead (ibid).

(24) There's **a new café** opened in town and I want to go there (ibid).

Explicit intervention like the aforementioned is particularly needed for learners who are at a higher proficiency level. It is only through deliberate, verbalized comparisons between noun phrases of the same or similar structure but different references that learners will be able to distinguish between the two concepts firmly and internalize their distinction. Explicit intervention will be more meaningful, and the concepts about (in)definiteness and (non)specificity will be more apparent, if the sentences for discussion are embedded in a communicative context, as in conversation (25).

(25) A: The shop at the corner which sold wine has recently closed.
      B: Maybe **a new café** will open there. We need a new café.
      A: But there's **a new café** opened in town and I want to go there instead.

Learners can also be encouraged to complete a table visualizing the (in)definite and (non-)specific references of the noun phrases under discussion as a way to supplement verbal discussions and to achieve more effective learning outcomes, as in Table 10.2.

Strengthening Learners' Awareness of the Definite Generic and Highlighting the Contexts for Expressing Genericity Using Different Articles

Despite the prevalence of learner problems with the use of articles for generic reference, most textbooks and teachers offer very little instruction in this aspect (Snape & Yusa, 2013). The definite generic, which is often regarded as very rare (Tarone & Parrish, 1988) and of which learners are often unaware, deserves particular pedagogical attention. Teachers can design teaching materials to guide learners to establish an appropriate context in which the definite generic can be used and to discover locations of a text where the structure is often found (e.g. for marking the topic of an essay in the scientific field, for noun phrases in subject position, for noun phrases in the first sentence of a paragraph, in introductions or in conclusions; Master, 1987).

Table 10.2 Noun phrases with different references

Noun Phrase	Definite (+/−)	Specific (+/−)
the cake which you bought for dessert	+	+
the cake with the most chocolate	+	-
a new café (will open there)	-	-
(There's) a new café (opened in town)	-	+

Just as what has been conducted by Snape, Umeda, Wiltshier and Yusa (2016), metalinguistic explanations targeting the different ways of representing generic reference other than the use of the definite generic (e.g. *a/an* + singular, *ZERO* + plural) can also be introduced to consolidate learners' understanding. Such explanations should aim to alert learners to the fact that the definite generic (e.g. sentence (26)) is used to refer to natural kinds (e.g. *The dodo*) with a kind-predicate (e.g. *be extinct*), whereas *a/an* + singular has a generic interpretation when the sentence (e.g. sentence (27)) describes a general property (e.g. *more expensive than a home phone*) of the noun phrase (e.g. *a mobile phone*), and that for both kinds of generics, *ZERO* + plural is also a suitable alternative (e.g. sentences (28) and (29)).

The + Singular
(26)   **The dodo** is extinct.

A/an + Singular
(27)   **A mobile phone** is more expensive than a home phone.

ZERO + Plural
(28)   **Dodos** are extinct.
(29)   **Mobile phones** are more expensive than home phones.

The most common problems learners have with the representation of generic reference should also be tackled. For example, the contexts in which a certain choice was inappropriate (e.g. sentence (30)), such as the inappropriate use of the definite generic (e.g. *the chocolate bar*) for describing a general property (e.g. *enjoyed by many people*) rather than a kind-predicate, should be highlighted.

(30)   ?**The chocolate bar** is enjoyed by many people (Snape, Umeda, Wiltshier & Yusa, 2016: 214).

Learners can be encouraged to compare desirable and undesirable sentences (e.g. sentences (26) and (30)) and discuss the most likely interpretations of the target noun phrases in the undesirable sentences, i.e. *the chocolate bar* in sentence (30) is more likely to have a definite interpretation than to have a generic interpretation.

The unacceptability of *the* + plural for generics (e.g. sentence (31)) and the ungrammatical structure of bare singular count nouns (e.g. sentence (32)) should also be brought up for explicit discussions in class.

(31)   *****The chocolate bars** are enjoyed by many people.
(32)   *****Dodo** is extinct.

A task requiring learners to judge the truth values of different sentences with different article + noun structures should be a useful follow-up exercise for enhancing learners' long-term understanding. Adapted from Ionin and Montrul's (2010) study, the task incorporates a story context (e.g. story (33)) where both the generic description and non-generic description of an entity (e.g. *kangaroo*) are included.

(33)   There are **two female kangaroos** in our zoo. They are very special. They carry their babies on their backs! But we all know that **a female kangaroo** normally carries its babies in its pouch.

Accompanying test statements containing different article + noun structures (e.g. *the female kangaroo, the female kangaroos, female kangaroos*) showing different references (e.g. generic, non-generic) are used to engage learners in truth-value judgements and subsequent discussions, such as statements (34–38).

(34)   The female kangaroo carries its babies in its pouch.   T/F
(35)   The female kangaroo carries its babies on its back.   T/F
(36)   The female kangaroos carry their babies on their backs.   T/F
(37)   Female kangaroos carry their babies on their backs.   T/F
(38)   Female kangaroos carry their babies in their pouches.   T/F

(Chan, 2019b: 869)

It is desirable for teachers to vary the structures for representing generic reference in different story contexts with different test statements to ensure a better effect for the task. For example, the generic description of an entity (e.g. *a/an* + singular in story (33)) could be replaced by *ZERO* + plural in other story contexts (e.g. *mobile phones* . . .); the corresponding test statements could have *a/an* + singular for generic reference (e.g. *a mobile phone* . . .). In the implementation of the task, learners should be encouraged to discuss the reasons for the truth values of the test statements by only referring to the given story context instead of relying on their common sense or world knowledge. Visual stimuli in the form of static or motion pictures depicting the situation described in the story can be used to supplement the written story for motivating learners' interest and strengthening their conceptualization of the contexts and the uses of the different structures.

Comparing English Articles With Similar but
Distinct Native Language Items

A contrastive analysis approach discussing the similarities and differences between similar but distinct language items in the native and target languages is worth implementing in a Chinese-Cantonese ESL language classroom. Similar but distinct language items include demonstratives (e.g. *this* or *that* in English and 嗰個 (that) or 嗰啲 (those) in Chinese-Cantonese). In English, noun phrases with demonstratives (e.g. *this book* in sentence (39)) can show definite reference in much the same way as noun phrases with *the* (e.g. *the book* in sentence (40)).

(39) **This book** is mine.
(40) **The book** is mine.

However, English articles and demonstratives are not totally interchangeable. Although English demonstratives can show proximity, the English definite article cannot (e.g. sentence (40)). Unlike the English definite article, English demonstratives cannot be used in generic contexts (e.g. sentence (41)).

(41) *__This dodo__ is extinct.

In Chinese-Cantonese, there are language items, such as determiners, that serve similar but distinct purposes as certain English articles. Chinese-Cantonese noun phrases with demonstratives also show definite reference and proximity (e.g. sentence (42)), although there are no functional equivalents of English articles in Chinese-Cantonese (see Chapter 2).

(42) 這　本　書　很　深奧。
　　　 this　CL　book　very　difficult
　　　 (This book is very difficult/The book is very difficult.)

Given that Chinese-Cantonese ESL learners may refer to the need for using an L1 demonstrative or not in their selection of English articles (see Chapter 5), a contrastive analysis approach should be useful in alerting learners to the subtle functional and semantic differences between these similar but distinct language items in the two languages. Not only are awareness-raising exercises comparing these items in the native and target languages needed, but language tasks encouraging learners themselves to verbalize the use of such language items in the two languages are also useful (Chan, 2019a), especially in classrooms with students from different language backgrounds, so that learners will be allowed to discover the correct and incorrect uses of different items in their native and target languages.

Conclusion

In this chapter, some approaches to the explicit teaching of grammar have been described, including an algorithmic approach to error correction and a discovery-based consciousness-raising technique, as well as the use of metalinguistic explanations. Concrete examples, including the correction of the pseudo-tough movement structure, the teaching of ergative verbs and the teaching of English articles, have also been used to illustrate how the proposed approaches can be implemented. It is argued that explicit grammar teaching and explicit error correction are important for helping ESL learners acquire target language structures and preventing them from having their errors fossilized. The pedagogical suggestions given in this chapter are by no means exhaustive, but they are some of the effective strategies that have been put forward in the literature. ESL teachers can experiment with the techniques and/or remedial instructional materials described in this chapter to help their students overcome persistent problems in their acquisition of English as a second language. The next chapter will present some pedagogical insights into the teaching of phonology.

Notes

1 Confusion between *-ed* and *-ing* participles are characterized by the substitution of an *-ed* participle for an *-ing* participle, or vice versa, as in **The book is **interested** (vs. interesting)* (Li & Chan, 2000).
2 The dangling modifier problem is characterized by the use of a subjectless nonfinite clause where the subject of the main clause cannot be interpreted as the underlying subject of the nonfinite clause, such as **Having finished our lunch, **the ship** departed* (Chan, Kwan & Li, 2002a).
3 The words/expressions in brackets at the end of a certain step are the expected answers to the questions.
4 The materials included in the section Use of Metalinguistic Explanations in the Teaching of Grammar are reproduced from Chan (2021), with some slight adaptations to ensure smooth integration of the reproduced materials into the current chapter.

11 The Teaching of Phonology to Cantonese ESL Learners

In Chapters 7 and 8, we examined the most common perception and production problems encountered by Cantonese ESL learners in their acquisition of English phonology. This chapter will provide some pedagogical insights into the teaching of phonology to Cantonese ESL learners. It will be argued that both speech perception and speech production should be given comparable pedagogical attention. ESL students should be guided not only to the observable articulatory features of L2 speech sounds, but also to the acoustic characteristics of the target sounds. The subtle differences between similar yet distinct L1 and L2 speech sounds should be attended to. Other specific speech perception and production teaching priorities and strategies enlightened by relevant research on ESL learner difficulties will also be discussed.

ESL Pronunciation Teaching Goals

As argued in Chapter 10, explicit teaching is important for learners' acquisition of grammar, but is explicit teaching on English phonology equally important? What should ESL pronunciation teaching goals be, and what should be taken as the norm of teaching for ESL teachers?[1]

Disputes Between Linguists and Educationalists

The speech phenomena discussed in Chapters 7 and 8 may create much debate between linguists and educationalists. From a linguist's point of view, not all spoken features are equally acceptable or equally unacceptable in all contexts. A spoken feature which is not acceptable in a formal, careful reading style may be deemed acceptable in other contexts, such as in an informal, casual conversational context. In formal contexts, language accuracy is often considered essential, and correct pronunciations are necessary for word differentiation. In informal contexts, "faulty" pronunciations are often ignored, so long as communication and/or understanding is not impeded. Noticeable deviations from the pronunciation norms may simply be regarded as idiosyncratic variations typical of a certain speaker's own desire to retain the speech features as a marker of his/her own identity.

On the other hand, educationalists are more adamant about "correct" usage and regard the attainment of accurate speech conforming to the native speaker's

DOI: 10.4324/9781003252498-11

norms as one of the main goals of second language learning. ESL teachers may be inclined to use a standard native variety, such as Received Pronunciation (RP) or General American (GA), as the model of "good" or" accurate" English pronunciation and expect their students to mimic such pronunciation models. Native models have indeed been adopted as the models for teaching by many ESL teachers irrespective of students' educational levels (primary, secondary or tertiary). Many teaching resources, including textbooks and dictionaries, are also based on these standard varieties (Pennington & Rogerson-Revell, 2019). When students' pronunciations deviate from the adopted model(s), the pronunciation features will be regarded as erroneous or problematic, and the speakers will be labelled as low-proficiency speakers lacking professionalism.

Models of Pronunciation

It is true that a model of pronunciation is needed for demonstration purposes, and a standard native accent, such as RP or GA, should be a desirable model for adoption, especially because these varieties are recognized as prestigious varieties worldwide. There have, however, often been arguments whether a standard native model should be taken as ESL learners' pronunciation goal and whether learners should aim at achieving native-like accuracy, especially in this new era where there are increasing multilingual orientations to pronunciation (Pennington, 2021). What is more, some pronunciation features discussed in the previous chapters, such as non-release of final plosives, devoicing of final voiced obstruents and vocalization of final /l/,[2] are also found in native speakers' speech, albeit to a lesser extent. It is inevitable that learners will be confronted with such speech phenomena of native speakers even after being taught the "correct" model. Should learners be discouraged to adopt these features, then? In the author's opinion, a standard native accent is the most desirable model to be adopted for ESL phonology teaching and learning, especially at the initial learning stages. However, learners who have reached a more sophisticated stage should also be alerted to the degree of variability of "correct" speech and the varying degrees of acceptability in different contexts.

Priorities of Phonology Teaching

Another area of concern that ESL teachers need to consider is the priorities of phonology teaching. What should or should not be taught in an ESL pronunciation classroom? What are the teaching focuses? Should all problematic sounds be attended to?

English as an International Language (EIL)/a Lingua Franca (ELF)

It has been argued that addressing phonological and phonetic features which are important for ensuring mutual intelligibility in EIL or ELF is more effective than tackling all interlanguage features of learner speech (Jenkins, 2002; Low, 2015), as achieving native-like proficiency is simply unrealistic for L2 learners (Low,

2021) and teachers should not spend excessive classroom time on "something that is not likely to pay off" (Levis, 2016: 4). A case in point is the English dental fricatives /θ/ and /ð/,[3] which have created notorious perception and production difficulties for ESL/EFL learners worldwide but which have been found to be very rare in the world's languages other than English (Maddieson, 1984). From the EIL and/or ELF perspectives, it is doubtful whether learner difficulties associated with these sounds are treatable and whether adopting these sounds as pronunciation learning targets is appropriate (Chan, 2011).

Learners' Own Learning Goals

Despite the aforementioned arguments from the EIL and/or ELF perspectives, in the consideration of teaching priorities, learners' own learning goals should carry the utmost concern. Although one important purpose of language learning is effective communication (Fernandez Amaya, 2008), some learners, especially advanced learners, do not learn English just for communicating in international settings. Their learning goals may be to achieve near-native standards, so they often strive to learn or imitate the "correct" pronunciations of a standard variety. To these students, imperfect control of the target language may undermine their professional image and may even result in undesirable stigmatization by peers. Given the varied learning goals of different students, ESL teachers should prioritize their teaching focuses to suit learners' needs.

In determining priorities of phonology teaching, teachers should strive to understand learners' learning purposes. What is their desired degree of mastery – to attain intelligibility, or to achieve native-like accuracy? If there are students who consistently do not speak in conformity with the native norm despite their strong desire to speak "good" English, teachers can safely conclude that the deviated forms are the results of their incompetence in producing accurate English pronunciations. Remedial measures targeting such problems should be devised (Chan, 2006b). On the other hand, if students can demonstrate tactful deployment of alternative speaking strategies in different speech contexts, teachers should acknowledge the variations in their students' speech. As such, adopting multiple pronunciation models instead of a single model for students may be necessary (Carrie, 2017).

Learners' age and L2 experience are also significant factors. Phonology training programmes targeting young-aged or elementary learners more often aim to avoid or pre-empt pronunciation problems, whereas training programmes targeting advanced or later-stage learners will aim to remediate pronunciation problems (Pennington, 2021). Whether remediation of errors or prevention of errors should be given priorities is thus an issue that ESL teachers need to consider.

Teaching of Individual Problematic Sounds vs. Teaching of Problematic Patterns

It has also been argued that not all problems are equally teachable, so pronunciation teaching focuses should be prioritized (Chan, 2011). Learner problems which show a systematic pattern should be given prior attention. This is not to nullify the gravity of learner problems associated with individual sounds, but pedagogical efforts on systematic learner problems are more worthy of pedagogical attention. Take devoicing of English voiced obstruents, especially final obstruents, as an example. Given the widespread devoicing of English voiced obstruents by Cantonese ESL learners (and other ESL learners worldwide), remedial activities can be designed to guide learners to discover the shared attributes of their mispronunciations of different sounds as well as the commonalities in the pronunciation habits of different learners (Chan, 2010a). Remediation of such systematic problem patterns can cover different sound categories (e.g. plosives, fricatives) and will thus be more cost-effective than pedagogical efforts on individual sounds.

Segmental vs. Suprasegmental Problems

Whether learners' segmental problems or suprasegmental problems should be prioritized in a phonology training programme is also another important concern. It has been noted in Chapter 7 that English prosody[4] presents a number of difficulties for many Cantonese ESL learners, yet being able to use prosody in a native-like way has been argued as important in fluent L2 speech (Wennerstrom, 2000). Prosody is important in indicating a speaker's attitude towards the audience. Whether a listener will pay attention to a message and put efforts in receiving a message also depends on the speaker's use of prosody (Pennington & Rogerson-Revell, 2019). In this sense, errors in prosody may have more detrimental effects on listeners' judgement of comprehensibility and L2 proficiency than errors in individual segments (Anderson-Hsieh, Johnson & Koehler, 1992; Munro & Derwing, 1995a). For learners with poor-quality segments, getting the prosody right is particularly important (Yenkimaleki & van Heuven, 2019).

Explicit prosody instruction has been found to result in nativelike spontaneous L2 speech (Derwing, Munro & Wiebe, 1998). If the prosodic patterns of the L1 and the target language are similar, there is not much need for the teaching of prosody. However, if the patterns of the two languages are different, then L2 prosody teaching is essential (Yenkimaleki & van Heuven, 2019). English and Cantonese differ significantly in their prosodic patterns, including rhythm, stress, intonation and the like (see Chapter 3). The teaching of English prosody to Cantonese ESL learners is, thus, an area which deserves attention. ESL teachers should decide whether to prioritize the teaching of segmentals or the teaching of suprasegmentals for their students.

Pre-Teaching Diagnosis

In Chapter 8, we have seen the intimate relations between speech perception and speech production. Although the ultimate goal of pronunciation learning for most learners is production, perception problems should not be ignored. A systematic and comprehensive phonology training programme should integrate speech perception and speech production. In the (remedial) teaching of pronunciation, both learners' perception problems and their production problems need to be addressed. Teachers need to shape their teaching activities in such a way as to target the resolution of both production and perception obstacles.

Teaching focuses, teaching strategies and teaching activities targeting perception problems can be very different from those targeting production problems, so before engaging students in remedial pronunciation learning activities, teachers should first diagnose learners' problems and unlock the sources of the problems: Are the problems perception-based or production-oriented? Not all English sounds are equally difficult for Cantonese ESL learners, and not all problems are equally grave. ESL teachers should recognize the predominant problems of their own students and identify individualized problems. Curriculum design should be informed by pre-teaching diagnosis, and teaching focuses need to cater for the needs and goals of different learners.

Diagnosis of Speech Perception Problems

As far as speech perception is concerned, pre-teaching diagnosis involves a distinction between discrimination of individual phones and identification of words. Discrimination is related to sensory detection, so it is related to learners' auditory and perceptual ability to differentiate between signals. Identification, on the other hand, is associated with pre-assumed word knowledge, so it is concerned with learners' ability to associate labels to acoustic signals based on the auditory content received. As discussed in Chapter 8, even if the acoustic differences (e.g. presence or absence of voicing) between a pair of contrasts can be detected, the corresponding segments (e.g. /v/ vs. /f/) and/or the corresponding words (e.g. *save* /seɪv/ vs. *safe* /seɪf/) may not be identified because of learners' incorrect labels associated with certain perceived speech signals. Perceptual diagnostic tests requiring learners to identify target sounds in isolation and in minimal pairs can be used in this regard. If it is found that a certain perception problem is discrimination-related, pedagogical efforts should be invested in helping students identify the articulatory and acoustic differences between confusable sound pairs. On the other hand, if it is found that a certain perception problem is identification-related, remedial efforts should be focused on helping students associate a certain label with a certain set of acoustic signals.

Diagnosis of Speech Production Problems

With regard to production problems, pre-teaching diagnosis involves teachers' recognition of learners' problems in producing a certain phonetic feature and their problems in actualizing the phonetic feature in continuous speech. For example, a learner may be able to produce a voiced sound in isolation (e.g. /z/), but he/she may have difficulties in actualizing the voicing feature in continuous speech, such as at the end of a word (e.g. *lose* /luːz/). Again, if a certain production problem is phonetically based, more teaching efforts should be invested in helping students produce the target sounds in isolation. On the other hand, if a certain production problem is concerned with learners' actualization of a target sound in continuous speech, remedial efforts should be focused on helping students produce sounds embedded in words.

It may be thought that pre-teaching diagnosis is laborious and time-consuming, especially when teachers want to elicit learners' natural speech by the use of specifically designed spontaneous speaking tasks such as picture description or storytelling. This is true, but pre-teaching diagnosis can also be simple. For speech production, simple diagnostic tests requiring students to read out isolated sounds or minimal pairs presented in word pairs or picture pairs can be used occasionally in class for identifying production problems. For speech perception, simple diagnostic tests with teachers producing some target sounds in isolation or in minimal pairs and students identifying the target sounds can be used sporadically in class for identifying perception problems. These diagnostic tests can be easily incorporated into regular teaching without affecting daily teaching routines, but they can be very useful in informing teachers, especially experienced teachers, of learners' genuine learning challenges.

More systematic diagnoses can be done with the use of computers. Many computer-assisted pronunciation training (CAPT) systems allow teachers to do pre-teaching pronunciation diagnoses, including both diagnoses for perception and those for production. ESL teachers can make use of these advanced and sophisticated systems for achieving their diagnostic goals, but they should also be alert to the possible demerits of such systems (see the section "Use of CAPT" later in this chapter).

Research-Driven Curriculum

There is often a gap between research and practice in phonology teaching (Derwing & Munro, 2015). A lack of connection between research and teaching will result in teachers' reliance on intuition when determining teaching priorities (Levis, 2005). They may not be able to determine whether a certain pronunciation feature is learnable in a classroom setting, whether a feature is more learnable or less learnable than other features, or even whether a certain chosen teaching priority suits the needs of their students (see earlier in this chapter). Pronunciation training programmes, especially those for advanced ESL learners, should therefore be research-driven (Chan, 2010a).

Take the production of English consonant clusters as an example. ESL teachers may tend to include many different consonant clusters, such as /str/ (as in the word *stray* /streɪ/), /pl/ (as in the word *play* /pleɪ/) or /lm/ (as in the word *film*/fɪlm/), as their teaching targets. However, we have seen in Chapter 7 that for Cantonese ESL learners, the segment composition of a consonant cluster determines the difficulty level of the cluster, in that certain segments (e.g. /r/ in /str/; /l/ in /lm/) are more problematic than other segments (e.g. /s/ in /str/; /m/ in /lm/) in the same cluster. Remedial pronunciation training programmes which are research-driven will focus on the problematic segment(s) of a cluster instead of the entire cluster itself, as the latter could be better handled after students have successfully mastered the former (Chan, 2006c).

In a similar fashion, research has shown that learners of higher proficiency levels adopt deletion and substitution more than vowel epenthesis in coping with complex onset clusters (see Chapter 7), so ESL teachers should prioritize deletion and substitution in their design of remedial pronunciation training for intermediate and advanced learners, while vowel epenthesis should be more the focus of training programmes targeting less advanced students.

In short, the source and exact nature of a learner problem needs to be carefully diagnosed before (remedial) teaching is to be given. Individualized learning programmes based on current research findings and teachers' own diagnostic findings should be more useful than general programmes which include learning items which do not cater to learners' needs.

Teaching Strategies

Upon understanding students' learning goals and deciding on the teaching priorities for respective groups of students, ESL teachers need to identify suitable teaching strategies. In this section, some principles and guidelines underlying the choice of teaching strategies will be offered. Some concrete examples will also be given to illustrate the suggestions. It will be argued that conducting L1–L2 contrastive comparisons and alerting learners' conscious attention to the correct model via different means are useful teaching strategies.

Conducting L1–L2 Contrastive Comparisons

Some form of L1–L2 contrastive comparisons should be conducted in an ESL phonology programme, especially in a programme for advanced learners. An awareness of L1–L2 differences can facilitate bilingual learners' pronunciation training (Hung, 1993), so contrastive comparisons are needed for both speech production and speech perception training. However, rather than focusing on the differences between the L1 and the L2 on the basis of inventory gaps (i.e. non-existence a target L2 sound in the L1 (e.g. English /θ/ or /v/)), the subtle *differences* between *similar* L1 and L2 sounds should be attended to (cf. Chapter 8). The ultimate purpose of contrastive comparisons is to help learners successfully discriminate similar native and non-native sounds so as to establish a new phonetic category for a target L2 sound to facilitate production.

For example, English /ɜː/ (as in the word *bird* /bɜːd/) and Cantonese /œ/(as in the word 唱 'sing' /tsœŋ/) are similar but different: While English /ɜː/ does not require lip rounding in production, Cantonese /œ/ does. On the other hand, while English /tʃ, dʒ/ require lip rounding, Cantonese /ts, dz/ do not. The differences between these L1–L2 sound pairs are readily correctible. Explicit comparisons of the articulatory and/or acoustic features of these similar L1–L2 sounds are useful in arousing learners' awareness of the subtle differences.

Helping Learners Observe Visual Articulatory Cues

Not only is learners' awareness of the differences between similar L1–L2 sounds important, but their being able to notice the differences between their own L2 productions and those of native/competent speakers' productions will also significantly enhance L2 acquisition (Olson, 2014). Deliberate comparisons between correct and incorrect pronunciations with special emphasis on the observable articulatory features of a target sound should, therefore, be a useful phonology teaching strategy (Chan, 2009b). Learners should be guided to notice both the salient articulatory features of target sounds and the discrepancies between the model and their own pronunciations.

The articulatory features of some English sounds are easily observable, such as the lowering of the jaw for the open vowel /æ/. If learners are alerted to the much greater degree of lowering of the jaw in the production of English /æ/ than that in the production of English /e/, then the confusion between this pair of target sounds (e.g. in minimal pairs such as *sat* /sæt/ and *set* /set/, or *bat* /bæt/ and *bet* /bet/) will be much more easily resolved. In a similar fashion, the articulatory differences between the English labio-dental fricative /v/ and its popular substitute /w/ are also easily observable: the former requires the "biting" of the lower lip with the upper teeth, whereas the latter requires the rounding of the lips. Learners who are alerted to such visual differences will be able to pay more conscious attention to the accurate articulation of these features in their own productions.

A useful technique in helping students notice the observable visual articulatory cues is the use of video clips or photos. For example, in highlighting the salient differences between /ʃ/ and /s/ (i.e. the protruding and rounding of the lips for the former, but an absence of such articulatory features in the latter), ESL teachers can make videos or shoot photos of their production of the target sounds and ask students to compare the video clips/photos by focusing on the observable differences in the lip shapes. More interactive and student-oriented activities can be introduced to invite students themselves to record videos or shoot photos of their own production of the target sounds. Comparisons between teachers' and students' video clips/photos, or among students' own videos/photos, can be made to identify discrepancies, deviations and correct practices. In this way, students themselves can become evaluators of each other and, where appropriate, models for each other. Engaging students in these interactive activities will create more fun and evoke some laughter in class without stifling the academic value of the teaching (Chan, 2015).

The use of observable visual cues is beneficial not just to speech production but also to speech perception (Hazan, Sennema, Faulkner, Ortega-Llebaria, Iba & Chung, 2006): If learners pay attention to the presence or absence of such observable features in their face-to-face encounters with English speakers, their discrimination and identification of the target sounds/words will be facilitated.

Helping Learners Observe Computer-Analysable Articulatory and/or Acoustic Properties

For advanced learners of English, visual cues are not limited to observable articulatory features. The articulatory features of some English sounds may not be easily observable, such as the raising of the back of the tongue in the production of dark [ɫ] or the lowering of the velum in the production of nasal sounds. For these sounds, observing computer-analysable properties is more feasible and achievable. Visual cues of these sounds can be provided in the form of a virtual teacher with an augmented-reality talking head display. Movements of the tongue shown with computer animations, together with concurrent explanations on associated articulatory movements, can be provided to help learners produce the target sounds (Engwall, 2012; Engwall & Bälter, 2007). When learners are simultaneously hearing and seeing speech articulations, both their perception and production of L2 sounds can be improved (Massaro, 1987) (see the section "Use of CAPT" later in this chapter).

Visual displays via spectrograms or waveform displays can also be used to alert learners to the acoustic features of a target sound and the acoustic differences between native speakers' speech and their own speech (Olson, 2014). For example, the major difference between initial voiceless plosives (e.g. [tʰ] in *tar* /tɑː/, or [pʰ] in *par* /pɑː/) and voiceless plosives after /s/ (e.g. [t] in *star* /stɑː/, or [p] in *spar* /spɑː/), namely presence of aspiration in the former but absence of such in the latter, can be clearly demonstrated by spectrographic or waveform analysis. By showing respective spectrograms or waveforms, teachers can alert students to the period of voicelessness between the release of the aspirated plosives (e.g. [tʰ] or [pʰ]) and the onset of voicing of the following vowels (e.g. /ɑː/) in words such as *tar* or *par*. Such a period of voicelessness is absent after the articulation of the unaspirated plosives [t] or [p] in *star* or *spar* and the absence can be clearly seen from the respective spectrograms or waveforms (see Figures 11.1 and 11.2 for a simplified visual display of *tar* and *star*).

Teachers can also encourage learners to subject their own speech to spectrographic and/or waveform analysis for comparison purposes. Though it may be more meaningful to teach pronunciations in meaningful units, such as in authentic conversations (Chela-Flores, 2001), the value of using visual cues to highlight

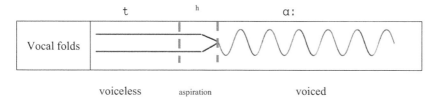

Figure 11.1 A simplified visual display of the plosive /t/ and the vowel /ɑː/ in *tar*

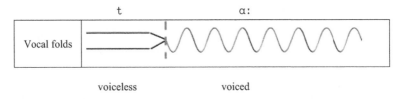

Figure 11.2 A simplified visual display of the plosive /t/ and the vowel /ɑː/ in *star*

significant acoustic or articulatory properties of individual sound segments is not to be ignored.

Arousing Learners' Awareness of Phonological Phenomena or Variations

Raising learners' awareness of relevant phonological phenomena or variations in the target language is also an important strategy for the teaching of pronunciations. Some speech production or perception problems may originate from learners' unawareness of certain (well-known) phonological phenomena. The absence of aspiration for English voiceless plosives after /s/ is again a case in point. Many ESL learners are not aware of the phonological phenomenon that voiceless plosives after /s/ are not aspirated, so they have simply preserved a familiar articulatory habit (i.e. aspirating initial voiceless plosives) in an inappropriate context (i.e. after /s/). Such inaccurate production habits can be easily rectified with learners' heightened awareness of the speech phenomenon. The use of spectrographic or waveform analysis, as discussed earlier, is again one effective awareness-raising technique.

Awareness-raising activities can also be introduced for tackling speech perception problems. One example is the differentiation between English voiced and voiceless obstruents. Recall that final voiced obstruents are often devoiced even by native speakers but that the vowel preceding an English voiced obstruent is longer than that preceding a voiceless obstruent (Roach, 2009). Awareness-raising activities highlighting such durational differences will advance learners' perception of voiced and voiceless obstruents in word pairs such as *bet* /bet/ and *bed* /bed/, or *leaf* /liːf/ and *leave* /liːv/ (Chan, 2011). Rather than focusing on the voicing contrast, which may not be actualized in authentic speech, learners who have enhanced awareness of the durational differences will focus more on the lengths of the preceding vowels when perceiving (or even producing) minimal pairs.

Use of CAPT

In this millennium, the use of digital technologies in teaching is ubiquitous and inevitable. Phonology teaching has also entered an era of technology. Early technologically based pronunciation programmes were typically restricted to the use of audio- and/or video-recording devices. Recent CAPT systems are increasingly sophisticated, with the adoption of technologies such as automated speech recognition (ASR) and artificial intelligence (AI), thus facilitating the provision of individualized feedback and providing more opportunities for language production (Rogerson-Revell, 2021).

CAPT can be used for pre-learning diagnosis, initial learning and/or remedial learning purposes. Different CAPT tools have been designed for different purposes. Zhao, Liu, Lu, Han and Li (2003), for instance, developed a system for teaching English pronunciation to Chinese students with demonstrations on individual phonemes, words and sentences. Learners can also take a speech test for diagnosis and receive feedback from the system. Qian, Soong and Meng (2010) proposed a discriminative training algorithm to minimize errors in mispronunciation detection and diagnosis errors, and Qian, Meng and Soong (2016) extended the work by having a two-pass framework to improve accuracy. Learners of all proficiency levels have been considered. Some CAPT systems, such as visual simulation-based systems, are more suitable for young learners, whereas systems which are comparative phonetics based are more suitable for adult learners who are fluent in their native languages (Agarwal & Chakraborty, 2019).

CAPT has been found to be effective not just in the production and/or perception learning and teaching of individual segments (e.g. Badin, Tarabalka, Elisei & Bailly, 2010; Lambacher, 1999; Molholt, 1988; Motohashi-Saigo & Hardison, 2009; Patten & Edmonds, 2015; Rahimi & Tavakoli, 2015) but also in the learning and teaching of suprasegmental features, including rhythm, stress, pitch and duration (e.g. Anderson-Hsieh, 1994; Coniam, 2002; Hardison, 2004; Hirata, 2004; Levis & Pickering, 2004; Ramírez-Verdugo, 2006; Yenkimaleki & van Heuven, 2019). Computer-based training allows the provision of a wide variety of spoken input from multiple speakers (Rogerson-Revell, 2021), and different programmes can be designed for different groups of learners. Technological advances, thus, "bring further benefits to pronunciation teaching and learning, especially if harnessed to the needs and priorities of learners and teachers" (Rogerson-Revell, 2021: 201).

Advanced though these systems are, they are not without problems. Incorrect error detection is sometimes found, such as inaccurately accepting a mispronounced sound or inaccurately rejecting a correct production. Errors in diagnosis are also common, such as incorrectly stating in what ways a mispronunciation is wrong. What is more, the same utterance correctly spoken by two speakers may be assigned different acoustic representations. Computers may also fall short of adaptability and perceptual accuracy, in such a way that their ability to provide appropriate feedback, especially when compared to human teachers, is undermined (Lee, Jang & Plonsky, 2015). To a more serious extent, some CAPT resources may be more technology-led than pedagogy-driven, as developers may prioritize technological attractiveness over pedagogical value.

Users' technological competence is also an issue. Interpretation of the visual displays produced by the computer systems often require a certain degree of expertise or even pre-training. It is important that ESL teachers be equipped with relevant knowledge and sophistication when adopting CAPT, but such knowledge and sophistication are often lacking in many ESL teachers, not to mention students who have to work without the guidance of a qualified teacher. If students are left to correct their mispronunciations randomly without enough guidance, they may ultimately get frustrated and their errors may possibly be further fossilized (Rogerson-Revell, 2021). CAPT resources may also put too much emphasis on nativelike language accuracy rather than intelligibility (Pennington & Rogerson-Revell, 2019), thus failing the expectations of teachers of EIL (see the section "Priorities of Phonology Teaching" earlier in this chapter). ESL teachers should, therefore, strike a balance between the use of technologies and cost-effectiveness, as well as between time and teaching/learning goals. Last but not least, they should have a correct evaluation of their own technological competence in using a chosen CAPT system.

Conclusion

In this chapter, we have examined some controversies about phonology training and have offered some principles and guidelines which are potentially beneficial to ESL phonology teaching and learning. It is observed that perception training and production training are equally important. While a speaker's production problems may give listeners a poor impression of his/her English proficiency, perception problems may cause misunderstanding and even embarrassment. Only through rectifying both areas of speech learning can ESL learners be groomed towards successful mastery of L2 phonology. ESL teachers should carefully diagnose the pronunciations of their students to understand features of learners' speech, so that they can uncover the nature of learners' pronunciation problems and the speaking strategies learners use to cope with problematic speech sounds.

Phonology learning is a long process. Learners need a large quantity of high-quality L2 input to achieve their articulatory and perceptual targets (Pennington, 2021). Many pronunciation errors are difficult to rectify but easy to fossilize. While successful phonology teaching needs to be carefully planned and systematically implemented, successful phonology learning presumes long-term endeavour by learners themselves and effective guidance by teachers. Phonology training should not be a peripheral component of an ESL programme: It should be a core component comprising research-driven curriculum and student-centred learning activities. The suggestions given in this chapter are not meant to be novel discoveries, but they are among the most important considerations that ESL teachers should pay attention to.

Notes

1 In this chapter, the terms "pronunciation teaching/teaching of pronunciations" and "phonology teaching/teaching of phonology" are used interchangeably, although phonology teaching has a wider scope and may cover more aspects than just pronunciations.
2 Vocalization of final /l/ is found even in RP speakers' speech, but such vocalization is typically limited to words with a labial articulation, such as *careful* or *people* (Cruttenden, 2001).

3 In Chapter 8, it was noted that /ð/ does not trigger significant perception problems for Cantonese ESL learners, despite the fact that in production, it is often confused with /d/. More research is needed to ascertain its level of difficulties for Cantonese ESL learners and other learners worldwide.

4 The terms "prosody" and "suprasegmentals" are often used interchangeably in the literature (e.g. Rasier & Hiligsmann, 2007; Trofimovich & Baker, 2006). These two terms are also used interchangeably in this chapter.

12 Conclusions

The Way Forward

In the previous chapters, the contrastive differences between English and Chinese-Cantonese grammar and those between English and Cantonese phonology have been analysed. The problems that Cantonese ESL learners often encounter in their acquisition of English grammar and phonology have been explored, the probable sources of learner problems have been examined, and pedagogical insights for the remediation of such problems have also been proposed. In this chapter, a summary of all the major findings and arguments discussed in the previous chapters will be given. This chapter will also recommend possible future theoretical and empirical research on the learning of English grammar and phonology by Cantonese ESL learners and on the teaching of such by ESL teachers.

A Brief Summary: Cantonese ESL Learners' Acquisition of Grammar and Phonology, Sources of Learner Problems and Pedagogical Insights

Cantonese ESL Learners' Acquisition of Grammar and Phonology

English and Chinese belong to two typologically distant language families with many structural disparities. Cantonese ESL learners often encounter difficulties in acquiring English grammar. Many errors can be attributed to L1 interference, such as serial verb constructions, incorrect placement of adverbs, pseudo-tough movement and many others. L1-related errors notwithstanding, there are also errors which are not necessarily results of L1 interference, including misuse of prepositions, non-parallel structures, and the like. English articles, some of the most common function words in English, also present a number of problems, not just in learners' productive use of articles but also in their interpretation of structures consisting of English articles. Learners are found to have different misconceptions about the English article system, including the functions, uses and reference representations of different articles.

As far as phonology is concerned, English and Cantonese differ not only in their phonemic inventories but also in the characteristics of the sounds, the distributions of the phonemes, the permissible syllable structures, and the rhythms. Cantonese ESL learners use different strategies to cope with sounds that they find

DOI: 10.4324/9781003252498-12

difficult to produce. At the segmental level, substitution of an inappropriate sound for the target, devoicing of voiced obstruents, and deletion of singleton final consonants or of one or two consonants in a consonant cluster (initial or final), are all common. Vowel epenthesis is also sometimes adopted for coping with consonant clusters. Suprasegmentally, Cantonese ESL learners have a tendency to use a syllable-timed rhythm characteristic of Cantonese in pronouncing English, stressing most syllables of an English word. Although it is often claimed that there is an intimate relationship between speech perception and speech production, the two areas of learning do not seem to bear a strict one-to-one relationship for Cantonese ESL learners. English speech sounds that cause perception problems may not necessarily cause speech production problems, and speech sounds that are easy to perceive may still cause production problems.

Sources of Learner Problems

L1 interference is without a doubt a major source of learner problems for both L2 grammar and phonology, but not all error/problems are attributed to L1 interference. As far as Cantonese ESL learners' acquisition of English grammar is concerned, other probable causes include overgeneralization, misapplication of L2 rules, lack of awareness of the native norms, and universal processes. There is often a complex interplay between L1 and non-L1-related factors, and many errors are the results of such interactions. With regard to phonology acquisition, other considerations such as universal markedness, perceived phonetic similarity between a pair of L1–L2 sounds, and developmental processes are also probable contributing factors. Thus, L1 transfer alone is not sufficient in accounting for learner problems in either aspect of L2 learning, but it remains one most important factor.

Pedagogical Insights

Given the prevalence of learner problems in both grammar and phonology acquisition, explicit teaching is important in helping learners overcome their problems. In terms of grammar teaching, consciousness-raising teaching approaches which aim at arousing learners' awareness of their problems as well as the characteristic features of the target learning items are particularly useful. For language items the correction of which can be broken down into small, proceduralized, cognitively manageable steps, an algorithmic approach to error correction is beneficial. For other errors which are not amenable to the use of an algorithmic approach, the use of metalinguistic explanations or discovery-based, consciousness-raising techniques can help advance learners' understanding of the target items.

Regarding the teaching of phonology, both perception training and production training are equally important. Learners need to be explicitly alerted to the specific phonological phenomena which may impinge on their perception and/ or production of English speech sounds, such as the absence of the aspiration feature of plosives after /s/. Not only should pronunciation errors which affect communication be targeted, but focus should also be placed on other mispronunciations which reflect learners' inadequate mastery of the target language. It is important to conduct L1–L2 contrastive analyses and help learners observe visual articulatory cues and computer-analysable articulatory and/or acoustic properties of problematic sounds. The use of computer-assisted pronunciation training is useful for pre-learning diagnosis, initial learning and/or remedial learning purposes.

The Way Forward

As argued in Chapter 1, it is important to understand the nature of learners' difficulties before effective remedial efforts are invested. The kinds of learner problems discussed in the previous chapters are not meant to be exhaustive among the target group of learners, nor are the proposed pedagogical insights meant to be the only effective strategies for remediation. Other learner problems not covered in this book may also be prevalent among Cantonese ESL learners, and there are also areas of investigation which are worth attending to. The following sections discuss some possible criticisms about the research findings and pedagogical insights discussed in this book, and they outline some issues that need to be tackled in future research and pedagogical endeavours.

L2 Grammar Learning, Teaching and Future Research

A number of issues are worth considering in the discussions of L2 grammar learning, teaching and future research. One important issue concerns the limited learner samples used in previous studies. Other issues include the contexts in which error correction should be situated, as well as the technological recency of teaching strategies.

Inclusion of Larger Learner Samples

No single research studies can yield an exhaustive list of learner errors. Though extracted from the findings of a number of relevant and interrelated research studies, the lists of grammatical problems discussed from Chapters 4 to 6 are far from exhaustive. One issue has to do with the pool of participants. It has been argued that most SLA research has placed excessive reliance on university-educated learners (Plonsky, 2017). University students also constituted the main pool of participants in some of the research studies from which the learner problems reported in this book came.[1] The problems identified are, thus, typical of a relatively more advanced learner sample. Problems which are characteristic of the elementary or intermediate groups may not have been fully represented, but they are important for a full understanding of L2 grammar acquisition by Cantonese ESL learners. As Collins and Ruivivar (2021: 419) suggest, it is illuminating to conduct "collaborative research focused on multi-site replications with participants from more diverse education and literacy backgrounds". Further research including participants at other proficiency levels is needed to yield a more comprehensive list of learner errors.

Contexts in Which Pedagogical Endeavours Can Be Situated

The teaching approaches advocated in Chapter 10, such as the use of an algorithmic approach to error correction, aim at eradicating common grammatical errors using isolated sentences. While such approaches can help focus learners' attention on the target errors, it may undermine the importance of situating the target language items in a larger discourse context. A discourse-based approach to the teaching of grammar, in which learners are provided with abundant examples of contextualized usages of a target language structure in authentic or simplified discourse, should be useful in promoting the establishment of form-meaning relationships (Celce-Murcia, 2002). Instead of merely viewing language as structure governed by rigid rules, learners could then realize the meanings of grammatical constructions within discourse (Strauss, Feiz & Xiang, 2018). Useful though a discourse-based approach could be, there has been a paucity of research on the use of such an approach targeting the problems discussed in this book. Further research can investigate how a discourse-based approach can be best adopted in the correction of, for example, pseudo-tough movement and pseudo-passive structures, among others.

Incorporation of Technological Advances

Another possible criticism about the pedagogical insights given in Chapter 10 is concerned with the modality of teaching. In this technology-driven era, the suggested teaching ideas may be considered "old-fashioned" or lacking in recency because of insufficient incorporation of new technological advances. Recent research has found that the use of multi-media input (e.g. audio + animation + captions/subtitles) can enhance L2 grammar learning, in that learners tend to pay more attention to the learning activities (Lee & Révész, 2020) and can be provided with more information about grammar (Pattemore & Muñoz, 2020). While such studies have provided new insights into the teaching of grammar, there is again a scarcity of research on how technology can help learners overcome the grammatical anomalies discussed in this book. Further research efforts can be invested in the examination of the effectiveness of using multi-media input for rectifying the identified problems.

Data-driven learning (DDL), or corpus-based language learning, is also one possible addition of technological advances in the teaching of grammar. In this context, students examine authentic samples of language, such as a concordance, to extract language patterns and/or to verify their hypotheses about certain language use or to correct their own errors (Collins & Ruivivar, 2021). Concordances allow both teachers and learners to obtain large numbers of examples of a target language structure. The use of a concordance also makes target language input salient because the search words are always highlighted and centred (Heift &

Vyatkina, 2017). DDL has been found to be useful in helping learners overcome persistent errors, such as the over-generated *be* problem (e.g. *be* + base form; see Chapter 4) (Moon & Oh, 2018), and other lexico-grammatical problems, such as the confusion between *say* and *tell* (e.g. **Many people **tell** that . . .*; **My teacher **says** me that . . .*) (Boulton, 2010). Chapter 10 also demonstrated how the use of concordances can help focus learners' attention on the countability of an English noun and the associated use/non-use of an English article. While DDL has been found to be useful for a subset of learner problems, it is important to conduct further research to investigate what error types are more amenable to such learning strategies and what are less amenable.

Another consideration about the use of DDL is the amount of teacher guidance. Research has found that learners who are engaged in DDL without teacher guidance make less effective use of the available data than students who receive guidance from teachers (Pérez-Paredes, Sánchez-Tornel, Calero & Jiménez, 2011). Learners may be overwhelmed by the large volume of data given in the concordances and may have difficulty knowing how to use a target feature appropriately (Geluso & Yamaguchi, 2014). Questions also arise about what kinds of teacher guidance should be given and how teachers can guide learners to the use of DDL in the correction of the learner problems identified in this book.

L2 Phonology Learning, Teaching and Future Research

With regard to L2 phonology learning, teaching and future research, there is also the concern about the representativeness of learner samples. The speech production and perception problems discussed in this book are also more characteristic of learners at a higher proficiency level, such as university English majors,[2] thus limiting the representativeness of the problems identified. Other areas of concern include the timeframes of data collection, the baseline adopted for comparisons and the learning preferences of learners themselves.

Timeframes of Data Collection

One limitation of the phonology research studies reported in this book is that none of the studies was longitudinal. The findings about perception, production and the relationships between perception and production all came from participants' performance in a few test sessions at some single points in time. The lack of correspondence or even contradictory relationships observed between Cantonese ESL learners' speech perception abilities and their speech production abilities (see Chapter 8) may be the result of such restricted timeframes of data collection. Unlike research conducted at some random time points, longitudinal research has the capability of detecting the change of perception-production links over time. Future research can adopt a longitudinal approach to the investigation of the perception-production link, such as the use of a time-varying approach in which perception is operationalized as a time-varying predictor of production (Nagle, 2021). With such research, new insights into the links between speech perception and production may be obtained, including the extent to which changes in perception over time guide changes in production, the relative rates of change in perception and production, and the extent of influence that perception exerts on production at different points of the learning process (Nagle, 2021). Perception and production processes do not occur sequentially. Instead, they are likely to overlap and influence one another over time. Categorical perception measures should be paired with categorical production measures longitudinally.

Baselines Adopted for Comparisons

Another concern about L2 phonology research is related to the baselines adopted for comparisons. Most perception-production research studies, including the ones reported in this book, use monolingual native speakers' norms as the baselines, and comparisons were made between learners' performance and native speakers' speech. Such comparisons have, however, been acknowledged to be inappropriate (Nagle & Baese-Berk, 2022). Instead, advanced L2 users who are highly intelligible and comprehensible should form a suitable comparison group in L2 pronunciation research (Sakai, 2018). Future research can move towards a bilingual baseline for perception and production comparisons so as to arrive at a more authentic description of L2 speech acquisition.

Learners' Preferences and Attitudes

As discussed in Chapter 11, one main concern regarding L2 phonology pedagogy lies in learners' preference for which accent to approximate. Their attitudes towards a certain widely accepted accent may affect their desire to learn Standard English. Some learners may opt for preserving their identity by retaining the accent which is typical of the group of learners with whom they identify themselves. For example, although many people in Hong Kong do not want to speak Hong Kong English (HKE), judging the accent negatively and preferring to follow native models such as British English or American English (Zhang, 2013), there are people who not only use HKE but also accept it as an accent portraying a Hong Kong identity in the region (Hansen Edwards, 2015). For these learners, it is doubtful whether a native model should be chosen as the model of teaching. On the other hand, for learners who aim at achieving native-like competence, a native model should better be used as the model of teaching. Attitudinal research exploring learners' preferences towards different accents of the target language, and most importantly, their preferences towards the standard models, should be conducted before the design and implementation of an L2 pronunciation programme.

Conclusion

Much research effort has been devoted to Cantonese ESL learners' acquisition of grammar and phonology. As informative and insightful as the findings are, the research studies are subjected to some methodological or implementational concerns. One is related to the representativeness of the samples collected, which should include not just university participants but also learners at other educational levels, such as primary and secondary levels. As far as L2 grammar is concerned, the contexts in which teaching strategies should be situated and the incorporation of technological advances are areas which future research can attend to. With regard to L2 phonology, the timeframes of data collection, the baselines adopted for comparisons as well as learners' own preferences for a pronunciation model are some major issues of consideration. Future research tackling such limitations will portray a more comprehensive and representative picture of L2 grammar and phonology. Further research is also needed to experiment with the pedagogical suggestions given in this book to confirm the contribution of the proposals to effective remediation. There also needs to be a good connection between research and pedagogy, with researchers providing rigorous data to help practitioners make informed decisions about the focus and ways of teaching, and practitioners considering the research base which supports their choices of teaching focuses and practices. Research and practice should be a two-way process (Pennington & Rogerson-Revell, 2019). This is true for both L2 grammar and L2 phonology not only for Cantonese ESL learners but also for ESL learners of other native languages.

Notes

1 Examples of research studies (on grammar acquisition) which exclusively focused on university students include Chan (2000, 2016, 2017a, 2017b, 2019a, 2019b).
2 Examples of research studies (on phonology acquisition) which exclusively focused on university students include Chan (2006b, 2006c, 2007, 2010a, 2010b, 2011, 2012, 2013, 2014).

References

Abercrombie, D. (1967). *Elements of general phonetics*. Edinburgh: Edinburgh University Press.

Agarwal, C., & Chakraborty, P. (2019). A review of tools and techniques for computer aided pronunciation training (CAPT) in English. *Education and Information Technologies*, 24(6), 3731–3743. https://doi.org/10.1007/s10639-019-09955-7

Akakura, M. (2012). Evaluating the effectiveness of explicit instruction on explicit and implicit L2 knowledge. *Language Teaching Research*, 16(1), 9–37. https://doi.org/10.1177/1362168811423339

Allan, K. (1980). Nouns and countability. *Language*, 56(3), 541–567. https://doi.org/10.2307/414449

Anderson-Hsieh, J. (1983). The difficulties of English syllable structure for Chinese ESL learners. *Language Learning and Communication*, 2(1), 53–61.

Anderson-Hsieh, J. (1994). Interpreting visual feedback on suprasegmentals in computer assisted pronunciation instruction. *CALICO Journal*, 11(4), 5–22. www.jstor.org/stable/24152754

Anderson-Hsieh, J., Johnson, R., & Koehler, K. (1992). The relationship between native speaker judgements of nonnative pronunciation and deviance in segmentals, prosody and syllable structure. *Language Learning*, 42(4), 529–555. https://doi.org/10.1111/j.1467-1770.1992.tb01043.x

Aoyama, K., Flege, J.E., Guion, S.G., Akahane-Yamada, R., & Yamada, T. (2004). Perceived phonetic dissimilarity and L2 speech learning: The case of Japanese /r/ and English /l/ and /r/. *Journal of Phonetics*, 32(2), 233–250. https://doi.org/10.1016/S0095-4470(03)00036-6

Avery, P., Ehrlich, S., Mendelson-Burns, I., & Archibald, J. (1987). Specific pronunciation problems. *TESL-Talk*, 17(1), 81–116.

Badin, P., Tarabalka, Y., Elisei, F., & Bailly, G. (2010). Can you "read" tongue movements? Evaluation of the contribution of tongue display to speech understanding. *Speech Communication*, 52(6), 493–503. https://doi.org/10.1016/j.specom.2010.03.002

Baker, W., Trofimovich, P., Mack, M., & Flege, J.E. (2002). The effect of perceived phonetic similarity on non-native sound learning by children and adults. *Proceedings of the Annual Boston University Conference on Language Development*, 26(1), 36–47.

Balas, A. (2018). English vowel perception by Polish advanced learners of English. *Canadian Journal of Linguistics/Revue canadienne de linguistique*, 63(3), 309–338. https://doi.org/10.1017/cnj.2018.5

Bauer, R.S. (1995). Syllable and word in Cantonese. *Journal of Asian Pacific Communication*, 6(4), 245–306.

Bauer, R.S., & Benedict, P.K. (1997). *Modern Cantonese phonology. Trends in linguistics: Studies and monographs 102*. Berlin: Mouton de Gruyter.

Becker, M. (2002). The development of the copula in child English. *Annual Review of Language Acquisition, 2*(1), 37–58. https://doi.org/10.1075/arla.2.03bec

Bell, N. (1992). The role of spoken error correction in second language acquisition: Issues in corrective technique. *ORTESOL Journal, 13*, 21–32.

Best, C.T. (1994). The emergence of native-language phonological influences in infants: A perceptual assimilation model. In J.C. Goodman & H.C. Nusbaum (Eds.), *The development of speech perception: The transition from speech sounds to spoken words* (pp. 167–224). Cambridge, MA: MIT Press.

Best, C.T., Goldstein, L., Tyler, M.D., & Nam, H. (2009). Articulating the perceptual assimilation model (PAM): Perceptual assimilation in relation to articulatory organs and their constriction gestures. *The Journal of the Acoustical Society of America, 125*(4), 2758. https://doi.org/10.1121/1.4784648

Best, C.T., McRoberts, G.W., & Goodell, E. (2001). Discrimination of non-native consonant contrasts varying in perceptual assimilation to the listener's native phonological system. *The Journal of the Acoustical Society of America, 109*(2), 775–794. https://doi.org/10.1121/1.1332378

Best, C.T., & Tyler, M.D. (2007). Nonnative and second-language speech perception: Commonalities and complementarities. In O.S. Bohn & M.J. Munro (Eds.), *Language experience in second language speech learning: In honor of James Emil Flege* (pp. 13–34). Amsterdam & Philadelphia: John Benjamins. https://doi.org/10.1075/lllt.17.07bes

Bhatia, T.K. (1995). Acquisition of voicing and aspiration in second language development. In V. Gambhir (Ed.), *The teaching and acquisition of South Asian languages* (pp. 183–196). Philadelphia: University of Pennsylvania Press.

Bloom, L. (1991). *Language development from two to three*. Cambridge: Cambridge University Press.

Bohn, O.S., & Flege, J.E. (1992). The production of new and similar vowels by adult German learners of English. *Studies in Second Language Acquisition, 14*(2), 131–158. https://doi.org/10.1017/S0272263100010792

Bolton, K. (2012). World Englishes and Asian Englishes: A survey of the field. In A. Kirkpatrick & R. Sussex (Eds.), *English as an international language in Asia: Implications for language education* (pp. 13–26). Dordrecht: Springer. https://doi.org/10.1007/978-94-007-4578-0_2

Bolton, K., & Kwok, H. (1990). The dynamics of the Hong Kong accent: Social identity and sociolinguistic description. *Journal of Asian Pacific Communication, 1*(1), 147–172.

Boulton, A. (2010). Data-driven learning: Taking the computer out of the equation. *Language Learning, 60*(3), 534–572. http://doi.org/10.1111/j.1467-9922.2010.00566.x

Brinton, L.J., & Brinton, D.M. (2010). *The linguistic structure of modern English*. Amsterdam: John Benjamins.

Brown, R. (1973). *A first language*. Cambridge, MA: Harvard University Press.

Budge, C. (1989). Plural marking in Hong Kong English. *Hong Kong Papers in Linguistics and Language Teaching, 12*, 39–47.

Carlisle, R.S. (1997). The modification of onsets in a markedness relationship: Testing the interlanguage structural conformity hypothesis. *Language Learning, 47*(2), 327–361. https://doi.org/10.1111/0023-8333.101997010

Carlisle, R.S. (1998). The acquisition of onsets in a markedness relationship: A longitudinal study. *Studies in Second Language Acquisition, 20*, 245–260.

Carrie, E. (2017). "British is professional, American is urban": Attitudes towards English reference accents in Spain. *International Journal of Applied Linguistics*, 27(2), 427–447. https://doi.org/10.1111/ijal.12139

Carroll, S., & Swain, M. (1993). Explicit and implicit negative feedback: An empirical study of the learning of linguistic generalizations. *Studies in Second Language Acquisition*, 15(3), 357–386. https://doi.org/10.1017/S0272263100012158

Carroll, S., Swain, M., & Roberge, Y. (1992). The role of feedback in adult second language acquisition: Error correction and morphological generalizations. *Applied Psycholinguistics*, 13(2), 173–198. https://doi.org/10.1017/S0142716400005555

Celce-Murcia, M. (2002). Why it makes sense to teach grammar in context and through discourse. In E. Hinkel & S. Fotos (Eds.), *New perspectives on grammar teaching in second language classrooms* (pp. 119–134). Mahwah, NJ: Erlbaum.

Chafe, W.L. (1976). Givenness, contrastiveness, definiteness, subjects, topics, and point of view. In C. Li (Ed.), *Subject and topic* (pp. 25–55). New York: Academic Press.

Chan, A.Y.W. (2000). A study of English non-parallel structures – Typology, causes and rectification. *EA Journal*, 18(2), 21–30.

Chan, A.Y.W. (2003). Alerting students to the correct use of *until* using an algorithmic approach. *The ORTESOL Journal*, 22, 69–78.

Chan, A.Y.W. (2004a). Although . . . but; because . . . so: Why can't they be used together? *Modern English Teacher*, 13(2), 24–25.

Chan, A.Y.W. (2004b). Noun phrases in Chinese and English: A study of English structural problems encountered by Chinese ESL students in Hong Kong. *Language, Culture and Curriculum*, 17(1), 33–47. https://doi.org/10.1080/07908310408666680

Chan, A.Y.W. (2004c). Syntactic transfer: Evidence from the interlanguage of Hong Kong Chinese ESL learners. *The Modern Language Journal*, 88(1), 56–74. https://doi.org/10.1111/j.0026-7902.2004.00218.x

Chan, A.Y.W. (2004d). The boy who Mary loves him is called John: A study of the resumptive pronoun problem and its correction strategies. *Hong Kong Journal of Applied Linguistics*, 9(1), 53–69.

Chan, A.Y.W. (2006a). An algorithmic approach to error correction: An empirical study. *Foreign Language Annals*, 39(1), 131–147. https://doi.org/10.1111/j.1944-9720.2006.tb02254.x

Chan, A.Y.W. (2006b). Cantonese ESL learners' pronunciation of English final consonants. *Language, Culture and Curriculum*, 19(3), 296–313. https://doi.org/10.1080/07908310608668769

Chan, A.Y.W. (2006c). Strategies used by Cantonese speakers in pronouncing English initial consonant clusters: Insights into the interlanguage phonology of Cantonese ESL learners in Hong Kong. *International Review of Applied Linguistics in Language Teaching*, 44(4), 331–355. https://doi.org/10.1515/IRAL.2006.015

Chan, A.Y.W. (2007). The acquisition of English word-final consonants by Cantonese ESL learners in Hong Kong. *Canadian Journal of Linguistics/Revue canadienne de linguistique*, 52(3), 231–253. https://doi.org/10.1017/S0008413100004291

Chan, A.Y.W. (2008, January). Ideas for teaching ergative verbs to ESL students. *Internet TESL Journal*, XIV(1). Retrieved from http://iteslj.org/Techniques/Chan-ErgativeVerbs.html

Chan, A.Y.W. (2009a). Does mother tongue influence have a greater effect on L2 speech perception or production? A study of the learning of English by Cantonese ESL learners in Hong Kong. In *Proceedings of the phonetics teaching and learning conference 2009* (pp. 31–34). London: University College London.

Chan, A.Y.W. (2009b). Helping Cantonese ESL learners overcome their difficulties in the production and perception of English speech sounds. *English Language Teaching World Online: Voices from the Classroom*, 1, 05.12.2009.

Chan, A.Y.W. (2010a). Advanced Cantonese ESL learners' production of English speech sounds: Problems and strategies. *System*, 38(2), 316–328. https://doi.org/10.1016/j. system.2009.11.008

Chan, A.Y.W. (2010b). An investigation into Cantonese ESL learners' acquisition of English initial consonant clusters. *Linguistics*, 48(1), 99–141. https://doi.org/10.1515/ LING.2010.003

Chan, A.Y.W. (2010c). Toward a taxonomy of written errors: Investigation into the written errors of Hong Kong Cantonese ESL learners. *TESOL Quarterly*, 44(2), 295–319. https://doi.org/10.5054/tq.2010.219941

Chan, A.Y.W. (2011). The perception of English speech sounds by Cantonese ESL learners in Hong Kong. *TESOL Quarterly*, 45(4), 718–748. https://doi.org/10.5054/ tq.2011.268056

Chan, A.Y.W. (2012). Cantonese English as a second language learners' perceived relations between "similar" L1 and L2 speech sounds: A test of the Speech Learning Model. *The Modern Language Journal*, 96(1), 1–19. https://doi.org/10.1111/j.1540-4781.2012.01291.x

Chan, A.Y.W. (2013). The discrimination of English vowels by Cantonese ESL learners in Hong Kong: A test of the Perceptual Assimilation Model. *Open Journal of Modern Linguistics*, 3(3), 182–189. https://doi.org/10.4236/ojml.2013.33025

Chan, A.Y.W. (2014). The perception and production of English speech sounds by Cantonese ESL learners in Hong Kong. *Linguistics*, 52(1), 35–72. https://doi.org/10.1515/ ling-2013-0056

Chan, A.Y.W. (2015). Making your phonetics and phonology lessons interesting. In *Proceedings of the phonetics teaching and learning conference 2015* (pp. 35–38). London: University College London.

Chan, A.Y.W. (2016). How much do Cantonese ESL learners know about the English article system? *System*, 56, 66–77. https://doi.org/10.1016/j.system.2015.11.005

Chan, A.Y.W. (2017a). The effectiveness of using a bilingualized dictionary for determining noun countability and article selection. *Lexikos*, 27, 183–213. https://doi. org/10.5788/27-1-1399

Chan, A.Y.W. (2017b). Why do Hong Kong Cantonese ESL learners choose a certain English article for use? *Asian Journal of Applied Linguistics*, 4(1), 16–29.

Chan, A.Y.W. (2019a). L1 influence on the acquisition of English articles by Cantonese ESL learners in Hong Kong: Presence or absence? *Journal of Language and Communication*, 6(1), 103–113.

Chan, A.Y.W. (2019b). Use and misuse of the English "the": A case of Hong Kong Cantonese ESL learners. *The Journal of Asia TEFL*, 16(3), 859–875. https://doi.org/10.18823/ asiatefl.2019.16.3.6.859

Chan, A.Y.W. (2021). Using metalinguistic explanations to help advanced ESL/EFL learners overcome their problems with the use of English articles and reference representation. *TESOL Journal*, 12(2), e559. https://doi.org/10.1002/tesj.559

Chan, A.Y.W. (2022). Typology and contexts of article errors: Investigation into the use of English articles by Hong Kong Cantonese ESL learners. *International Review of Applied Linguistics in Language Teaching*, 60(2), 197–227. https://doi.org/10.1515/iral-2018-0268

Chan, A.Y.W., Kwan, B.S.C., & Li, D.C.S. (2002a). An algorithmic approach to error correction: Correcting three common errors at different levels. *JALT Journal*, 24(2), 201–216.

Chan, A.Y.W., Kwan, B.S.C., & Li, D.C.S. (2002b). Helping students overcome the *somewhere has something* Problem. *Guidelines*, 4(1), 14–18.

Chan, A.Y.W., Kwan, B.S.C., & Li, D.C.S. (2003). Tackling the "independent clause as subject" problem. *Asian Journal of English Language Teaching*, 13, 107–117.

Chan, A.Y.W., & Li, D.C.S. (2000). English and Cantonese phonology in contrast: Explaining Cantonese ESL learners' English pronunciation problems. *Language, Culture and Curriculum*, 13(1), 67–85. https://doi.org/10.1080/07908310008666590

Chan, A.Y.W., & Li, D.C.S. (2002). Form-focused remedial instruction: An empirical study. *International Journal of Applied Linguistics*, 12(1), 24–53. https://doi.org/10.1111/1473-4192.00023

Chan, A.Y.W., Li, D.C.S., & Kwan, B.S.C. (2003). Misplacement and misuse of *very*: Helping students overcome the *very + VERB* problem. *The English Teacher: An International Journal*, 6(2), 125–132.

Chan, C.P.H. (2001). The perception (and production) of English word-initial consonants by native speakers of Cantonese. *Hong Kong Journal of Applied Linguistics*, 6(1), 26–44.

Chao, Y.R. (1947). *Cantonese primer*. Cambridge, MA: Harvard University Press.

Chao, Y.R. (1968). *A grammar of spoken Chinese*. Berkeley: University of California Press.

Chappell, H. (1986). Formal and colloquial adversity passives in standard Chinese. *Linguistics*, 24(6), 1025–1052. https://doi.org/10.1515/ling.1986.24.6.1025

Chela-Flores, B. (2001). Pronunciation and language learning: An integrative approach. *International Review of Applied Linguistics in Language Teaching*, 39(2), 85–101. https://doi.org/10.1515/iral.39.2.85

Chen, C.Y. (1976). Pronunciation of English by students from the Chinese stream in Singapore: Some salient features. *RELC Journal*, 7(2), 54–60. https://doi.org/10.1177/003368827600700214

Cheng, L.L.S., & Sybesma, R. (1999). Bare and not-so-bare nouns and the structure of NP. *Linguistic Inquiry*, 30(4), 509–542. https://doi.org/10.1162/002438999554192

Cheng, L.L.S., & Sybesma, R. (2005). Classifiers in four varieties of Chinese. In G. Cinque & R.S. Kayne (Eds.), *The Oxford handbook of comparative syntax* (pp. 259–292). Oxford: Oxford University Press. https://doi.org/10.1093/oxfordhb/9780195136517.013.0007

Chierchia, G. (1998). Reference to kinds across language. *Natural Language Semantics*, 6, 339–405. https://doi.org/10.1023/A:1008324218506

Collins, L., & Ruivivar, J. (2021). Research agenda: Researching grammar teaching and learning in the second language classroom. *Language Teaching*, 54(3), 407–423. https://doi.org/10.1017/S0261444821000070

Comrie, B. (1976). *Aspect: An introduction to the study of verbal aspects and related problems*. Cambridge: Cambridge University Press.

Comrie, B. (1985). *Tense*. Cambridge: Cambridge University Press.

Coniam, D. (2002). Technology as an awareness-raising tool for sensitising teachers to features of stress and rhythm in English. *Language Awareness*, 11(1), 30–42. https://doi.org/10.1080/09658410208667044

Corder, S.P. (1967). The significance of learner's errors? *International Review of Applied Linguistics in Language Teaching*, 5(4), 161–170. https://doi.org/10.1515/iral.1967.5.1-4.161

Corder, S.P. (1978). Language-learner language. In J.C. Richards (Ed.), *Understanding second and foreign language learning: Issues and approaches* (pp. 71–93). Rowley, MA: Newbury House.

Corder, S.P. (1981). *Error analysis and interlanguage*. Oxford: Oxford University Press.

Cruttenden, A. (2001). *Gimson's pronunciation of English* (6th Edition). London: Arnold.

Dayal, V. (2004). Number marking and (in)definiteness in kind terms. *Linguistics and Philosophy*, 27(4), 393–450. https://doi.org/10.1023/ B:LING.0000024420.80324.67

DeCapua, A. (2008). *Grammar for teachers: A guide to American English for native and non-native speakers*. New York: Springer.

DeFrancis, J. (1984). *The Chinese language: Fact and fantasy*. Honolulu: University of Hawaii Press.

DeFrancis, J. (1989). *Visible speech: The diverse oneness of writing systems*. Honolulu: University of Hawaii Press.

Demirezen, M. (2016). Perception of nuclear stress in vocabulary items in teacher education in terms of shadow listening. *Procedia – Social and Behavioral Sciences*, 232, 537–546. https://doi.org/10.1016/j.sbspro.2016.10.074

Derwing, T.M., & Munro, M.J. (2015). *Pronunciation fundamentals: Evidence-based perspectives for L2 teaching and research*. Amsterdam: John Benjamins.

Derwing, T.M., Munro, M.J., & Wiebe, G.E. (1998). Evidence in favor of a broad framework for pronunciation instruction. *Language Learning*, 48(3), 393–410. https://doi.org/10.1111/0023-8333.00047

Deterding, D., & Kirkpatrick, A. (2006). Emerging South-East Asian Englishes and intelligibility. *World Englishes*, 25(3/4), 391–409. https://doi.org/10.1111/j.1467-971X.2006.00478.x

Deterding, D., Wong, J., & Kirkpatrick, A. (2008). The pronunciation of Hong Kong English. *English World-Wide*, 29(2), 148–175. https://doi.org/10.1075/eww.29.2.03det

Doughty, C. (1991). Second language instruction does make a difference: Evidence from an empirical study of SL relativization. *Studies in Second Language Acquisition*, 13(4), 431–469. https://doi.org/10.1017/S0272263100010287

Doughty, C., & Varela, E. (1998). Communicative focus on form. In C. Doughty & J. Williams (Eds.), *Focus on form in classroom SLA* (pp. 114–138). Cambridge: Cambridge University Press.

Downing, A. (2015). *English grammar: A university course* (3rd Edition). London: Routledge.

Duanmu, S. (1998). Wordhood in Chinese. In J. Packard (Ed.), *New approaches to Chinese word formation: Morphology, phonology and the lexicon in modern and ancient Chinese* (pp. 135–196). Berlin & New York: Mouton de Gruyter. https://doi.org/10.1515/9783110809084.135

Dziemianko, A. (2012). *Noun and verb codes in English monolingual dictionaries for foreign learners: A study of usefulness in the Polish context*. Poznań: Wydawnictwo Naukowe UAM.

Eckman, F.R. (1977). Markedness and the contrastive analysis hypothesis. *Language Learning*, 27(2), 315–330. http://dx.doi.org/10.1111/j.1467-1770.1977.tb00124.x

Eckman, F.R. (1981a). On predicting phonological difficulty in second language acquisition. *Studies in Second Language Acquisition*, 4(1), 18–30. https://doi.org/10.1017/S0272263100004253

Eckman, F.R. (1981b). On the naturalness of interlanguage phonological rules. *Language Learning*, 31(1), 195–216. https://doi.org/10.1111/j.1467-1770.1981.tb01379.x

Eckman, F.R. (1984). Universals, typologies and interlanguage. In W.E. Rutherford (Ed.), *Language universals and second language acquisition* (pp. 79–105). Amsterdam: John Benjamins. https://doi.org/10.1075/tsl.5.08eck

Eckman, F.R. (1991). The structural conformity hypothesis and the acquisition of consonant clusters in the interlanguage of ESL learners. *Studies in Second Language Acquisition*, 13(1), 23–41. https://doi.org/10.1017/S0272263100009700

Eckman, F.R. (1996). A functional-typological approach to second language acquisition theory. In W.C. Ritchie & T.K. Bhatia (Eds.), *Handbook of second language acquisition* (pp. 195–211). San Diego: Academic Press.

Eckman, F.R. (2004). From phonemic differences to constraint rankings: Research on second language phonology. *Studies in Second Language Acquisition*, 26(4), 513–549. https://doi.org/10.1017/S027226310404001X

Eckman, F.R. (2008). Typological markedness and second language phonology. In J.G. Hansen Edwards & M.L. Zampini (Eds.), *Phonology and second language acquisition* (pp. 95–115). Amsterdam: John Benjamins.

Eckman, F.R., Bell, L., & Nelson, D. (1988). On the generalization of relative clause instruction in the acquisition of English as a second language. *Applied Linguistics*, 9(1), 1–20. https://doi.org/10.1093/applin/9.1.1

Edge, B.A. (1991). The production of word-final voiced obstruents in English by L1 speakers of Japanese and Cantonese. *Studies in Second Language Acquisition*, 13(3), 377–393. https://doi.org/10.1017/S0272263100010032

Eisenberg, S.L., Guo, L.Y., & Germezia, M. (2012). How grammatical are 3-year-olds? *Language, Speech, and Hearing Services in Schools*, 43(1), 35–52. https://doi.org/10.1044/0161-1461(2011/10-0093)

Ellis, N.C. (1995). Consciousness in second language acquisition: A review of field studies and laboratory experiments. *Language Awareness*, 4(3), 123–146. https://doi.org/10.1080/09658416.1995.9959876

Ellis, R. (2002). Does form-focused instruction affect the acquisition of implicit knowledge? A review of the research. *Studies in Second Language Acquisition*, 24(2), 223–236. https://doi.org/10.1017/S0272263102002073

Engwall, O. (2012). Analysis of and feedback on phonetic features in pronunciation training with a virtual teacher. *Computer Assisted Language Learning*, 25(1), 37–64. https://doi.org/10.1080/09588221.2011.582845

Engwall, O., & Bälter, O. (2007). Pronunciation feedback from real and virtual language teachers. *Computer Assisted Language Learning*, 20(3), 235–262. https://doi.org/10.1080/09588220701489507

Escudero, P. (2005). *Linguistic perception and second language acquisition: Explaining the attainment of optimal phonological categorization*. PhD thesis, LOT Dissertation Series 113, Utrecht University.

Escudero, P. (2009). The linguistic perception of similar L2 sounds. In P. Boersma & S. Hamann (Eds.), *Phonology in perception* (pp. 151–190). Berlin, NY: Mouton de Gruyter.

Fernandez Amaya, L. (2008). Teaching culture: Is it possible to avoid pragmatic failure? *Revista Alicantina de Estudios Ingleses*, 21, 11–24. https://doi.org/10.14198/raei.2008.21.02

Flege, J.E. (1987a). Effects of equivalence classification on the production of foreign language speech sounds. In A. James & J. Leather (Eds.), *Sound patterns in second language acquisition* (pp. 9–40). Dordrecht, Holland: Foris. https://doi.org/10.1515/9783110878486-003

Flege, J.E. (1987b). The production of "new" and "similar" phones in a foreign language: Evidence for the effect of equivalence classification. *Journal of Phonetics*, 15(1), 47–65. https://doi.org/10.1016/S0095-4470(19)30537-6

Flege, J.E. (1995). Second language speech learning: Theory, findings and problems. In W. Strange (Ed.), *Speech perception and linguistic experience: Issues in cross-language research* (pp. 233–277). Timonium, MD: York Press.

Flege, J.E., & Bohn, O.S. (2021). The revised speech learning model (SLM-r). In R. Wayland (Ed.), *Second language speech learning: Theoretical and empirical progress* (pp. 3–83). Cambridge: Cambridge University Press. https://doi.org/10.1017/9781108886901.002

Flege, J.E., & Mackay, I.R.A. (2004). Perceiving vowels in a second language. *Studies in Second Language Acquisition*, 26(1), 1–34. https://doi.org/10.1017/S0272263104026117

Fok Chan, Y.Y. (1974). A perceptual study of tones in Cantonese. *Centre of Asian studies occasional papers and monographs*, No. 18. University of Hong Kong Press.

Forbes, D. (1993). Singlish. *English Today*, 9(2), 18–22. https://doi.org/10.1017/S0266078400000304

Fromkin, V., Rodman, R., & Hyams, N. (2017). *An introduction to language* (10th Edition). Boston: Cengage.

Fry, D.B. (1979). *The physics of speech*. Cambridge: Cambridge University Press.

Gamkrelidze, T. (1978). On the correlation between stops and fricatives in a phonological system. In J.H. Greenberg, C.A. Ferguson, & E.A. Moravcsik (Eds.), *Universals of human language, Vol. 2: Phonology* (pp. 9–46). Stanford: Stanford University Press.

Gass, S.M. (1979). Language transfer and universal grammatical relations. *Language Learning*, 29(2), 327–344. https://doi.org/10.1111/j.1467-1770.1979.tb01073.x

Gass, S.M. (1983). Second language acquisition and language universals. In R. DiPietro, W. Frawley, & A. Wedel (Eds.), *The first Delaware symposium on language studies* (pp. 249–260). Newark, DE: University of Delaware Press.

Gass, S.M., Behney, J., & Plonsky, L. (2013). *Second language acquisition: An introductory course* (4th Edition). New York: Routledge.

Geluso, J., & Yamaguchi, A. (2014). Discovering formulaic language through data-driven learning: Student attitudes and efficacy. *ReCALL*, 26(2), 225–242. https://doi.org/10.1017/S0958344014000044

Gimson, A.C., & Ramsaran, S. (1989). *An introduction to the pronunciation of English* (4th Edition). London: Edward Arnold.

Gisborne, N. (2002). Relative clauses in Hong Kong English. In K. Bolton (Ed.), *Hong Kong English: Autonomy and creativity* (pp. 141–160). Hong Kong: Hong Kong University Press.

Goriot, C., McQueen, J.M., Unsworth, S., Hout, R., & Broersma, M. (2020). Perception of English phonetic contrasts by Dutch children: How bilingual are early-English learners? *PLoS ONE*, 15(3), e0229902. https://doi.org/10.1371/journal.pone.0229902

Green, C. (1991). Typological transfer, discourse accent and the Chinese writer of English. *Hong Kong Papers in Linguistics and Language Teaching*, 14, 51–63.

Greenberg, J. (1966). *Language universals: With special reference to feature hierarchies*. Mouton: The Hague.

Greenberg, J. (1978). Some generalizations concerning initial and final consonant clusters. In J.H. Greenberg, C.A. Ferguson, & E.A. Moravcsik (Eds.), *Universals of human language, Vol. 2: Phonology* (pp. 243–279). Stanford: Stanford University Press.

Guion, S.G., Flege, J.E., Akahane-Yamada, R., & Pruitt, J.C. (2000). An investigation of current models of second language speech perception: The case of Japanese adults' perception of English consonants. *The Journal of the Acoustical Society of America*, 107, 2711–2724. https://doi.org/10.1121/1.428657

Guion, S.G., Harada, T., & Clark, J.J. (2004). Early and late Spanish-English bilinguals' acquisition of English word stress patterns. *Bilingualism: Language and Cognition*, 7(3), 207–226. https://doi.org/10.1017/S1366728904001592

Gussenhoven, C., & Jacobs, H. (2017). *Understanding phonology* (4th Edition). New York: Routledge.

Hall, C.J. (2002). The automatic cognate form assumption: Evidence for the parasitic model of vocabulary development. *International Review of Applied Linguistics in Language Teaching*, 40(2), 69–87. https://doi.org/10.1515/iral.2002.008

Hall, C.J., Schmidtke, D., & Vickers, J. (2013). Countability in world Englishes. *World Englishes*, 32(1), 1–22.

Halliday, M.A.K. (2004). *An introduction to functional grammar* (3rd Edition). London: Edward Arnold.

Han, H. (2019). Effect of topic-prominent features of Mandarin Chinese on English writing. *Journal of Language Teaching and Research*, 10(2), 353–362. http://doi.org/10.17507/jltr.1002.18

Han, N.R., Chodorow, M., & Leacock, C. (2006). Detecting errors in English article usage by non-native speakers. *Natural Language Engineering*, 12(2), 115–129. https://doi.org/10.1017/s1351324906004190

Han, S.J., & Koh, L.H. (1976). Aural discrimination difficulties of Hong Kong, Malaysian and Singaporean Chinese. *RELC Journal*, 7(1), 53–63. https://doi.org/10.1177/003368827600700107

Han, Z. (2000). Persistence of the implicit influence of NL: The case of the pseudo-passive. *Applied Linguistics*, 21(1), 78–105. https://doi.org/10.1093/applin/21.1.78

Hansen Edwards, J.G. (2001). Linguistic constraints on the acquisition of English syllable codas by native speakers of Mandarin Chinese. *Applied Linguistics*, 22(3), 338–365. https://doi.org/10.1093/applin/22.3.338

Hansen Edwards, J.G. (2004). Developmental sequences in the acquisition of English L2 syllable codas: A preliminary study. *Studies in Second Language Acquisition*, 26(1), 85–124. https://doi.org/10.1017/S0272263104026142

Hansen Edwards, J.G. (2006). *Acquiring a non-native phonology: Linguistic constraints and social barriers*. London: Continuum.

Hansen Edwards, J.G. (2011). Deletion of /t, d/ and the acquisition of linguistic variation by second language learners of English. *Language Learning*, 61(4), 1256–1301. https://doi.org/10.1111/j.1467-9922.2011.00672.x

Hansen Edwards, J.G. (2014). Developmental sequences and constraints in second language phonological acquisition: Balancing language-internal and language-external factors. In J. Levis & A. Moyer (Eds.), *Social dynamics in second language accent* (pp. 53–73). Boston & Berlin: De Gruyter Mouton.

Hansen Edwards, J.G. (2015). Hong Kong English: Attitudes, identity, and use. *Asian Englishes*, 17(3), 184–208, https://doi.org/10.1080/13488678.2015.1049840

Hansen Edwards, J.G. (2016a). Sociolinguistic variation in Asian Englishes: The case of coronal stop deletion. *English World-Wide*, 37(2), 138–167. https://doi.org/10.1075/eww.37.2.02han

Hansen Edwards, J.G. (2016b). The deletion of /t, d/ in Hong Kong English. *World Englishes*, 35(1), 60–77. https://doi.org/10.1111/weng.12166

Hansen Edwards, J.G. (2019). TH variation in Hong Kong English. *English Language & Linguistics*, 23(2), 439–468. https://doi.org/10.1017/S1360674318000035

Hardison, D.M. (2004). Generalization of computer-assisted prosody training: Quantitative and qualitative findings. *Language Learning & Technology*, 8(1), 34–52.

Harnsberger, J.D. (2001). On the relationship between identification and discrimination of non-native nasal consonants. *The Journal of the Acoustical Society of America*, 110(1), 489–503. https://doi.org/10.1121/1.1371758

Hartmann, R.R.K. (1994). Bilingualised versions of learner's dictionaries. *Fremdsprachen Lehren und Lernen*, 23, 206–220.

Hazan, V., Sennema, A., Faulkner, A., Ortega-Llebaria, M., Iba, M., & Chung, H. (2006). The use of visual cues in the perception of non-native consonant contrasts. *The Journal of the Acoustical Society of America*, 119, 1740–1751. https://doi.org/10.1121/1.2166611

Hazen, K. (2011). Flying high above the social radar: Coronal stop deletion in modern Appalachia. *Language Variation and Change*, 23(1), 105–137. https://doi.org/10.1017/S0954394510000220

He, N. (2010). Rush to learn English fuels quality issues. *China Daily*. Retrieved April 20, 2022 from www.chinadaily.com.cn/china/2010-08/05/content_11098499.htm

Heift, T., & Vyatkina, N. (2017). Technologies for teaching and learning L2 grammar. In C.A. Chapelle & S. Sauro (Eds.), *The handbook of technology and second language teaching and learning* (pp. 26–44). Hoboken, NJ: Wiley Blackwell.

Hirata, Y. (2004). Computer assisted pronunciation training for native English speakers learning Japanese pitch and durational contrasts. *Computer Assisted Language Learning*, 17(3–4), 357–376. https://doi.org/10.1080/0958822042000319629

Hodges, J.C., Horner, W.B., Webb, S.S., & Miller, R.K. (1994). *Harbrace college handbook* (12th Edition). Harcourt Brace College Publisher.

Howatt, A.P.R. (1984). *A history of English language teaching*. Oxford: Oxford University Press.

https://www.collinsdictionary.com/dictionary/english/on-the-contrary (2000).

https://www.collinsdictionary.com/dictionary/english/until (2000).

https://www.english-corpora.org/bnc/ (2000).

Hu, J.H., Pan, H.H., & Xu, L.J. (2001). Is there a finite vs. nonfinite distinction in Chinese? *Linguistics*, 39(6), 1117–1148.

Huebner, T. (1983). *A longitudinal analysis of the acquisition of English*. Ann Arbor, MI: Karoma.

Hume, E. (2004). Deconstructing markedness: A predictability-based approach. *Berkeley linguistics society: Proceedings of the annual meeting 2004*, Department of Linguistics, University of California, Berkeley, pp. 182–198.

Hung, T.T.N. (1993). The role of phonology in the teaching of pronunciation to bilingual students. *Language, Culture and Curriculum*, 6(3), 249–256. https://doi.org/10.1080/07908319309525155

Hyltenstam, K. (1984). The use of typological markedness conditions as predictors in second language acquisition. In R. Andersen (Ed.), *Second languages: A cross-linguistic perspective* (pp. 39–58). Rowley, MA: Newbury House.

Ingram, J.C.L., & Park, S.G. (1997). Cross-language vowel perception and production by Japanese and Korean learners of English. *Journal of Phonetics*, 25(3), 343–370. https://doi.org/10.1006/jpho.1997.0048

Ingvalson, E.M., McClelland, J.L., & Holt, L.L. (2011). Predicting native English-like performance by native Japanese speakers. *Journal of Phonetics*, 39(4), 571–584. https://doi.org/10.1016/j.wocn.2011.03.003

Ionin, T. (2003). *Article semantics in second language acquisition*. Doctoral dissertation, MIT, Cambridge, MA.

Ionin, T. (2006). *This* is definitely specific: Specificity and definiteness in article systems. *Natural Language Semantics*, 14(2), 175–234. https://doi.org/10.1007/s11050-005-5255-9

Ionin, T., Baek, S., Kim, E., Ko, H., & Wexler, K. (2012). *That*'s not so different from *the*: Definite and demonstrative descriptions in second language acquisition. *Second Language Research*, 28(1), 69–101. https://doi.org/10.1177/0267658311432200

Ionin, T., Ko, H., & Wexler, K. (2004). Article semantics in L2-acquisition: The role of specificity. *Language Acquisition*, 12(1), 3–69. https://doi.org/10.1207/s15327817la1201_2

Ionin, T., & Montrul, S. (2010). The role of L1 transfer in the interpretation of articles with definite plurals in L2 English. *Language Learning*, 60(4), 877–925. https://doi.org/10.1111/j.1467-9922.2010.00577.x

Ionin, T., Montrul, S., Kim, J.H., & Philippov, V. (2011). Genericity distinctions and the interpretation of determiners in second language acquisition. *Language Acquisition*, 18(4), 242–280. https://doi.org/10.1080/10489223.2011.610264

Ionin, T., Zubizarreta, M.L., & Maldonado, S.B. (2008). Sources of linguistic knowledge in the second language acquisition of English articles. *Lingua*, 118(4), 554–576. https://doi.org/10.1016/j.lingua.2006.11.012

Jackson, H., & Amvela, E.Z. (2007). *Words, meaning and vocabulary: An introduction to modern English lexicology* (2nd Edition). London & New York: Continuum.

James, C. (1998). *Errors in language learning and use: Exploring error analysis*. London: Longman.

James, G. (1994). Towards a typology of bilingualized dictionaries. In G. James (Ed.), *Meeting points in language studies: A festschrift for Ma Tailai: Working papers* (pp. 184–196). Hong Kong: Hong Kong University of Science and Technology Language Center.

Jenkins, J. (2002). A sociolinguistically based, empirically researched pronunciation syllabus for English as an international language. *Applied Linguistics*, 23(1), 83–103. https://doi.org/10.1093/applin/23.1.83

Jones, I. (1979). Some cultural and linguistic considerations affecting the learning of English by Chinese children in Britain. *ELT Journal*, 34(1), 55–61. https://doi.org/10.1093/elt/34.1.55

Jones, R. (1995). Emma has an enemy. In M.C. Pennington (Ed.), *New ways in teaching grammar* (pp. 127–128). Alexandria, VA: Teachers of English to Speakers of Other Languages, Inc.

Kankaanranta, A., & Lu, W. (2013). The evolution of English as the business lingua franca: Signs of convergence in Chinese and Finnish professional communication. *Journal of Business and Technical Communication*, 27(3), 288–307. https://doi.org/10.1177/1050651913479919

Keenan, E.L., & Comrie, B. (1977). Noun phrase accessibility and universal grammar. *Linguistic Inquiry*, 8(1), 63–99. www.jstor.org/stable/4177973

Kellerman, E. (1979). Transfer and non-transfer: Where we are now? *Studies in Second Language Acquisition*, 2(1), 37–57. https://doi.org/10.1017/S0272263100000942

Kenworthy, J. (1986). *Teaching English pronunciation*. Hong Kong: Longman.

Kirkpatrick, A., & Xu, Z. (2012). *Chinese rhetoric and writing: An introduction for language teachers*. Fort Collins, CO: Parlor Press. https://doi.org/10.37514/PER-B.2012.2393

Kleinmann, H.H. (1977). Avoidance behavior in adult second language acquisition. *Language Learning*, 27(1), 93–107. https://doi.org/10.1111/j.1467-1770.1977.tb00294.x

Ko, H., Ionin, T., & Wexler, K. (2010). The role of presuppositionality in the second language acquisition of English articles. *Linguistic Inquiry*, 41(2), 213–254. https://doi.org/10.2307/40606838

Krashen, S. (1982). *Principles and practice in second language acquisition*. New York: Pergamon.

Krashen, S. (1985). *The input hypothesis: issues and implication*. New York: Longman.

Krifka, M., Pelletier, F.J., Carlson, G.N., ter Meulen, A., Link, G., & Chierchia, G. (1995). Genericity: An introduction. In G.N. Carlson & F.J. Pelletier (Eds.), *The generic book* (pp. 1–124). Chicago: University of Chicago Press.

Kuhl, P.K. (2000). A new view of language acquisition. *Proceedings of the National Academy of Science*, 24, 11850–11857. http://doi.org/10.1073/pnas.97.22.11850

Kuhl, P.K., Conboy, B.T., Coffey-Corina, S., Padden, D., Rivera-Gaxiola, M., & Nelson, T. (2008). Phonetic learning as a pathway to language: New data and native language magnet theory expanded (NLM-e). *Philosophical Transactions of the Royal Society B: Biological Sciences*, 363, 979–1000. https://doi.org/10.1098/rstb.2007.2154

Kuhl, P.K., & Iverson, P. (1995). Linguistic experience and the perceptual magnet effect. In W. Strange (Ed.), *Speech perception and linguistic experience: Issues in cross-language research* (pp. 121–154). Timonium, MD: York Press.

Kwan, B.S.C., Chan, A.Y.W., & Li, D.C.S. (2003). "According to X, X said . . ." A consciousness-raising approach to helping Cantonese speakers overcome problems in topic-comment structures. *Asia Pacific Journal of Language in Education*, 5(2), 87–94.

Lai, Y.H. (2010). English vowel discrimination and assimilation by Chinese-speaking learners of English. *Concentric: Studies in Linguistics*, 36(2), 157–182.

Lambacher, S. (1999). A CALL tool for improving second language acquisition of English consonants by Japanese learners. *Computer-Assisted Language Learning*, 12(2), 137–156. https://doi.org/10.1076/call.12.2.137.5722

Lando, J. (1998). Grammatical instruction and implicational features: Evidence from an experiment. *ITL Review of Applied Linguistics*, 119/120, 65–78. https://doi.org/10.1075/itl.119-120.05lan

Larsen-Freeman, D., & Long, M. (1991). *An introduction to second language acquisition research*. London: Longman.

Larson-Hall, J. (2004). Predicting perceptual success with segments: A test of Japanese speakers of Russian. *Second Language Research*, 20(1), 33–76. https://doi.org/10.1191/0267658304sr230oa

Laufer, B. (1997). The lexical plight in second language reading: Words you don't know, words you think you know, and words you can't guess. In J. Coady & T. Huckin (Eds.), *Second language vocabulary acquisition: A rationale for pedagogy* (pp. 20–34). Cambridge: Cambridge University Press.

Lee, J., Jang, J., & Plonsky, L. (2015). The effectiveness of second language pronunciation instruction: A meta-analysis. *Applied Linguistics*, 36(3), 345–366. https://doi.org/10.1093/applin/amu040

Lee, M.S. (1976). Pronunciation problems different and similar among Cantonese and Mandarin speakers. *TESL Reporter*, 9(4), 3–6.

Lee, M.S., & Révész, A. (2020). Promoting grammatical development through captions and textual enhancement in multimodal input-based tasks. *Studies in Second Language Acquisition*, 42(3), 625–651. https://doi.org/10.1017/S0272263120000108

Leech, G.N. (1983). *Principles of pragmatics*. London: Longman.

Lenzing, A. (2015). Exploring regularities and dynamic systems in L2 development. *Language Learning*, 65(1), 89–122. https://doi.org/10.1111/lang.12092

Levis, J.M. (2005). Changing contexts and shifting paradigms in pronunciation teaching. *TESOL Quarterly*, 39(3), 369–377. https://doi.org/10.2307/3588485

Levis, J.M. (2016). The interaction of research and pedagogy. *Journal of Second Language Pronunciation*, 2(1), 1–7. https://doi.org/10.1075/jslp.2.1.001lev

Levis, J.M., & Pickering, L. (2004). Teaching intonation in discourse using speech visualization technology. *System*, 32(4), 505–524. https://doi.org/10.1016/j.system.2004.09.009

Li, C.N., & Thompson, S. (1974). Co-verbs in Mandarin Chinese: Verbs or prepositions? *Journal of Chinese Linguistics*, 2(3), 253–278.

Li, C.N., & Thompson, S. (1981). *Mandarin Chinese: A functional reference grammar*. Berkeley, CA: University of California Press.

Li, D.C.S. (1999). The functions and status of English in Hong Kong: A post-1997 update. *English World-Wide*, 20(1), 67–110. https://doi.org/10.1075/eww.20.1.03li

Li, D.C.S., & Chan, A.Y.W. (1999). Helping teachers correct structural and lexical English errors. *Hong Kong Journal of Applied Linguistics*, 4(1), 79–102.

Li, D.C.S., & Chan, A.Y.W. (2000). Form-focused negative feedback: Toward a pedagogically sound model of remedial instruction. In D.C.S. Li, A. Lin, & W.K. Tsang (Eds.), *Language and education in postcolonial Hong Kong* (pp. 333–351). Hong Kong: Linguistic Society of Hong Kong.

Li, D.C.S., & Chan, A.Y.W. (2001). Form-focused negative feedback: Correcting three common errors. *TESL Reporter*, 34(1), 22–34.

Li, D.C.S., & Luk, Z.P.S. (2017). *Chinese-English contrastive grammar: An introduction*. Hong Kong: Hong Kong University Press.

Lightbown, P.M., & Spada, N. (1990). Focus-on-form and corrective feedback in communicative language teaching: Effects on second language learning. *Studies in Second Language Acquisition*, 12(4), 429–448. https://doi.org/10.1017/S0272263100009517

Lightbown, P.M., & Spada, N. (2021). *How languages are learned* (5th Edition). Oxford: Oxford University Press.

Liu, D., & Gleason, J.L. (2002). Acquisition of the article *the* by nonnative speakers of English: An analysis of four nongeneric uses. *Studies in Second Language Acquisition*, 24(1), 1–26. https://doi.org/10.1017/S0272263102001018

Lock, G. (1995). Doers and causers. In M.C. Pennington (Ed.), *New ways in teaching grammar* (pp. 129–133). Alexandria, VA: Teachers of English to Speakers of Other Languages, Inc.

Lock, G. (1996). *Functional English grammar: An introduction for second language teachers*. Cambridge: Cambridge University Press.

Long, M.H. (1991). Focus on form: A design feature in language teaching methodology. In K. de Bot, R. Ginsberg, & C. Kramsch (Eds.), *Foreign language research in cross-cultural perspective* (pp. 39–52). Amsterdam: John Benjamins. http://doi.org/10.1075/sibil.2.07lon

Long, M.H. (1996). The role of linguistic environment in second language acquisition. In W.C. Ritchie & T.K. Bhatia (Eds.), *Handbook of second language acquisition* (pp. 413–468). San Diego: Academic Press.

Lopez, E. (2019). Teaching the English article system: Definiteness and specificity in linguistically-informed instruction. *Language Teaching Research*, 23(2), 200–217. https://doi.org/10.1177/1362168817739649

Low, E.L. (2015). *Pronunciation for English as an international language: From research to practice*. London: Routledge.

Low, E.L. (2021). EIL pronunciation research and practice: Issues, challenges, and future directions. *RELC Journal*, 52(1), 22–34. https://doi.org/10.1177/0033688220987318

Lowie, W., & Verspoor, M. (2015). Variability and variation in second language acquisition orders: A dynamic reevaluation. *Language Learning*, 65(1), 63–88. https://doi.org/10.1111/lang.12093

Luk, Z.P.S., & Shirai, Y. (2009). Is the acquisition order of grammatical morphemes impervious to L1 knowledge? Evidence from the acquisition of plural -s, articles, and possessive's. *Language Learning*, 59(4), 721–754. https://doi.org/10.1111/j.1467-9922.2009.00524.x

Maddieson, I. (1984). *Patterns of sounds*. New York: Cambridge University Press.

Major, R.C. (2001). *Foreign accent: The ontogeny and phylogeny of second language phonology*. Mahwah, NJ: Lawrence Erlbaum Associates.

Major, R.C. (2008). Transfer in second language phonology: A review. In J.G. Hansen Edwards & M.L. Zampini (Eds.), *Phonology and second language acquisition* (pp. 63–94). Amsterdam: John Benjamins.

Major, R.C., & Faudree, M.C. (1996). Markedness universals and the acquisition of voicing contrasts by Korean speakers of English. *Studies in Second Language Acquisition,* 18(1), 69–90. https://doi.org/10.1017/S0272263100014686

Major, R.C., & Kim, E. (1999). The similarity differential rate hypothesis. *Language Learning,* 49(Supplement 1), 151–183. https://doi.org/10.1111/0023-8333.49.s1.5

Marello, C. (1998). Hornby's bilingualized dictionaries. *International Journal of Lexicography,* 11(4), 292–314.

Massaro, D.W. (1987). *Speech perception by ear and eye: A paradigm for psychological enquiry.* Hillsdale, NJ: Lawrence Erlbaum.

Master, P. (1987). Generic the in scientific American. *English for Specific Purposes,* 6(3), 165–186. https://doi.org/10.1016/0889-4906(87)90002-0

Master, P. (2002). Information structure and English article pedagogy. *System,* 30(3), 331–348. https://doi.org/10.1016/S0346-251X(02)00018-0

Matthews, S., & Yip, V. (2011). *Cantonese: A comprehensive grammar* (2nd Edition). London: Routledge.

Miller, J.L., & Eimas, P.D. (1995). Speech perception: From signal to word. *Annual Review of Psychology,* 46, 467–492. https://doi.org/10.1146/annurev.ps.46.020195.002343

Mizuno, H. (1986). *Interlanguage analysis of article errors in English among Japanese adult learners in an acquisition poor environment.* Doctoral dissertation of Teachers College Columbia University, USA.

Mizuno, M. (1999). Interlanguage analysis of the English article system: Some cognitive constraints facing the Japanese adult learners. *International Review of Applied Linguistics in Language Teaching,* 37(2), 127–152. https://doi.org/10.1515/iral.1999.37.2.127

Mohamed, N. (2004). Consciousness-raising tasks: A learner perspective. *ELT Journal,* 58(3), 228–237. https://doi.org/10.1093/elt/58.3.228

Molholt, G. (1988). Computer-assisted instruction in pronunciation for Chinese speakers of American English. *TESOL Quarterly,* 22(1), 91–111. https://doi.org/10.2307/3587063

Moon, S., & Oh, S.Y. (2018). Unlearning overgenerated be through data-driven learning in the secondary EFL classroom. *ReCALL,* 30(1), 48–67. https://doi.org/10.1017/S0958344017000246

Motohashi-Saigo, M., & Hardison, D.M. (2009). Acquisition of L2 Japanese geminates: Training with waveform displays. *Language Learning & Technology,* 13(2), 29–47.

Munro, M.J., & Derwing, T.M. (1995a). Foreign accent, comprehensibility, and intelligibility in the speech of second language learners. *Language Learning,* 45(1), 73–97. https://doi.org/10.1111/j.1467-1770.1995.tb00963.x

Munro, M.J., & Derwing, T.M. (1995b). Processing time, accent, and comprehensibility in the perception of native and foreign-accented speech. *Language and Speech,* 38, 289–306. https://doi.org/10.1177/002383099503800305

Muranoi, H. (2000). Focus on form through interaction enhancement: Integrating formal instruction into a communicative task in EFL classrooms. *Language Learning,* 50, 617–673. https://doi.org/10.1111/0023-8333.00142

Murphy, S. (1997). *Knowledge and production of English articles by advanced second language learners.* PhD thesis, University of Texas at Austin.

Nagle, C.L. (2021). Revisiting perception – production relationships: Exploring a new approach to investigate perception as a time-varying predictor. *Language Learning,* 71(1), 243–279. https://doi.org/10.1111/lang.12431

Nagle, C.L., & Baese-Berk, M.M. (2022). Advancing the state of the art in L2 speech perception-production research: Revisiting theoretical assumptions and methodological practices. *Studies in Second Language Acquisition*, 44(2), 580–605. https://doi.org/10.1017/S0272263121000371

Nattinger, J. (1988). Some current trends in vocabulary teaching. In R. Carter & M. McCarthy (Eds.), *Vocabulary and language teaching* (pp. 62–82). London: Longman.

Nelson, G., & Greenbaum, S. (2016). *An introduction to English grammar* (4th Edition). New York: Routledge.

Newbrook, M. (1988). Relative clauses, relative pronouns and Hong Kong English. *Working Papers in Linguistics and Language Teaching*, 11, 25–41.

Newson, D. (1998). Translation and foreign language learning. In K. Malmkjær (Ed.), *Translation and language teaching: Language teaching and translation* (pp. 63–68). Manchester: St Jerome Publishing.

Norouzian, R., & Eslami, Z.R. (2016). Critical perspectives on interlanguage pragmatic development: An agenda for research. *Issues in Applied Linguistics*, 20(1), 25–50. https://doi.org/10.5070/L4200012868

Odlin, T. (1989). *Language transfer: Cross-linguistic influence in language learning*. Cambridge: Cambridge University Press.

Ogihara, T. (1989). *Temporal reference in English and Japanese*. PhD dissertation, University of Texas at Austin.

Olson, D.J. (2014). Benefits of visual feedback on segmental production in the L2 classroom. *Language Learning and Technology*, 18(3), 173–192.

Ortega, L. (2009). *Understanding second language acquisition*. London: Hodder.

Ouertani, Y. (2013). Errors in the use of English articles among 1st and 4th year EFL students at the Higher Institute of Languages of Tunis (ISLT). *Journal of Teaching and Education*, 2(4), 353–363.

Oyama, R. (2017). Effects of cognitive comparison during focus-on-form instruction on Japanese EFL learners' acquisition of grammar. *Journal of Asia TEFL*, 14, 1–15. http://doi.org/10.18823/asiatefl.2017.14.1.1.1

Pan, Y.C., & Pan, Y.C. (2010). The use of L1 in the foreign language classroom. *Columbian Applied Linguistics Journal*, 12(2), 87–96. https://doi.org/10.14483/22487085.85

Parrish, B. (1987). A new look at methodologies in the study of article acquisition for learners of ESL. *Language Learning*, 37(3), 361–383. https://doi.org/10.1111/j.1467-1770.1987.tb00576.x

Pater, J. (2003). The perceptual acquisition of Thai phonology by English speakers: Task and stimulus effects. *Second Language Research*, 19(3), 209–223. https://doi.org/10.1191/0267658303sr220oa

Pattemore, A., & Muñoz, C. (2020). Learning L2 constructions from captioned audiovisual exposure: The effect of learner-related factors. *System*, 93(4), 102303. https://doi.org/10.1016/j.system.2020.102303

Patten, I., & Edmonds, L.A. (2015). Effect of training Japanese L1 speakers in the production of American English /r/ using spectrographic visual feedback. *Computer Assisted Language Learning*, 28(3), 241–259. https://doi.org/10.1080/09588221.2013.839570

Peng, L., & Setter, J. (2000). The emergence of systematicity in the English pronunciations of two Cantonese-speaking adults in Hong Kong. *English World-Wide*, 21(1), 81–108. https://doi.org/10.1075/eww.21.1.05pen

Pennington, M.C. (2021). Teaching pronunciation: The state of the art 2021. *RELC Journal*, 52(1), 3–21. https://doi.org/10.1177/00336882211002283

Pennington, M.C., & Rogerson-Revell, P. (2019). *English pronunciation teaching and research: Contemporary perspectives*. London: Palgrave Macmillan.

Pérez-Paredes, P., Sánchez-Tornel, M., Calero, C.J.M., & Jiménez, P.A. (2011). Tracking learners' actual uses of corpora: Guided vs non-guided corpus consultation. *Computer Assisted Language Learning*, 24(3), 233–253. https://doi.org/10.1080/09588221.2010.539978

Pica, T. (1985). The selective impact of classroom instruction on second-language acquisition. *Applied Linguistics*, 6(3), 214–222. https://doi.org/10.1093/applin/6.3.214

Pienemann, M. (1984). Psychological constraints on the teachability of languages. *Studies in Second Language Acquisition*, 6(2), 186–214. https://doi.org/10.1017/S0272263100005015

Pienemann, M. (1985). Learnability and syllabus construction. In K. Hyltenstam & M. Pienemann (Eds.), *Modelling and assessing second language acquisition* (pp. 23–75). Clevedon: Multilingual Matters.

Pienemann, M. (1998). *Language processing and second language development: Processability theory*. Amsterdam: John Benjamins. https://doi.org/10.1075/sibil.15

Pilus, Z. (2003). *Second language speech: Production and perception of voicing contrasts in word-final obstruents by Malay speakers of English*. Madison, WI: University of Wisconsin-Madison.

Plonsky, L. (2017). Quantitative research methods in instructed SLA. In S. Loewen & M. Sato (Eds.), *The Routledge handbook of instructed second language acquisition* (pp. 505–521). New York: Routledge. https://doi.org/10.4324/9781315676968

Proctor, M. (2004). Production and perception of AusE vowels by Vietnamese and Japanese ESL learners. *Paper presented at 2004 Australian linguistic society annual conference*, University of Sydney, Sydney, Australia, 13–15 July 2004.

Qian, X., Meng, H., & Soong, F. (2016). A two-pass framework of mispronunciation detection and diagnosis for computer-aided pronunciation training. *IEEE/ACM Transactions on Audio, Speech, and Language Processing*, 24(6), 1020–1028.

Qian, X., Soong, F., & Meng, H. (2010). Discriminative acoustic model for improving mispronunciation detection and diagnosis in computer-aided pronunciation training (CAPT). *Proceedings of the eleventh annual conference of the international speech communication association*, pp. 757–760. https://doi.org/10.21437/Interspeech.2010-278

Quirk, R., Greenbaum, S., Leech, G., & Svartvik, J. (1985). *A comprehensive grammar of the English language*. London: Longman.

Rahimi, M., & Tavakoli, M. (2015). The effectiveness of CALL in helping Persian L2 learners produce the English vowel /ɒ/. *Gema Online Journal of Language Studies*, 15(3), 17–30.

Ramírez-Verdugo, M. (2006). A study of intonation awareness and learning in non-native speakers of English. *Language Awareness*, 15(3), 141–159. https://doi.org/10.2167/la404.0

Rasier, L., & Hiligsmann, P. (2007). Prosodic transfer from L1 to L2. Theoretical and methodological issues. *Nouveaux Cahiers de Linguistique Française*, 28, 41–66.

Rato, A., & Carlet, A. (2020). Second language perception of English vowels by Portuguese learners: The effect of stimulus type. *Ilha Desterro*, 73(3), 205–226. https://doi.org/10.5007/2175-8026.2020v73n3p205

Redford, M.A., & Diehl, R.L. (1996). The relative perceptibility of initial and final consonants. *The Journal of the Acoustical Society of America*, 100, 2693–2693. https://doi.org/10.1121/1.417050

Richards, J.C. (1971). A non-contrastive approach to error analysis. *ELT Journal*, 25(3), 204–219. https://doi.org/10.1093/elt/XXV.3.204

Richards, J.C., & Rodgers, T.S. (1986). *Approaches and methods in language teaching: A description and analysis*. Cambridge: Cambridge University Press.

Richards, J.C., & Schmidt, R. (2010). *Longman dictionary of language teaching and applied linguistics* (4th Edition). Harlow & New York: Longman.

Roach, P. (2009). *English phonetics and phonology: A practical course* (4th Edition). Cambridge & New York: Cambridge University Press.

Robertson, D. (2000). Variability in the use of the English article system by Chinese learners of English. *Second Language Research*, 16(2), 135–172. https://doi.org/10.1191/026765800672262975

Rochet, B. (1995). Perception and production of second-language speech sounds by adults. In W. Strange (Ed.), *Speech perception and linguistic experience: Issues in cross-language speech research* (pp. 379–410). Timonium, MD: York Press.

Rogerson-Revell, P.M. (2021). Computer-assisted pronunciation training (CAPT): Current issues and future directions. *RELC Journal*, 52(1), 189–205. https://doi.org/10.1177/0033688220977406

Rutherford, W., & Sharwood Smith, M. (1988). Consciousness raising and universal grammar. In W. Rutherford & M. Sharwood Smith (Eds.), *Grammar and second language teaching: A book of readings* (pp. 107–116). New York: Newbury House.

Sakai, M. (2018). Moving towards a bilingual baseline in second language phonetic research. *Journal of Second Language Pronunciation*, 4(1), 11–45. https://doi.org/10.1075/jslp.00002.sak

Sapir, E. (1921). *Language: An introduction to the study of speech*. New York: Harcourt, Brace & Company.

Schachter, J. (1974). An error in error analysis. *Language Learning*, 24(2), 205–214. http://doi.org/10.1111/j.1467-1770.1974.tb00502.x

Schmid, P.M., & Yeni-Komshian, G.H. (1999). The effects of speaker accent and target predictability on perception of mispronunciations. *Journal of Speech, Language, and Hearing Research*, 42(1), 56–64. https://doi.org/10.1121/1.408755

Schmidt, R. (1990). The role of consciousness in second language learning. *Applied Linguistics*, 11(2), 129–158. https://doi.org/10.1093/applin/11.2.129

Schmidt, R. (1992). Psychological mechanisms underlying second language fluency. *Studies in Second Language Acquisition*, 14(4), 357–385. https://doi.org/10.1017/S0272263100011189

Sharifi, S., Sabet, M.K., & Tahriri, A. (2018). A study on the way in which words are organized in Iranian EFL learners' mental lexicon. *International Journal of Applied Linguistics and English Literature*, 7(6), 80–85. http://doi.org/10.7575/aiac.ijalel.v.7n.6p.80

Shintani, N. (2013). The effect of focus on form and focus on forms instruction on the acquisition of productive knowledge of L2 vocabulary by young beginning-level learners. *TESOL Quarterly*, 47(1), 36–62. https://doi.org/10.1002/tesq.54

Simargool, N. (2008). Interlanguage passive construction. *Pan-pacific Association of Applied Linguistics*, 12(1), 97–103.

Singler, J.V. (1988). The homogeneity of the substrate as a factor in pidgin/creole genesis. *Language*, 64(1), 27–51.

Singleton, D. (1987). Mother and other tongue influence on learner French. *Studies in Second Language Acquisition*, 9(3), 327–345. www.jstor.org/stable/44487419

Snape, N. (2013). Japanese and Spanish adult learners of English: L2 acquisition of generic reference. *Studies in Language Sciences: Journal of the Japanese Society for Language Sciences*, 12, 70–94.

Snape, N. (2018). Definite generic vs. definite unique in L2 acquisition. *Journal of the European Second Language Association*, 2(1), 83–95. https://doi.org/10.22599/jesla.46

Snape, N., Umeda, M., Wiltshier, J., & Yusa, N. (2016). Teaching the complexities of English article use and choice for generics to L2 learners. In D. Stringer, J. Garrett, B. Halloran, & S. Mossman (Eds.), *Proceedings of the 13th generative approaches to second language acquisition conference GASLA 2015* (pp. 208–222). Somerville, MA: Cascadilla Proceedings Project.

Snape, N., & Yusa, N. (2013). Explicit article instruction in definiteness, specificity, genericity and perception. In M. Whong, K. H. Gil, & H. Marsden (Eds.), *Universal grammar and the second language classroom* (pp. 161–183). Dordrecht, Netherlands: Springer.

Snow, D. (2004). *Cantonese as written language: The growth of a written Chinese vernacular*. Hong Kong: Hong Kong University Press.

Spada, N., & Tomita, Y. (2010). Interactions between type of instruction and type of language feature: A meta-analysis. *Language Learning*, 60(2), 263–308. https://doi.org/10.1111/j.1467-9922.2010.00562.x

Stibbard, R. (2004). The spoken English of Hong Kong: A study of co-occurring segmental errors. *Language, Culture and Curriculum*, 17(2), 127–142. https://doi.org/10.1080/07908310408666688

Stockman, I.J., & Pluut, E. (1992). Segment composition as a factor in the syllabification errors of second-language speakers. *Language Learning*, 42(1), 21–45. https://doi.org/10.1111/j.1467-1770.1992.tb00699.x

Strange, W., & Shafer, V.L. (2008). Speech perception in second language learners: The re-education of selective perception. In J.G. Hansen Edwards & M.L. Zampini (Eds.), *Phonology and second language acquisition* (pp. 153–191). Amsterdam: John Benjamins. https://doi.org/10.1075/sibil.36.09str

Strauss, S., Feiz, P., & Xiang, X. (2018). *Grammar, meaning, and concepts: A discourse-based approach to English grammar*. New York: Routledge. https://doi.org/10.4324/9781315767970

Sun, L., & van Heuven, V.J. (2007). Perceptual assimilation of English vowels by Chinese listeners. Can native-language interference be predicted? In B. Los & M. van Koppen (Eds.), *Linguistics in the Netherlands 2007* (pp. 150–161). Amsterdam: John Benjamins. https://doi.org/10.1075/avt.24.15sun

Swain, M. (1993). The output hypothesis: Just speaking and writing aren't enough. *Canadian Modern Language Review*, 50(1), 158–164. https://doi.org/10.3138/cmlr.50.1.158

Tabain, M. (1998). Non-sibilant fricatives in English: Spectral information above 10 kHz. *Phonetica*, 55(3), 107–130. https://doi.org/10.1159/000028427

Tang, M. (2020). Crosslinguistic influence on Chinese EFL learners' acquisition of English finite and nonfinite distinctions. *Cogent Education*, 7(1), 1721642. https://doi.org/10.1080/2331186X.2020.1721642

Tang, S.W., Fan, K., Lee, T.H.T., Lun, C., Luke, K.K., Tung, P., & Cheung, K.H. (2002). 鄧思穎, 范國, 李行德, 藺蓀, 陸鏡光, 童哲生, 張群顯 (2002). 粵語拼音字表 (第二版) *Cantonese romanization character list* (2nd Edition). Hong Kong: Linguistic Society of Hong Kong.

Tarone, E., Cohen, A.D., & Dumas, G. (1976). A closer look at some interlanguage terminology: A framework for communication strategies. *Working Papers on Bilingualism*, 9, 76–90.

Tarone, E., & Parrish, B. (1988). Task-related variation in interlanguage: The case of articles. *Language Learning*, 38(1), 21–44. https://doi.org/10.1111/j.1467-1770.1988.tb00400.x

Thomas, M. (1989). The acquisition of English articles by first- and second-language learners. *Applied Psycholinguistics*, 10(3), 335–355. https://doi.org/10.1017/s0142716400008663

Tobin, Y. (2005). Teaching phonetics to speech clinicians and audiologists according to the theory of phonology as human behaviour. *Paper presented at Phonetics teaching and learning conference 2005*, University College, London, 27–30, July 2005. Retrieved from www.researchgate.net/publication/237740590_Teaching_Phonetics_to_Speech_Clinicians_and_Audiologists_According_to_the_Theory_of_Phonology_as_Human_Behavior

Tomasello, M., & Herron, C. (1988). Down the garden path: Inducing and correcting over-generalization errors in the foreign language classroom. *Applied Psycholinguistics*, 9(3), 237–246. https://doi.org/10.1017/S0142716400007827

Trenkic, D. (2008). The representation of English articles in second language grammars: Determiners or adjectives? *Bilingualism: Language and Cognition*, 11(1), 1–18. https://doi.org/10.1017/S1366728907003185

Trenkic, D., Mirkovic, J., & Altmann, G.T.M. (2014). Real-time grammar processing by native and non-native speakers: Constructions unique to the second language. *Bilingualism: Language and Cognition*, 17(2), 237–257. https://doi.org/10.1017/S1366728913000321

Trofimovich, P., & Baker, W. (2006). Learning second language suprasegmentals: Effect of L2 experience on prosody and fluency characteristics of L2 speech. *Studies in Second Language Acquisition*, 28(1), 1–30. https://doi.org/10.1017/S0272263106060013

Tyler, M.D., Best, C.T., Faber, A., & Levitt, A.G. (2014). Perceptual assimilation and discrimination of non-native vowel contrasts. *Phonetica*, 71(1), 4–21. https://doi.org/10.1159/000356237

Umeda, M., Snape, N., Yusa, N., & Wiltshier, J. (2019). The long-term effect of explicit instruction on learners' knowledge on English articles. *Language Teaching Research*, 23(2), 179–199. https://doi.org/10.1177/1362168817739648

van Leussen, J.W., & Escudero, P. (2015). Learning to perceive and recognize a second language: The L2LP model revised. *Frontiers in Psychology*, 6, Article 1000. https://doi.org/10.3389/fpsyg.2015.01000

VanPatten, B. (1996). *Input processing and grammar instruction in second language acquisition*. Norwood, NJ: Ablex.

Walker, J.A. (2012). Form, function, and frequency in phonological variation. *Language Variation and Change*, 24(3), 397–415. https://doi.org/10.1017/S0954394512000142

Waltraud, P. (2005). Adjectival modification in Mandarin Chinese and related issues. *Linguistics*, 43(4), 757–793. https://doi.org/10.1515/ling.2005.43.4.757

Wang, Q. (2007). The national curriculum changes and their effects on English language teaching in the People's Republic of China. In J. Cummins & C. Davison (Eds.), *International handbook of English language teaching* (pp. 87–105). New York, NY: Springer.

Wang, Y. (2020). A contrastive study of the stative feature in English. *Journal of Language Teaching and Research*, 11(1), 115–120. http://doi.org/10.17507/jltr.1101.13

Webster, M., & Lam, W.C.P. (1991). Further notes on the influence of Cantonese on the English of Hong Kong students [Special issue]. *ILE Journal*, 2, 35–42.

Webster, M., Ward, A., & Craig, K. (1987). Language errors due to first language interference (Cantonese) produced by Hong Kong students of English. *ILE Journal*, 3, 63–81.

Wei, R., & Su, J. (2012). The statistics of English in China: An analysis of the best available data from government sources. *English Today*, 28(3), 10–14. https://doi.org/10.1017/S0266078412000235

Wennerstrom, A. (2000). The role of intonation in second language fluency. In H. Riggenbach (Ed.), *Perspectives on fluency* (pp. 102–127). Ann Arbor: University of Michigan Press.

White, L. (1991). Adverb placement in second language acquisition: Some effects of positive and negative evidence in the classroom. *Second Language Research*, 7(2), 133–161. https://doi.org/10.1177/026765839100700205

White, L., Spada, N., Lightbown, P.M., & Ranta, L. (1991). Input enhancement and L2 question formation. *Applied Linguistics*, 12(4), 416–432. https://doi.org/10.1093/applin/12.4.416

Wisniewski, E.J., Lamb, C.A., & Middleton, E.L. (2003). On the conceptual basis for the count and mass noun distinction. *Language and Cognitive Processes*, 18(5–6), 583–624. https://doi.org/10.1080/01690960344000044

Wu, Y., & Bodomo, A. (2009). Classifiers ≠ Determiners. *Linguistic Inquiry*, 40(3), 487–503. https://doi.org/10.1162/ling_a_00109

Xiao, R., & McEnery, T. (2010). *Corpus-based contrastive studies of English and Chinese*. New York: Routledge. https://doi.org/10.4324/9780203847954

Yao, Y., & Du-Babcock, B. (2020). English as a lingua franca in mainland China: An analysis of intercultural business communicative competence. *International Journal of Business Communication*, first published on January 3, 2020. https://doi.org/10.1177/2329488419898221

Yenkimaleki, M., & van Heuven, V.J. (2019). The relative contribution of computer assisted prosody training vs. instructor based prosody teaching in developing speaking skills by interpreter trainees: An experimental study. *Speech Communication*, 107(C), 48–57. https://doi.org/10.1016/j.specom.2019.01.006

Yip, V. (1995). *Interlanguage and learnability: From Chinese to English*. Amsterdam: John Benjamins.

Yip, V., & Matthews, S. (1991). Relative complexity: Beyond avoidance. *CUHK Papers in Linguistics*, 3, 112–124.

Yip, V., & Matthews, S. (1995). I-interlanguage and typology: The case of topic-prominence. In L. Eubank, L. Selinker, & M. Sharwood Smith (Eds.), *The current state of interlanguage: Studies in honor of William E. Rutherford* (pp. 17–31). Amsterdam & Philadelphia: John Benjamins.

Yoon, K.K. (1993). Challenging prototype descriptions: Perception of noun countability and indefinite vs. zero article use. *International Review of Applied Linguistics in Language Teaching*, 31(4), 269–290. https://doi.org/10.1515/iral.1993.31.4.269

Yu, V.W.S., & Atkinson, P.A. (1988a). An investigation of the language difficulties experienced by Hong Kong secondary school students in English-medium schools I: The problems. *Journal of Multilingual and Multicultural Development*, 9(3), 267–284. https://doi.org/10.1080/01434632.1988.9994336

Yu, V.W.S., & Atkinson, P.A. (1988b). An investigation of the language difficulties experienced by Hong Kong secondary school students in English-medium schools II: Some causal factors. *Journal of Multilingual and Multicultural Development*, 9(4), 307–322. https://doi.org/10.1080/01434632.1988.9994339

Yule, G. (2017). *The study of language* (6th Edition). Cambridge: Cambridge University Press.

Zampini, M.L. (2008). L2 speech production research: Findings, issues and advances. In J.G. Hansen Edwards & M.L. Zampini (Eds.), *Phonology and second language acquisition* (pp. 219–249). Amsterdam: John Benjamins.

Zdorenko, T., & Paradis, J. (2012). Articles in child L2 English: When L1 and L2 acquisition meet at the interface. *First Language*, 32(1–2), 38–62. https://doi.org/10.1177/0142723710396797

Zee, E. (1993). A phonetic and phonological analysis of Cantonese vowels and diphthongs. In *Abstracts, the fourth international conference on Cantonese and other Yue dialects* (p. 98). Hong Kong: Linguistic Society of Hong Kong.

Zhang, H. (2007). Numeral classifiers in Mandarin Chinese. *Journal of East Asian Linguistics*, 16(1), 43–59. https://doi.org/10.1007/s10831-006-9006-9

Zhang, L., & Zhang, S. (1987). *Guoyin Yuyin Suoyin Zihui ('A Chinese word list ordered by Mandarin and Cantonese pronunciations')*. Hong Kong: Chung Hwa Bookstore.

Zhang, Q. (2013). The attitudes of Hong Kong students towards Hong Kong English and Mandarin-accented English? *English Today*, 29(2), 9–16. https://doi.org/10.1017/S0266078413000096

Zhao, T., Liu, J., Lu, Y., Han, S., & Li, C. (2003). An automatic pronunciation teaching system for Chinese to learn English. *Proceedings of the IEEE International Conference on Robotics Intelligent Systems and Signal Processing*, 2, 1157–1161. https://doi.org/10.1109/RISSP.2003.1285754

Zobl, H. (1980). The formal and developmental selectivity of L1 influence on L2 acquisition. *Language Learning*, 30(1), 43–57. https://doi.org/10.1111/j.1467-1770.1980.tb00150.x

Zsiga, E. (2013). *The sounds of language: An introduction to phonetics and phonology*. Maiden, MA: Wiley-Blackwell.

Index

Note: The locators followed by 'n' refer to notes and locators in **bold** refer to tables.

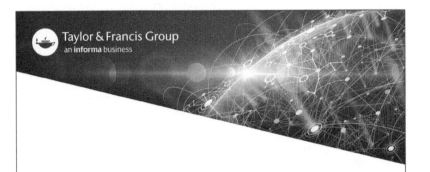